William James Gordon-Gorman

Converts to Rome Since the Tractarian Movement to May, 1899

William James Gordon-Gorman

Converts to Rome Since the Tractarian Movement to May, 1899

ISBN/EAN: 9783744664561

Printed in Europe, USA, Canada, Australia, Japan

Cover: Foto ©ninafisch / pixelio.de

More available books at **www.hansebooks.com**

CONVERTS TO ROME

SINCE THE TRACTARIAN MOVEMENT TO MAY, 1899

BY

W. GORDON GORMAN

FOURTH EDITION—REVISED AND ENLARGED

LONDON
SWAN SONNENSCHEIN & CO., Lim.
PATERNOSTER SQUARE
1899

"Before the storm I will not quail,
   From heights or depths I will not shrink,
Yet, gentle Lord, should courage fail
   Stretch forth Thy hand before I sink."

—The late Father BRIDGETT, C.SS.R.
(*Written on his death-bed.*)

PREFACE TO THE FOURTH EDITION.

In the present month this compilation attains its majority, for it was in June, 1878, that the lists bearing the title of "Rome's Recruits" first appeared in the columns of the *Whitehall Review*.

Since that date, and especially since that of the edition of 1892, the constant flow of conversions to Holy Church (the real old English Church, the Church that alone could be recognised by an Augustine, a Bede, a Dunstan, an à Becket or a Langton, could they but visit this land of 300 sects), and lastly the present acute crisis which is taking place in our midst in religious matters, have impelled me to issue a new and greatly enlarged edition of *Converts to Rome*.

Having been repeatedly asked how I became connected with this publication, I deem this a fitting occasion to satisfy the legitimate curiosity of my kind correspondents. While at college I took a keen interest in the return of England to the Old Faith, and I am pleased to admit that that feeling was fostered in me by my old tutor, the late Rev. E. G.

Kirwan Browne, a convert and author of the *Annals of the Tractarian Movement*. I can still picture the dear old man with his snow-white locks and gentle voice, and better still can I remember how he often discoursed to us—in a style peculiarly his own—on the stirring episodes of that period when the Church of England as by law established had that shock which a great statesman has so graphically depicted.

It will not be surprising then to my readers to imagine that, when the then editor of the *Whitehall Review* invited me to superintend the production of the present work in pamphlet form, I eagerly accepted a task which has ever since been to me a labour of love.

During the last twenty years I have been in receipt of thousands of letters from converts in all parts of the world. These letters have deeply impressed me, for they have all been couched in language which suggested that their authors had— as Cardinal Newman said—left the City of Confusion for the Mother of Saints, and had at length obtained a happiness and a peace of soul which they could never have expected here below.

It is often said that you may hurt an Englishman in many ways with impunity, but that he never allows his pecuniary interests and comforts to be assailed. When I scan the list of converts now before me, when I note the names of the many who have been real martyrs for the cause of Truth, I for one cannot acquiesce in the application of such a charge. How many a noble dame of ancient lineage has forsaken home, family and fortune, laid her coronet aside, and assumed the veil in some humble convent? How many an Anglican clergyman has left his snug parsonage and rich living and begun life afresh, and struggled on joyfully to the end of his days on a pittance equivalent to that of Goldsmith's country rector? And more than all, how many have died in those establishments for the poor, rendered necessary by the " Blessed " Reformation, deserted by all dear to them by the ties of kindred, and yet blessing God to the last for having found the True Fold? Many such cases are known to me, and must be familiar to many who read these lines.

Some of us born Catholics, failing to appreciate the possibility of abandoning the religion of one's parents, or remembering only the days of penal laws and intolerance, and priding ourselves on the fact that our ancestors were never traitors to the See of Peter, are apt at times to be cool and distant to converts. This should not be, and we have noble examples set us by our Holy Father Pope Leo XIII. and his Eminence Cardinal Vaughan, who have done and are doing much for the welfare, spiritual and temporal, of our new brethren. The establishment and endowment of the Collegio Beda at Rome, whose *alumni* are to be converted Anglican clergymen (fourteen are there in residence at the present moment), clearly demonstrate the Holy Father's ardent wish for the conversion of England, and his great affection for this country. The Cardinal Archbishop of Westminster has been no laggard in the same noble cause, if we judge him by his many letters to the Faithful, and the interest he takes in the Converts' Aid Society. The offices of that most excellent institution are at 42 Gerrard Street, Soho, London, W. I should deem it a favour if all those who derive any pleasure from the perusal of my book would kindly send a subscription to the Hon. Secretary, John B. Corney, Esq.

At this point I cannot refrain from alluding to the grand work that is being accomplished by the Rev. Philip Fletcher and Mr. Lister Drummond in connection with the Guild of Our Lady of Ransom for the Conversion of England, of which they are the founders. These gentlemen are working with a zeal only comparable to that which animated the late Father Ignatius Spencer of saintly memory. I have ample evidence to prove that many conversions are due to their untiring efforts.

Last year I had the pleasure of meeting for the first time a young gentleman of an old and distinguished Kentish family. During the course of an interesting conversation he told me that he owed his conversion, some six years previously, to a series of sermons he heard at an Anglican church, given by the Rev. B. W. Maturin; this, I trust, will be pleasing news to the good Father, and let us hope that he may be with us soon as a true Pastor, working to bring others to the Fold, as are doing the Revv. Fathers Croke Robinson, C. H. Moore, Sydney Smith, S.J., and many other devoted convert priests by their sermons and their beautiful written expositions of the doctrines of the Church of their adoption.

Neither are the laity found wanting when their services are needed from the platform or from the pen. I have only to mention, among others, the names of Messrs. James Britten, K.S.G., W. Vance Packman, Dudley Baxter, Robert Dell, and W. Mowbray to prove my assertion.

I would call special attention to the fact that this list is not official, for I did not apply to nor have had the slightest assistance from any of our Bishops. Neither must I be exuberant in my acknowledgments to our clergy, for to my 500 applications for information I was honoured by *thirty replies*. The names have been culled from the columns of the Catholic and Protestant papers, or have been supplied to me by the converts themselves or their friends.

I trust the new arrangement may give general satisfaction, and that the statistics, now introduced for the first time, may prove interesting.

I am withholding hundreds of names of relatives of clergymen and of others who wish me to do so for family reasons.

As the number of converts in England now amount to nearly 10,000 per annum, it will be

STATISTICS OF THE LIST.

Authors, Poets and Journalists 162

Public Officials 90

Oxford University 445

All Souls' College	4	New Inn Hall	2
Balliol College	30	New College	16
Brasenose College	22	Oriel College	33
Charsley Hall	1	Pembroke College	9
Christ Church	55	Queen's College	18
Corpus Christi College	5	St. Alban's Hall	3
Exeter College	45	St. Edmund's Hall	8
Hertford College	3	St. John's College	15
Jesus College	6	Trinity College	14
Keble College	13	University College	20
Lincoln College	8	Wadham College	9
Magdalen College	22	Worcester College	16
Magdalen Hall	11	Graduates whose Col-	
St. Mary's Hall	11	leges are unknown to	
Merton College	19	the compiler	27

Cambridge University 213

Caius College	8	Magdalene College	4
St. Catherine's College	3	Pembroke College	4
St. Catherine's Hall	1	St. Peter's College	10
Christ College	7	Queens' College	9
Clare College	4	Selwyn College	1
Corpus Christi College	6	Sidney Sussex College	4
Downing College	3	Trinity College	79
Emmanuel College	8	Trinity Hall	6
Jesus College	11	Graduates whose Col-	
St. John's College	28	leges are unknown to	
King's College	2	the compiler	15

Trinity College, Dublin 23

London University 11

STATISTICS OF THE LIST.

DURHAM UNIVERSITY	10
ABERDEEN UNIVERSITY	1
ST. ANDREW'S UNIVERSITY	2
EDINBURGH UNIVERSITY	4
GLASGOW UNIVERSITY	2
KING'S COLLEGE, LONDON	10

POSTSCRIPT.

REV. LUKE RIVINGTON, D.D.

JUST as I am revising the last proof-sheets of this work the melancholy intelligence reaches me of the sudden death of one of our most important converts—the Rev. Luke Rivington, D.D. I can never forget the kindly assistance and encouragement he has given me in connection with this production.

Doubtless he has done more than any living English priest, by his learned works and sermons, to bring back his countrymen to the Faith of his forefathers. His loss will be deeply felt, and Holy Church is deprived of a champion by his untimely death.—*R.I.P.*

ABADAM, Miss Alice, daughter of the late Edward Abadam, of Middleton Hall, Carmarthenshire, High Sheriff for that county. (1880.)

Abbott, Mrs. J. B., wife of J. B. Abbott, solicitor.

Abbott, Miss, M.A., of Deal.

Abbott, Mrs. R. B., wife of R. B. Abbott, barrister. (1866.)

à Beckett, Arthur.

à Beckett, Gilbert, sub-editor of *Punch*.

à Beckett, Mrs. Gilbert, his wife.

Abingdon (Montagu), eighth Earl of, Lieutenant-Colonel of the Berkshire Militia and President of the Portsmouth Voluntary School Association. (1858.)

Abraham, The late Edwin, of the Record Office, uncle to the Very Rev. Canon Augustus P. Bethell. (1849.)

Acheson, Lady Annabella, daughter of the second Earl of Gosford. (1845.)

Acheson, Lady Olivia, daughter of the second Earl of Gosford. (1845.)

Acklend, Miss May, of Plymouth.

à Court, The Hon. Mrs. Arthur W. Holmes, daughter of the late Hon. T. B. H. Berkeley, C.M.G. (1888.)

Adair, Major, of the Royal Engineers, of Dover.

Adair, Mrs., wife of the above.

Adams, Mrs. Elizabeth, of Lancaster.

Adams, Walter Marsham, M.A. and Fellow of New College, Oxford, son of the late Assistant Judge, Mr. Serjeant Adams; author of various works.

Adderley, Mrs. Edmund, sister-in-law to Lord Norton.

Adey, W. More, M.A. of Keble College, Oxford, author and translator of Ibsen and Balzac. (1880.)

Agnett, Miss, a Carmelite Nun.

Agnew, Miss, daughter of Sir Stair Agnew, Bart., authoress of *Geraldine*, etc.

Ainsworth, The late John Lees, of Oldham. (1850.)

Ainsworth, The late Mrs. J., wife of the above, granddaughter of Sir Thomas Hanmer, Bart., of Hanmer Hall, Flintshire; a Redemptorist Nun at Drumcondra, Dublin. (1850.)

Ainsworth, The Misses, daughters of the above; both nuns. (1850.)

Akers, George, M.A. of Oriel College, Oxford, for some years the Rev. F. G. Lee's coadjutor and curate at Aberdeen, and then at St. George's Mission under the late Rev. Charles Lowder, uncle to the Right Hon. Aretas Akers-Douglas, M.P. for East Kent, and First Commissioner of Works. A priest, Canon of Westminster, till lately President of St. Edmund's College, Ware, now at St. Mary and St. Michael, London, E. (1868.)

Albemarle, William, eighth Earl of, P.C., K.C.M.G., F.R.G.S., Under-Secretary of State for War (1878-80 and 1885-86), Lieutenant-Colonel of the

12th Middlesex, R.V.C., eldest son of the seventh Earl who fought at Waterloo. (1879.)

Alderson, Mrs. Mary E., widow of an Anglican clergyman.

Aldrich, Mrs. A. P., niece of Dr. Poynter, V.A.

Alexander, Henry, barrister.

Algar, Commander.

Algar, J., M.A. and Fellow of University College, Oxford, late a clergyman of the English Church.

Algar, John, M.A. of Trinity College, Cambridge. (1848.)

Alger, The late F., solicitor.

Alington, Alan John, B.A. of Worcester College, Oxford, son of the late Rev. Marmaduke Alington, M.A., Rector of Bensworth, Lincolnshire. (1898.)

Allcard, Miss Mary, formerly an Anglican Nun.

Allchin, Arthur, a Jesuit Priest at Holy Cross, St. Helen's, Lancashire.

Allen, Dr., of Longford House, Acton, London, W.

Allen, Mrs. George, of Oxford.

Allen, The late Major-General Stewart, of the Bengal Army.

Alleyne, Mrs. J., wife of the Rev. Joseph Alleyne, M.A., and her two sons.

Alleyne, Miss, her daughter.

Allies, T. W., M.A. and Fellow of Wadham College, Oxford, and formerly Rector of Launton, Oxon., chaplain to the Bishop of London; Knight Commander of St. Gregory the Great, author of *The Church of England Cleared from* the *Charge of Schism, The See of Peter, A Life's Decision, The Formation of Christendom Series,* etc. (1851.)

Allies, Mrs., wife of the above. (1851.)

Allnatt, Charles Francis F., B.A. Trinity College, Dublin, son of the late Charles Blake Allnatt, of Shrewsbury; barrister and author.

Allnut, Mrs., of Birmingham.

Alston, George, at one time monk of Llanthony Abbey, and formerly a member of the Cowley Brotherhood; now a postulant at Downside Benedictine Monastery. (1898).

Ames, Linden. (1891.)

Ames, Mrs. Margaret W., wife of the above, and cousin of the Hon. and Rev. Monsignor Stanley. (1875.)

Anderdon, The late Rev. William Henry, M.A. and Bennett Scholar of University College, Oxford, formerly Vicar of St. Margaret's, Leicester; a Jesuit Priest, and author of *Via Crucis* and of various controversial works. (1850.)

Anderson, Arthur, M.A. Trinity Hall, Cambridge, late curate of St. John's, East Dulwich. (1892.)

Anderson, Mrs. E., of Liverpool.

Anderson, Miss, her daughter.

Anderson, W. D., of Ardsheal, Ballachulish, Argyllshire. (1897.)

Andrews, Arthur E. J., of London. (1895.)

Andrews, Colonel, of Plymouth.

Andrews, Mrs. wife of the above, and sister-in-law of the Rev. G. R. Prynne, of Plymouth.

Andrews, Mrs., of Camberwell.

Andrews, Mrs., wife of a Suffolk rector. (1867.)

Andrews, Septimus, M.A. and student of Christ Church, Oxford, formerly Vicar of Market Harborough. A priest (Oblate of St. Charles) at St. Mary of the Angels, Bayswater, London, W. (1869.)

Angelo, Miss, of Brighton.

Anglesea, Lilian Florence, Marchioness of, wife of the fifth Marquis and daughter of Sir George Chetwynd, Bart., and of the Marchioness of Hastings. (1896.)

Angus, George, M.A., S.C.L. St. Edmund's Hall, Oxford, formerly curate of Prestbury, Gloucestershire. A priest, at one time Chaplain of the Catholic University College, Kensington; now at St. James's, St. Andrews, Fife, N.B. (1873.)

Annaly, The Lady.

Anstey, The late Chisholm, sometime M.P., and Attorney-General of Hong-Kong. (1846.)

Anstice, Mrs. J., wife of the late Rev. Joseph Anstice, M.A., of King's College, London.

Anstruther, Mrs., granddaughter of the last Lord Seaforth.

Anstruther, Miss Lloyd; now a nun.

Antrobus, Frederick I., son of the late Sir Edmund Antrobus, sixth Bart., formerly *attaché* at the British Embassy, Paris; a priest at the Brompton Oratory, London, S.W., author of *The Excellencies of the Congregation of the Oratory*, etc. (1869.)

Arbuthnott, The Hon. Mrs.

Arbuthnott, The Misses, her daughters.
Arbuthnott, Henry Donald, son of the eighth Viscount Arbuthnott.
Arbuthnott, Mrs., the authoress.
Archer, Miss Margaret, of Wexford. (1870.)
Archer, Mrs., of Clifton.
Arden, The late Rev. Henry Alban; a Dominican Priest at St. Dominic's Priory, London, N.W. (1850.)
Argyll, Anne, Duchess of, wife of the seventh Duke.
Arkwright, Mrs., wife of the Vicar of Latton.
Arkwright, The Misses, her four daughters, one a nun.
Arkwright, Mrs., wife of Robert Wigram Arkwright, of Normanton Turville Hall, Leicestershire.
Arkwright, W. P., of Sutton Scarsdale, Chesterfield, Derbyshire. (1881.)
Armstrong, Miss, daughter of the Rev. J. Armstrong, M.A., an Anglican clergyman.
Arnold, Charles, of Cambridge.
Arnold, Damien, a Passionist Priest at St. Joseph's Retreat, Highgate, London, N.
Arnold, Miss, his sister, a nun.
Arnold, H. Coape, of Wolvey Hall, Warwickshire.
Arnold, Thomas, M.A. University College, Oxford, and Fellow of the Royal University of Ireland, late Professor of English at the Catholic University College, Dublin, second son of the late celebrated Dr. Arnold, of Rugby School; brother of Matthew Arnold, and father of Mrs. Humphrey Ward.
Arnold, Mrs., wife of the above and daughter of James Benison of Slieve Russell, Co. Cavan, Ireland.

Arnold-Morris, Herbert, the artist. (1876.)
Arnold-Morris, Miss, his sister. (1876.)
Arnott, A. P., M.A. Trinity College, Oxford; now of Bath.
Arnott, J., M.A. Oxon., late clergyman of the Anglican Church.
Arnott, Mrs., widow of an Anglican clergyman.
Arthur, Miss, sister of Sir Frederick Arthur, Bart.
Arundell, Mrs., wife of A. Tagg Arundell, M.C.S., late President of the Madras Municipality. (1891.)
Arundell of Wardour, The Lady, sister of the first Duke of Buckingham and Chandos, and wife of the tenth Lord Arundell of Wardour.
Ashborne, Mrs., of Oxford.
Ashborne, Miss, her daughter.
Ashburnham, Bertram, fifth Earl of, J.P., D.L., Knight of St. John of Jerusalem, Knight Grand Cross of the Order of Pius, and Knight Grand Cross of the Order of Malta. (1872.)
Ashby, Miss, of Cambridge. (1896.)
Ashley, Edward, of Oxford.
Ashley, Miss E., of Oxford.
Ashley, Henry, of Oxford.
Ashley, M. M., of Oxford.
Ashley, Robert, of Clapham, London, S.W.
Aspinall, The late John Bridge, Q.C., Recorder of Liverpool, son of the late Rev. James Aspinall, M.A., Rector of Althorpe, Lincolnshire. (1848.)
Aspland, W. B., of Spilsby, Lincolnshire. (1897.)
Asselbourg, Madame (*née* Newnham), now of Lille, France.

Astley, Miss F., now Prioress of Colwith. (1872.)

Aston, Mr., of the Oaklands, Edgbaston, Birmingham.

Aston, Mrs., wife of the above.

Athy, Mrs., of Renville, Co. Galway, Ireland. (1876.)

Atkinson, Miss, now a nun at the Convent of the Sacred Heart, Roehampton, London, S.W. (1884.)

Atkinson, Miss E., now a nun at the Convent of the Sacred Heart, Armagh, Ireland. (1883.)

Atkinson, Frederick Walton, LL.B. of London University, solicitor.

Atkinson, The late Rev. Joseph, a priest of the Order of Charity, at St. Etheldreda's, Holborn, London, E.C.

Atkinson, Miss Madeline, of Eustace Street, Dublin. (1888.)

Atkinson, Miss Susan, relative of Mrs. Anne Ramsden Bennett, cousin of the late Right Hon. W. E. Gladstone and of Sir Thomas Gladstone, Bart. (1874.)

Atkinson-Grimshawe, Mrs. Charles, of Bruges, Belgium. (1889.)

Atlee, Albert, son of the late Falconer Atlee, C.M.G.

Atlee, The late Falconer, C.M.G., for fifty years Consul and Secretary at the British Embassy, Paris.

Atlee, Mrs., wife of the above.

Atlee, The Misses, their daughters.

Atwood, Lieutenant Arthur, of the Royal Navy, son of the Rev. Francis Atwood, of Boscombe, Bournemouth.

Atwood, The late E. W., B.A. Jesus College, Oxford, late curate of St. Leonard, Shoreditch, London, E.C.

Atwood, Miss Hilda, daughter of the Rev. Francis Atwood, of Boscombe, Bournemouth; now a Benedictine nun.

Auchinleck, David, of Newhaven House, Edinburgh.

Auckland, The Lady, daughter of Colonel George Hutton, C.B., of Gate Burton, Lincolnshire. (1897.)

Audry, Mrs. Joseph, of Ludington. (1888.)

Auger, Miss Emma, of Walthamstow. (1892.)

Auger, Thomas à Beckett, of Walthamstow. (1892.)

Aveling, A. P., of Keble College, Oxford. (1896.)

Ayer-Carr, A., of Heslington, Yorkshire. (1880.)

Aylmer, The late Sir Arthur, Bart. (1893.)

Ayres, Miss Alice, of Colchester. (1895.)

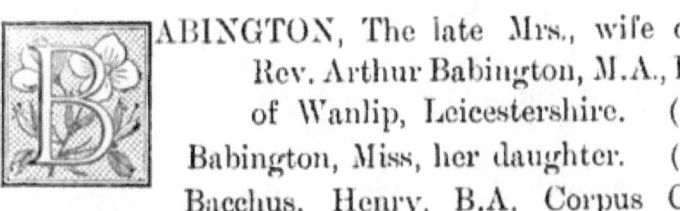

ABINGTON, The late Mrs., wife of the Rev. Arthur Babington, M.A., Rector of Wanlip, Leicestershire. (1881.)

Babington, Miss, her daughter. (1881.)

Bacchus, Henry, B.A. Corpus Christi College, Cambridge. (1846.)

Bacchus, Mrs., daughter of the late Rev. Professor Cumming, M.A. of Trinity College, Cambridge, and Rector of North Runcton.

Bacon, Francis, formerly lay-worker at St. Peter's, London Docks. A Jesuit Priest at St. Aloysius', Glasgow, N.B.

Bacon, Mrs., of Ipswich.

Badeley, The late Edward, Q.C., and M.A. of Brasenose College, Oxford. (1852.)

Bagshawe, Miss Henrietta, of Rome.

Baigent, William J., a priest at All Saints, Hassop, Derbyshire. (1872.)

Bailey, Captain Farmer, D.L., Kent.

Bailey, Mrs. John, of Bridgwater.

Bailey, M. G., of Liverpool.

Bailey, T. R., of Arundel.

Baillie, The late Evan, M.A. Trinity College, Oxford, late Rector of Lawshall ; lineal descendant of Sir William Wallace, the Scottish patriot. (1850.)

Baine, Captain.

Baines, Miss Rosa, of Solihull, Warwickshire. (1885.)

Baisall, The late Mrs., niece of the late Sir Walter Scott, Bart., the poet and novelist. (1846.)

Baker, Arnold S., of Exeter College, Oxford. A priest (Oblate of St. Charles) at the Church of Our Lady of the Holy Souls, Kensal New Town, London, W.

Baker, Charles, of Plymouth.

Baker, Edward, of Plymouth.

Baker, Edward Bernard, of Midford. (1840.)

Baker, Henry Sherston, M.A. Exeter College, Oxford, father of Sir George Edward Dunstan Baker, Bart.

Baker, John, of Oxford.

Baker, John Sherston, M.A., barrister.

Baker, Miss Mary, of Plymouth.

Baker, Miss M. A., of Cottles, Wilts. (1874.)

Baker, Oscar, of Boston Park Road, Brentford, W.

Bale, Miss, of Ipswich.

Ball, James, of Burton.

Ball, Miss, of Octagon House, Bideford. (1886.)

Ballantine, Miss, daughter of the late Mr. Serjeant Ballantine.

Ballard, The late Rev. Edward H., M.A. and Fellow of Wadham College, Oxford. A priest and Chaplain to H.M.S. *Melampus*, Southsea. (1850.)

Ballard, George Frederick, M.A. Worcester College, Oxford, formerly a barrister; a priest, Canon of Portsmouth, and till recently of the Church of the Immaculate Conception and St. Joseph, Christchurch, Hants. (1850.)

Ballard, Major. (1848.)

Balston, The late Rev. F. R., M.A. Christ Church, Oxford, formerly an Anglican clergyman; a priest at West Grinstead, Horsham, Sussex. (1850.)

Bamfield, Miss Mary, of Bristol.

Bampfield, G. F. L., B.A. and late Scholar of Lincoln College, Oxford, First Class in Classics, formerly an Anglican clergyman; a priest, and director of the Barnet Schools, Herts. (1865.)

Bampton, The late Rev. George, at one time clergyman of the English Church; a Jesuit Priest.

Barclay, Miss Emma, sister of the Rev. John Barclay, M.A., Hon. Canon of Chester, Rural Dean and Vicar of Runcorn, Cheshire

Barclay, Miss Fanny, her sister.

Barff, The late Rev. Professor Frederick Settle, F.C.S., Royal Academy, M.A. Christ College, Cambridge, formerly curate of Holy Trinity, Hull; late Professor at St. Edmund's College, Ware, and Professor of Chemistry at Beaumont College, Old Windsor; author of several scientific works and text-books. (1851.)

Barham, The late Lady Caroline, sister to the Earl of Thanet.

Barham, Mrs. Gaggiotti, daughter of the above.

Barker, G. T., of Liverpool.

Barker, Henry, of Liverpool.

Barker, Miss, of Worthing.

Barker, Robert, of Hull.

Barllett, John, of Liverpool.

Barllett, Mrs., his wife.

Barlow, Miss, formerly an Anglican Nun at All Saints', Margaret Street, London, W.

Barlow, T. W., M.A., late Vicar of Little Bowden.

Barnard, E. J., M.A. Merton College, Oxford.

Barnes, Arthur Stapylton, M.A. University College, Oxford, formerly curate of St. Agnes, Kennington Park, London, S.E., late Rector of St. Ives, Hunts; a priest at Ilford, Essex. (1895.)

Barnes, Captain.

Barnes, J. G. H., B.A. Wadham College, Oxford.

Barnes, The late Mrs., of Gilling Castle, Yorkshire.

Barnes, Miss, her daughter.

Barnes, Thomas, B.A. New College, Oxford, late curate of St. Peter's, Vauxhall, London. (1898.)

Barnes, William, of Cottles, Wilts. (1864.)

Barraud, Clement; a Jesuit Priest in America.

Barrett, Miss Ella, now a nun at the Convent of the Sacred Heart, Armagh. (1885.)

Barrett, Ernest Michael, of Northampton; a Benedictine Priest at St. Benedict's Abbey, Fort Augustus, N.B.

Barrett, Miss Lily, now a nun at the Convent of the Sacred Heart, Armagh. (1885.)

Barrett, Lady Maud, younger daughter of the ninth Earl of Cavan.

Barrett, The Misses, of Plymouth.

Barrie, Miss Dorothea, relative of Admiral Sir Robert Barrie.

Barrie, Miss Georgina, her sister, a nun who nursed the wounded at Scutari.

Barrie, The late Captain William, R.N., son of Admiral Sir Robert Barrie.

Barrow, The late Rev. John, D.D., and Principal of St. Edmund's Hall, Oxford, formerly an Anglican clergyman. A Jesuit. (1864.)

Barrow, Sir John Croker, Bart., M.A. University College, Oxford, formerly an Anglican clergyman; now a barrister. (1859.)

Barrow, Lady, wife of the above. (1859.)

Barrow, Miss, their daughter; a Franciscan nun. (1859.)

Barrows, Henry, of Oxford.

Barry, M. J., of Liverpool.

Bartlett, Charles, of Plymouth.

Bartlett, John, of Clifton.

Bartlett, Joseph Henry, a Dominican Priest, and Prior of St. Thomas's Priory, Rugeley, Staffordshire.

Bartlett, Miss, of Clifton.

Barton, Miss Emily, daughter of the late Rev. J Barton, an Irish clergyman. (1898.)

Barton, Miss Polly, her sister. (1898.)

Barton, Miss, of Rochestown, Co. Tipperary, Ireland (now Madame Schemanski).

Barton, William, of Aldershot. (1879.)

Barton-Webber, Mrs. Pitcairn, of Bideford.

Bashford, Miss Edith, of Brighton, daughter of Colonel Bashford, A.D.C. to Her Majesty Queen Victoria.

Baslick, William, of Exeter.

Baslick, Mrs., his wife.

Basstone, Mrs., of Clifton.

Bastard, Captain, of the Royal Navy.

Bastard, Edmund R. P., M.A. and double First-Class of Balliol College, Oxford, of Kitley, Devonshire, (1850.)

Bateman, Mrs., wife of Dr. Bateman, of Folkestone.

Bateman, W. J., of Marville Road, London, S.W.

Bates, Miss A. M., of Oxford.

Bates, Cadwallader, M.A. Jesus College, Cambridge.

Bates, Frederick, of Oxford.

Bates, Henry, of Birmingham.

Bates, Mrs., of Oxford.

Bathurst, Captain, of the Royal Navy.

Bathurst, Stuart Eyre, M.A. and Fellow of Merton College, Oxford, late Rector of Kibworth Beauchamp, son of the late General Sir James Bathurst, K.C.B., and grandson of the late Lord Bishop of Norwich. A priest, Canon of Birmingham, at St. Michael's, Aston, Stone, Staffordshire. (1850.)

Baugh, John, of Plymouth.

Baumgardt, Mrs., wife of Major-General J. G. Baumgardt, C.B.

Baxter, Dudley, B.A. University College, Oxford, a descendant of the great Nonconformist divine, Richard Baxter; founder and secretary of the Catholic Newspaper Guild; author. (1896.)

Baxter, J., B.A. St. John's College, Cambridge. (1846.)

Baxter, Mrs. J., his wife. (1846.)

Baxter, Stafford E., brother to Dudley Baxter, B.A.

Bayley, The late Rev. Henry Marmaduke, B.A. Trinity College, Cambridge. A priest (Oblate of St. Charles) at St. Mary's, Bayswater, London, W. (1857.)

Baylis, Miss, formerly an Anglican Nun and Mother Superior of St. Wilfrid's Home, Exeter. (1896.)

Bayly, Francis, of King's College, London. A priest at St. Francis de Sales, Tottenham, London, N.

Beacham, Mrs., now a nun.

Beale, Mrs. F. H. A., of Mount Mellick, Queen's County.

Beale, H. Ignatius, a priest at St. Edward's, Blue Bell Hill, Nottingham. (1877.)

Beamish, Mrs., of Clonakilty, Co. Cork. (1891.)

Beard, Mrs., wife of the Rev. Edward Beard, Methodist minister at Cambridge.

Beardsley, The late Aubrey Vincent, artist. (1897.)

Bearne, David, a Jesuit priest at the Oratory of the Sacred Heart, Bournemouth.

Beauchamp, A., B.A., late an Anglican clergyman. (1889.)

Beaufort, Miss Mary E., of London, E.C.

Beaumont, The ninth Lord (Henry Stapleton), of the 1st Life Guards, Knight Grand Cross of the Holy Sepulchre and Knight of Malta, J.P. for West Riding of Yorkshire, D.L. for Middlesex, had Military Orders from the King of Bavaria and the Grand Dukes of Mecklenburg and Baden. (1869.)

Beaumont, The tenth Lord (Miles Stapleton), brother of the above, Lieutenant-Colonel commanding the 20th Hussars, served in Bechuanaland (1884-85), also in the Soudan. (1880.)

Beaumont, Lady Isabella, daughter of the third Lord Kilmaine and mother of the ninth and tenth Lords Beaumont. (1872.)

Beaumont, Mrs., of Guildford.

Beck, Egerton William, B.A. Sidney Sussex College, Cambridge; barrister.

Beckwith, Mrs., wife of General Beckwith.

Beckworth, Mrs., of Silkworth Hall.

Bedford, Henry, M.A. of St. Peter's College, Cambridge, formerly curate of Christ Church, Hoxton, London; author of *Life of St. Vincent de Paul*, etc., editor of *All-Hallows Annual*. (1851.)

Beere, Mrs., wife of Major Beere, of Southampton.

Beesley, Charles, of Birmingham.

Beesley, John, of Birmingham.

Beesley, Mrs., of Birmingham

Beesley, Thomas, of Birmingham.

Belaney, Robert, M.A. of St. Catherine's College, Cambridge, late Vicar of Arlington. A priest in the Archdiocese of Westminster. (1852.)

Belcher, M.A. of Oxford.

Bell, E. Ingress, architect, of the War Office.

Bell, Mrs. E. Ingress, his wife, and children.

Bell, William, M.A. of St. John's College, Cambridge, formerly an Anglican clergyman.

Bellairs, Miss, daughter of Edmund Bellairs, British Vice-Consul at Biarritz, and niece of General William Bellairs. (1886.)

Bellairs, Miss Ada, sister of Lady Louth. (1895.)

Bellamy, H. E., of Oxford.

Bellasis, The late Mr. Serjeant Edward, son of the late Rev. George Bellasis, vicar of Basilden, Berks. (1850.)

Bellasis, Mrs., wife of the above, and daughter of the late William Garnett, of Peel Park, Salford, and children. (1851.)

Bellew, Evelyn, son of the late J. C. M. Bellew, S.C.L. Oxon., the celebrated elocutionist.

Bellew, Harold Kyrle, his brother, the actor.

Bellew, The late J. C. M., S.C.L., of St. Mary's Hall, Oxford, formerly an Anglican clergyman and a celebrated elocutionist.

Bellew, Mrs., wife of the above.

Bellingham, Sir Henry, Bart., M.A., S.C.L., Exeter College, Oxford, barrister, formerly M.P. for Co. Clare, Ireland, Private Chamberlain to His Holiness Pope Leo XIII; author. (1873.)

Bellingham, The Hon. Lady, second wife of the above, daughter of Captain Clifton and of the late Baroness Grey de Ruthyn.

Belloc, Madame (*née* Bessie Rayner Parkes, a Unitarian), descendant of Dr. Priestley, and a well-known writer.

Belton, Carmichael, M.A. Trinity College, Dublin, formerly a Cowley Brother. (1879.)

Benison, Miss Emily Mary, daughter of James Benison, of Slieve Russell, Co. Cavan, Ireland, sister-in-law of Thomas Arnold, M.A., son of the late Rev. Dr. Arnold.

Benison, Miss Henrietta, sister of the above.

Benjamin, George Whitefield, D.D., late curate of the English Church at Rome. (1877.)

Bennet, Lord, eldest son of the Earl of Tankerville. (1879.)

Bennett, Mrs. Anne Ramsden, cousin of the Right Hon. W. E. Gladstone and of Sir Thomas Gladstone. (1870.)

Bennett, Arthur Wentworth, M.A. Pembroke College, Cambridge, late curate-in-charge of St. Gabriel's, Bromley-by-Bow, London, E. (1898.)

Bennett, John, related to the Tichborne family.

Bennett, Mrs., of Peterborough.

Bennett, Mrs. Leigh, eldest daughter of Sir George Pocock, Bart. (1896.)

Bennett, T. Morden, M.A. Exeter College, Oxford, son of the Vicar of Bournemouth and formerly curate in the Anglican Church. (1888.)

Bennett, Mrs. T. Morden, wife of the above. (1888.)

Bennett, The late Colonel W. H.

Benson, Miss Anne, of Fleetwood.

Benson, John, of Fleetwood.

Bentley, George, of King's College, London.
Bentley, John Francis, the architect of the new Westminster Cathedral. (1862.)
Benton, Miss Anne Eliza, formerly Sister of the Anglican Order of St. Etheldreda. (1874.)
Beresford, Francis G., of the War Office, member of the Council of the Portsmouth Voluntary School Association.
Beresford, Miss, niece of the first Marquis of Waterford.
Beresford, Miss E., niece of the late Most Rev. Lord Decies, late Lord Archbishop of Tuam.
Berdoe, Edward, F.R.C.S., of London, author. (1889.)
Berger, Lewis, of Homerton, London. (1881.)
Berkeley, The late Swinburne, son of the Hon. Fitzhardinge-Berkeley, M.P., and grandson of the fifth Earl Berkeley.
Berlyn, Frederick, of Brixton, London, S.W.
Berlyn, L., brother of the above.
Bernard, Lieutenant-Colonel J. W., of the Royal Artillery, son of the Rev. S. E. Bernard, M.A.; now Private Chamberlain to His Holiness Pope Leo XIII.
Bernard, Mrs., wife of the above, and daughter of General H. Hamilton, C.B.
Bernard, Hon. F. L.
Berney, George, son of Sir John Berney, seventh Bart.
Berney, Miss, daughter of Commander John Berney, and granddaughter of Sir J. Berney, Bart.
Berry, Henry, of Oxford.
Berthon, Captain F., son of the Vicar of Ramsey.

Bertie, Hon. Charles, late of the 47th Regiment, fifth son of the sixth Earl of Abingdon. (1877.)

Bertie, Lady Elizabeth, daughter of the sixth Earl of Abingdon. (1874.)

Bertie, Lady Frances E., her sister, a nun.

Besant, W., late curate of St. Michael's, Shoreditch, London. (1891.)

Best, Mrs. H., of Huddersfield.

Beste, Mrs. R. Digby, wife of Richard Digby Beste, of Botleigh Grange, Hants.

Bethell, Mrs. C. J., daughter of the late Charles J. Manning, brother of the late Cardinal Manning. (1850.)

Bethell, Miss Coralie Mary, a nun, and Superioress of the Convent of the Holy Child, St. Leonards-on-Sea.

Bethell, Mrs. Henry, daughter of the Rev. A. J. Macleane, M.A., editor of *Horace*, etc., and first Principal of Brighton College. (1861.)

Bethell, Mrs. Hugh Nicholas Fitzgerald (née O'Callaghan). (1878.)

Bethell, Miss Jane Rose (now Mrs. F. P. Koe).

Bethell, Mrs. John, daughter of R. Abraham, architect, and sister of the first Lady Westbury. (1847.)

Betteris, Miss Clara, of Oxford.

Betteris, Miss E., her sister.

Bevan, Miss, of Clifton.

Bevan, Mrs., of Queen's Gate Terrace, London.

Bewicke, Mrs. Emma, daughter of the late Rev. Calverley John Bewicke, of Hallaton Hall,

Leicestershire, and wife of the late Calverley Richard Bewicke, of Ripple House, Ripple, Kent. (1877.)

Bewicke, Miss M. Harvey, second daughter of the above. (1892.)

Bewicke, Miss M. Honoria, her cousin, daughter of the late Calverley Bewicke, of Madeira; now a Sister of Charity. (1870.)

Biden, The late F. M., son of the late Sir Christopher Biden, of the Civil Service, Madras. (1839.)

Biden, The late Rev. John, M.A. University College, Oxford; a Jesuit Priest. (1842.)

Biggar, The late Joseph Gillis, late M.P. for Co. Cavan, Ireland, formerly Chairman of the Belfast Water Commissioners. (1876.)

Biggs, Lieutenant-Colonel, of the 60th Rifles.

Billington, Mrs., wife of Major B. Billington. (1877.)

Bingham, The Hon. Albert Edward, fifth son of the fourth Earl of Lucan and godson of H.R.H. the Prince of Wales. (1898.)

Bingham, The Hon. Mrs., wife of the above. (1898.)

Bird, Captain W. C. (1891.)

Birt, William Radcliff, F.R.A.S.

Birks, The late Rev. B. H., M.A. of St. Catherine's Hall, Cambridge, and formerly curate of Arley, Northwich. A priest. (1848.)

Bishop, Charles, solicitor, and Registrar of the Oxford County Court.

Bishop, Mrs., his wife.

Bishop, Miss, her daughter.

Bishop, Edmund, the historian. (1877.)

Bishop, The late Mrs. (*née* O'Connor Morris).

Bishop, L. E., of Oxford.

Bisshop, James Francis Wedderburn, of Bramdean House, Hants.

Bisshop, Philip G. Crosbie, brother of the above.

Bittleston, The late Rev. Henry, M.A. of St. John's College, Oxford, formerly curate of All Saints', Margaret Street, London, W. A priest at SS. Alban and Stephen, St. Albans, Herts. (1849.)

Black, Miss Grace, of the Carl Rosa Opera Company. (1893.)

Blackburn, The late J. W. Vernon, barrister.

Blacklock, Ralph, of Queen's College, Oxford. (1893.)

Blackman, Mrs., of Arundel.

Blackstock, A. M. J., of Liverpool.

Blackwell, Mrs., of Eaton Rise, Ealing, London, W., wife of a barrister. (1894.)

Blair, Miss E., of Twickenham.

Blake, Andrew, J.P. of Galway, Ireland.

Blake, The late Dr. C. Carter, F.G.S., formerly Lecturer on Comparative Anatomy and Zoology at Westminster Hospital, London.

Blake, Edwin, of Birmingham.

Blake, J., of Galway, Ireland. (1845.)

Blakeney, Captain Edward, of the Army Service Corps, cousin of the late Field-Marshal Edward Blakeney, formerly Commander of the Irish Forces. (1892.)

Blakiston, Ralph, of Waterloo, Liverpool, engineer of the Palatine Engineering Company, Liverpool, son of J. R. Blakiston, H.M.I.C.S., late Chief Inspector of Schools. (1880.)

Bleckley, Mrs., wife of an Anglican clergyman, and her children.

Blennerhassett, The late Sir Arthur, third Bart.

Bliss, W. H., M.A. Magdalen College, Oxford, late Rector of Hincksey, late sub-librarian of the Bodleian Library; sometime tutor to H.R.H. the Prince of Naples, K.G.

Bliss, Mrs. W. H., his wife.

Blomfield, Mrs., niece to Lady Matthews.

Blood, Howell Pattison Lewis, M.A. St. Peter's College, Cambridge, late Rector of West Bergholt; now Assistant Diocesan Inspector of Schools in the Archdiocese of Westminster. (1891.)

Bloom, Mark J., L.D.S., R.C.S.I., Surgeon-dentist, of Dublin.

Bloxam, Henry, of Arundel.

Bloxam, Mrs., his wife.

Bloxam, Miss E., their daughter.

Blunden, A., son of Sir D. Blunden, Bart.

Blunt, Lady Anne Isabella, daughter of the eighth Earl of Lovelace, granddaughter of Lord Byron and wife of Wilfrid Scawen Blunt, of Crabbetts Park.

Blunt, Major Francis Scawen, of the Rifle Brigade.

Blunt, Miss N. G., niece of the late E. G. Kirwan Browne, formerly curate of Bawdsey, Suffolk.

Blunt, Mrs., wife of General Blunt, and sister-in-law of the late Vicar of Old Windsor.

Blunt, Mrs., of Crabbetts, near Crawley, Sussex, mother of Major Francis and Wilfrid Blunt.

Blunt, Miss, daughter of the British Consul at Smyrna.

Blunt, Wilfrid Scawen, of Crabbetts Park.

Blyth, Mrs., wife of the Rev. Frederic Cavan Blyth, M.A., curate of Kew-with-Petersham and Chaplain of the Richmond Workhouse, Surrey.

Blythe, Mrs., wife of Captain Blythe.

Board, Mrs., of Cannington.

Bocock, Mrs. W., of Kirtling, Newmarket.

Bodley, William Hamilton, M.A. of Queens' College, Cambridge, formerly Chaplain of Archbishop Tenison's Chapel, Regent Street, London, W. A priest at Our Lady and St. Margaret, Oxburgh, Stoke Ferry, Suffolk. (1851.)

Boetler, Captain.

Boetler, Mrs., his wife.

Bogle, M. J., of Bath.

Bolton, E. M., of Oxford.

Bolton, Captain Gerald.

Bond, The late Rev. J. J., grandson of William Bond of St. Mangan, Cornwall. A priest at the Church of Our Lady and St. Thomas of Canterbury, Dudley.

Bond, The late William Bond, of St. Mangan, Cornwall, with his four sons (all priests) and his four daughters (all nuns).

Bond, The late W. P., a priest.

Bond, The Misses.

Booth, Mrs., of Ashby Manor, Lincoln.

Boothby, Herbert, B.A. Christ Church, Oxford, late curate of St. Augustine's, Stepney, London, E. Now a Trappist Monk at Notre Dame du Lac, Montreal, Canada. (1891.)

Borden, Mrs., wife of Admiral Borden.

Bostock, Arthur Reid, Coroner for West Sussex. (1882.)

Bostock, Mrs., of Cheltenham.

Bostock, The Misses, her daughters.

Boulderson, Captain Joseph, late of the 68th Light Infantry.

Boulderson, Mrs. Clare, his wife, and daughter of the late J. C. M. Bellew, S.C.L.

Boulger, Professor G. S., of Ladbroke Grove, London, W.

Boulton, Harold, of Balliol College, Oxford, journalist and author of *Songs of the North*, etc.

Bovill, Arthur, nephew of the late Lord Justice Bovill.

Bowden, The late Captain Henry, of the Guards, founder of the Catholic Church (St. Mary's) at Chislehurst, Kent.

Bowden, The late Mrs., wife of John William Bowden and fourth daughter of the late Sir John Swinburne, Bart.

Bowden, Charles Henry, son of the late J. W. Bowden. A priest of the Brompton Oratory, London, S.W.

Bowden, The late Miss, daughter of Captain Bowden, a nun.

Bowden, Miss Emily, her sister.

Bowden, Henry G. S., son of Captain Bowden, late captain in the Scots Fusilier Guards. A priest and for sometime Superior of the Brompton Oratory, London, S.W., author and translator of Hettinger.

Bowden, The late Rev. John Edward, son of the late J. W. Bowden. A priest of the Brompton Oratory, author of *Memoirs of the late Rev. F. W. Faber, D.D., M.A. Oxon.*

Bowden, The late Rev. William J., formerly lieutenant 97th Regiment, son of Captain Bowden; a priest of the Brompton Oratory.

Bowdler, T., M.A., late curate of Tenison's Chapel, Regent Street, London, W.

Bower, Commander Graham, late of the Royal Navy, son of Admiral Bower.

Bowles, Miss Alice, sister of the Rev. F. S. Bowles. (1892.)

Bowles, Miss Emily, authoress, sister of the Rev. J. C. B. Bowles, an Anglican clergyman. (1843.)

Bowles, Frederick S., B.A. Exeter College, Oxford, formerly an Anglican clergyman. A priest at Harrow.

Bown, The late Rev. Frederick, Associate of King's College, London, and late curate of St. Philip's, Clerkenwell, London. A priest at St. Anne's, Little Albany Street, Regent's Park, London, N.W. (1865.)

Bowrie, Thomas, of Barnhill House, Lanark, N.B.

Bowrie, The late Mrs. T.

Bowring, Algernon, cousin of Lord Ashcombe.

Bowring, The late Rev. C. A., B.A. Trinity College, Cambridge, son of the late Sir John Bowring. A Jesuit Priest. (1830.)

Bowring, Lewin, C.B., son of the late Sir John Bowring of the Bengal Civil Service, Private Secretary to the late Lord Canning. (1830.)

Bowring, The late Miss, daughter of the late Sir John Bowring, a nun. (1830.)

Bowyer, The late Sir George, Bart., D.C.L. of Oxford, Knight of the Order of St. John of Jerusalem, Knight Grand Cross of the Order of St. Gregory the Great, Knight Commander of the Order of Pius, President of the League of St. Sebastian for the Recovery of the Temporal Power of the Pope, Vice-President of the Aged Poor Society, late M.P. for County Wexford and a barrister. (1850.)

Bowyer, Mrs., sister-in-law of the late Sir George Bowyer, Bart. (1851.)

Boyce, Mrs., wife of the Rev. W. Boyce, M.A. of Cheltenham College.

Boycott, Mrs. Digby.

Boycott, Essex Digby.

Boycott, Mrs. Essex Digby.

Boycott, Comtesse Geraldine Digby, Canoness of the Royal Chapter of St. Anne, Münich.

Boycott, Mrs. Mabel Digby, a nun.

Boyd, Miss C., of Kilburn Orphanage. (1894.)

Boyd, R. C. A., B.A. Corpus Christi College, Cambridge.

Boyd, Mrs., wife of Colonel Boyd of Jersey, and family.

Boyle, E., of Brighton.

Boyle, Lady.

Boynton, Miss Alice, daughter of the Rev. Griffith Boynton, M.A., Rector of Bramiston, Yorkshire, a nun.

Boynton, Captain G. H. L., late of the 17th Lancers, son of Sir Henry Boynton, ninth Bart., of Bramston, and brother of the Rev. Griffith Boynton, M.A.

Boynton, Mrs., his wife.
Boys, The late Miss Catherine, foundress of The Orphanage, Middle Street, Deal, Kent. (1852.)
Bradish, Henry B., son of General Bradish. (1891.)
Bradley, The Misses, of Newton, Queen's County, Ireland.
Bradley, William, of Oxford.
Bradney, John, son of an Anglican clergyman.
Bradshaw, Miss Jane, of Fleetwood.
Bradshaw, John, of Fleetwood.
Bradshaw, Joseph, of Fleetwood.
Bradshaw, Mark, of Fleetwood.
Bradshaw, Peter, of Fleetwood.
Bradshaw, Richard, of Fleetwood.
Bradshaw, William, of Fleetwood.
Bradshaw, Mrs., wife of John Bradshaw, Inspector of Schools, Madras, and sister-in-law to Thomas Arnold, M.A., son of the late Rev. Dr. Arnold.
Bradshawe, George, sometime assistant-master at St. Joseph's College, Clapham, London, S.W. (1871.)
Bradshaw-Isherwood, H., B.A. of Trinity Hall, Cambridge, barrister at law, eldest son of H. Bradshaw-Isherwood, of Marple Hall, Stockton, and of Bradshaw Hall, Lancashire. (1889.)
Bradstreet, The late Sir John Valentine, Bart., of Castilla, Clontarf, Co. Dublin, President of the Dublin Council of the Society of St. Vincent de Paul. (1855.)
Bradstreet, Miss, daughter of the late Sir S. Bradstreet, Bart. (1855.)

Brady, The late William Mazière, D.D., M.A. of Trinity College, Dublin, Chaplain to a former Lord-Lieutenant of Ireland, Chamberlain to H.H. Pope Leo XIII., author. (1865.)

Brady, The late Mrs. W. M., wife of the above. (1865.)

Braine, Miss, of Buckfast Abbey, Devonshire.

Brampton, Lord (Sir Henry Hawkins) late Judge of the Queen's Bench Division. (1898.)

Brand, George Henry, of King's College, London, and London University, Surgeon to Nazareth House, Northampton, the asylum for aged poor, also Surgeon to the Foresters, Oddfellows, and Governor of the Northampton Nursing Association. (1892.)

Brand, Mrs., his wife. (1892.)

Brand, The late Miss, sister of Viscount Hampden, late Speaker of the House of Commons. (1854.)

Brasnell, H. G. J., late curate of Brastide, Kent. (1852.)

Bray, F., "Father Dunstan," of the Norwich Community, under " Father Ignatius ". (1879.)

Bray, Mrs., of Derby.

Braye (Alfred Thomas Townshend Verney-Cave), fifth Lord, M.A. Christ Church, Oxford, formerly captain 3rd Battalion Leicestershire Regiment, J.P. and D.L. for Leicestershire and Northamptonshire, Knight of Malta. (1870.)

Brenan, Mrs., wife of Colonel Brenan, of Clontarf, Dublin.

Brenan, Mrs. W. H., of Coolbawn, Castle Comer.

Breton, A. Gordon, solicitor.

Brevens, late William E., of Oreux, Gallicra. (1898.)

Brewer, H. W., architect.
Brewer, Mrs., wife of Colonel Brewer.
Brewer, William, solicitor.
Brewer, Mrs., his wife.
Brice, Albert Edward, of Hanover Square, London, W., Assistant Secretary of the Japan Society.
Brice, E. C., of Bridgwater.
Bridgeman, Mrs., of Frogmore, Herefordshire.
Bridgeman, The late Mrs., cousin of the Right Rev. Dr. Patterson, Bishop of Emmaus.
Bridger, Miss F. H., of Albion Place, Grantham, Lincolnshire. (1897.)
Bridger, Mrs. F. L., mother of the above. (1892.)
Bridges, Mrs., wife of the well-known Positivist writer. (1896.)
Bridges, The late C. B., M.A. of Oriel College, Oxford, formerly an Anglican clergyman. (1845.)
Bridges, Matthew, of Magdalen Hall, Oxford, formerly an Anglican clergyman, and a contributor to the *Edinburgh Review*. (1850.)
Bridgett, Charles, son of the late Joseph Bridgett, of Derby.
Bridgett, Gregson, his brother.
Bridgett, Assistant-Commissary-General G.
Bridgett, The late Rev. Roland, brother of the late Rev. T. E. Bridgett, a Redemptorist Priest; British Consul at Buenos Aires. (1855.)
Bridgett, The late Rev. Thomas Edward, of St. John's College, Cambridge, a Redemptorist Priest at St. Mary's, Clapham, London, S.W., author of *Life*

of the Blessed John Fisher, Our Lady's Dowry, Ritual of the New Testament, etc. (1850.)

Bridgman, The late F. Orlando, relative of the Earl of Bradford.

Bridson, Miss, daughter of Colonel Bridson, vicar's churchwarden of St. John's, Torquay. (1890.)

Briggs, A., of Sheffield.

Briggs, Hugh Currer, M.A. of Worcester College, Oxford, late curate of St. Stephen's, Devonport, and of All Saints', Plymouth. (1893.)

Briggs, The late Sir John Henry, chief clerk to the Admiralty. (1896.)

Brindle, Miss Ellen, of Fleetwood.

Brinkman, Sidney, late Associate of the English Church Union, Llantarnam. (1886.)

Bristow, Miss, daughter of Captain Bristow.

Bristow, Miss F., her sister.

Britten, James, F.L.S., formerly of the Natural History Museum, now Honorary Secretary of the Catholic Truth Society, and Knight of St. Gregory; author.

Britten, Major T. E., of the Bengal Staff Corps.

Brockman, Colonel, of Folkestone.

Brodie, Caithness, M.A. Trinity College, Cambridge, brother of Brodie of Brodie, late curate of St. Stephen's, Kensington, London, W.

Bromage, R. Raikes, M.A. Clare College, Cambridge, and late rector of Christ Church, Frome, Somerset. (1894.)

Bromby, Charles Hamilton, M.A. St. Edmund's Hall, Oxford, a barrister, and formerly Attorney-

General of Tasmania ; son of the Anglican Bishop Bromley.

Bromhead, Miss, daughter of Sir E. F. Bromhead, Bart.

Bromley, H. W., of Queen's College, Oxford ; a priest at Our Lady Star of the Sea, Ilfracombe.

Broughton, George, of Stamford.

Brown, The late Rev. Algernon, son of Dr. Brown of Brighton; a priest of the Paulist Community, New York.

Brown, Mrs. Andrew, cousin of the late Protestant bishop, the Right Rev. Dr. Forbes.

Brown, C. E., one of the leading merchants of Rangoon. (1894.)

Brown, Mrs. D., wife of Captain David Brown, 14th Light Dragoons.

Brown, Francis C. G., son of the late Rev. J. C. Brown, M.A., vicar of Great Clacton, Essex ; a priest at Leyton, Essex. (1883.)

Brown, Frederick D. H., brother of the above; a priest at Leyton, Essex. (1886.)

Brown, Frederick, late of the East India Company's Service.

Brown, George, of Liverpool,

Brown, Henry, of the East India Company's Service.

Brown, John, of Fleetwood.

Brown, Joseph M. Sherer, M.A. St. John's College, Cambridge, late curate at Penkridge and Clewer, son of the late Rev. J. C. Brown, M.A., for many years vicar of Great Clacton, Essex ; a priest (Oblate of St. Charles) at St. Mary's, Bayswater, London, W. (1882.)

Brown, Hon. Mrs., granddaughter of the late Most Rev. Lord Decies, Lord Archbishop of Tuam.

Brown, W., B.L. of Glasgow University, formerly secretary to Colonel Olcutt, the Theosophist. (1886.)

Brown, W. A., of Manchester. (1886.)

Brown, William, of Liverpool.

Brown, W. H., B.A. of the London University.

Brown, Mrs. William, of Devonshire. (1898.)

Brown, W. Kenworthy, of Calne, Wilts, B.A. of Exeter College, Oxford. (1882.)

Brown, Miss, of Ridgeway, Devonshire. (1886.)

Brownbill, John, M.A. St. John's College, Cambridge.

Browne, Miss Ada, of Colchester. (1892.)

Browne, Hon. Arthur, brother of Lord Kilmaine. (1881.)

Browne, Miss Catherine, of Colchester. (1893.)

Browne, The late Edward G. Kirwan, B.A. Trinity College, Dublin, formerly curate of Bawdsey, Suffolk, nephew of the late Sir W. Nott, K.C.B.; author of *Annals of the Tractarian Movement, Trials of Faith*, etc., formerly Professor of Classics at Trinity College, Dublin, and also at St. Joseph's College, Clapham, London, S.W. (1845.)

Browne, The late Mrs., wife of the above. (1845.)

Browne, Captain E. F. Madder, author.

Browne, Mrs., his wife.

Browne, E. G. Stanley, B.A. of St. Edmund's Hall, Oxford.

Browne, Henry B., M.A. New College, Oxford, son of J. Wilson Browne, of Birmingham; a Jesuit Priest, and Professor of University College, Dublin, Fellow of the Royal University of Ireland. (1874.)

Browne, James, LL.D.

Browne, James, of Brownville, Co. Galway.

Browne, Joseph M., grandson of Captain Browne, R.N., of Sligo.

Browne, Mrs. J. Wilson, of Solihull, Warwickshire. (1890.)

Browne, The late Mrs., wife of the late Major Browne, and mother of the late E. G. Kirwan Browne, B.A., late curate of Bawdsey, Suffolk. (1846.)

Browne, R. J., of Liverpool.

Browne, Valentine, C.E.

Browne, W. J. Carr, M.A., late curate of Dudley, Lickfold.

Browne, William Percy Wilson, son of J. Wilson Browne, of Birmingham, and brother of the Rev. Henry Browne, S.J. (1897.)

Brownlow, Rev. William Robert, M.A. Trinity College, Cambridge, formerly curate of Marychurch, Torquay. Now Bishop of Clifton.

Bruce, Eric Stuart, M.A. of Exeter College, Oxford, F.R.Met.S., Inventor of the Bruce War Balloon.

Bruce, The late General Michael, of the Coldstream Guards, served in the Crimea with the Grenadier Guards. (1883.)

Bruce, Mrs. Millicent Knight.

Brundritt, The late Rev. R. W., M.A. Christ College, Cambridge, formerly an Anglican clergyman ; a priest.

Bryden, J. S., of Stafford.

Buchan, The late David, Earl of.

Buchan, The late Elizabeth, Countess of, widow of the twelfth Earl.

Buchanan, A. M., of Edinburgh.

Buckingham, Leicester, author of *The Bible in the Middle Ages*, etc.

Buccleuch, The late Charlotte, Duchess of, daughter of the second Marquis of Bath. (1860.)

Buckle, Colonel.

Buckle, Mrs., his wife.

Buckle, The late Rev. Walter, M.A. of Exeter College, Oxford ; a priest.

Buckle, W. H., Controller of Customs.

Buckler, Albert, D.D., S.T.M., a Dominican Priest at the Dominican Priory, Woodchester, Stroud, Gloucestershire. (1845.)

Buckler, Charles Alban, his brother, architect and Surrey Herald Extraordinary. (1844.)

Buckler, Edmund, his brother, a Dominican Priest at the Dominican Priory, Newcastle-on-Tyne. (1845.)

Buckler, Reginald, his brother, a Dominican Priest at the Dominican Priory, Haverstock Hill, London, N.W. (1845.)

Buckridge, George, a Jesuit Priest, now in Australia.

Bulfield, A. P., of Springbank, Lancaster, and family.

Bulford, Miss Caroline Mary, of Leamington. (1897.)

Bull, Gilbert Vincent, of Tenby, late of Highgate, London, N.; a Gilbertine Monk at Spilsby Priory, Lincolnshire.

Bullen, Mrs., of Boulogne.

Bullen, Miss, her daughter.

Buller, Captain William Edward, late of the 14th Light Dragoons.

Bulley, J., B.A. Magdalen College, Oxford.

Bullivant, T. P., B.A. Balliol College, Oxford, of Homewood, Beckenham; a priest at the Collegio Beda, Rome. (1885.)

Bulmer, John, M.A., B.D., Mus. Bac., and Fellow of Durham University, late Chaplain of the Proprietary Chapel of Gibside, Northumberland. (1891.)

Bunn, Alfred, the librettist.

Burchett, Philip, author of well-known works on geometry.

Burchett, Richard, late Head Master of the South Kensington Art Schools.

Burder, The late Rev. G., M.A. Magdalen Hall, Oxford, formerly curate at Ruardean. A Cistercian Abbot. (1846.)

Burder, Mrs. H., sister-in-law of the Right Rev. Bishop Burder.

Burgoyne, Captain J. O.

Burke, Miss Caroline, daughter of Sir John Burke, second Baronet, of Marble Hill, Galway. (1855.)

Burke, Lady, daughter of the late Right Hon. J. Calcraft. (1855.)

Burke, Major.

Burke, Philip, of Oxford.
Burn, Mrs. Isabel, of Grange-over-Sands.
Burn, Miss, daughter of the above.
Burn, W. P., M.A. Downing College, Cambridge, late incumbent near Rotherham.
Burnand, Francis Cowley, B.A. Trinity College, Cambridge. Author of *Happy Thoughts*, etc., now editor of *Punch*.
Burnand, Mrs., his wife, and family.
Burnell, Miss M., of Cannington.
Burnell, Miss R., of Cannington.
Burnett, Captain.
Burnett, Mrs., wife of the above.
Burnham, A., of Oxford.
Burnham, H., of Cannington.
Burns, The late James, publisher, of Paternoster Row and Granville Mansions, Orchard Street, London, W. (1846.)
Burns, The late Mrs. Margaret Jean, wife of the above, formerly a Presbyterian and then a member of the English Church. (1846.)
Burns, The Misses, her five daughters, all nuns.
Burrell, Mrs., of Bolton Hall, Alnwick, sister of Major Browne, of Callaly Castle, Northumberland. (1893.)
Burrows, G. R., M.A. of Queen's College, Oxford, formerly an Anglican clergyman, and Head Master of Coleford Grammar School, Forest of Dean. (1878.)
Burrows, Mrs., great-granddaughter of the late Most

Rev. Lord Decies, D.D., Lord Archbishop of Tuam.

Burton, J. Harris, of Glenalmond College, Scotland, late Incumbent of St. John's, Selkirk, N.B.

Burton, The late Rev. Thomas, M.A. of Cambridge University, late curate of St. James's, Enfield: a priest.

Bushell, J., of East Dulwich, S.E.

Busk, Miss S., author of *Sages from the Far East, Contemporary Annals of Rome, Folklore of Rome*, etc.

Buswell, Miss, of Clifton.

Butcher, Miss Ives, fourth daughter of the late Lieutenant-Colonel Butcher, H.E.I.C.S., cousin of the late Right Rev. the Bishop of Meath and of the Provost of King's College, Cambridge, a Congregationalist; now a nun at Bristol.

Butcher, P., of Fleetwood.

Bute, The third Marquis of (John Patrick Crichton-Stuart), LL.D., and M.A. Christ Church, Oxford, K.T., Knight Grand Cross of the Holy Sepulchre, Knight of the Order of St. Gregory the Great, and Hereditary Keeper of Rothesay Castle. (1869.)

Butland, Benjamin J., B.A. Trinity College, Cambridge; a priest at St. John the Baptist, Great Hayward, Staffordshire. (1844.)

Butler, David, of Fleetwood.

Butler, Miss Gertrude, sister of the President of Trinity College, Cambridge, for many years an Anglican sister. (1896.)

Butler, Colonel James, of Dublin, late of the 26th Madras Infantry. (1895.)

Butler, Pierce, of Cahirciveen.

Butler, Mrs. Pierce, his wife.

Butler, Robert, M.A. Brasenose College, Oxford, formerly an Anglican clergyman, and Warden of the House of Charity, Soho, London.

Butler, Theobald, son of Colonel Butler. (1884.)

Butler, Lady, daughter of the late T. J. Thompson, M.A. Trinity College, Cambridge, and wife of Lieutenant-General Sir William Butler, K.C.B., Commanding the Forces in South Africa; painter of "The Roll Call," etc.

Butler, Captain W. H.

Butterfield, H. S., son of the Rev. H. Butterfield, M.A., Rector of Fulmer, Bucks.

Byford, A. M., of Redcar. (1895.)

Byford, Mrs., wife of the above. (1895.)

Byles, Roussel Davids, B.A. and late Scholar of Balliol College, Oxford, now Professor at St. Edmund's College, Ware, Herts. (1894.)

Byles, William Esdale, nephew of W. P. Byles, proprietor of the *Bradford Observer.*

Byrne, The late Mrs. Julia Clara Pitt, granddaughter of the late Sir Wadsworth Busk, Attorney-General of the Isle of Man, daughter of the late celebrated Hans Busk, and wife of the late William Pitt Byrne, son of the founder of *The Morning Post;* author of various esteemed works. (1860.)

Cahill, Mrs., wife of Major Cahill, of the Bombay Staff Corps.

Calcutt, Francis Macnamara, formerly M.P. for Co. Clare, Ireland.

Calman, Alfred J., B.A. of Worcester College, Oxford, father of the Rev. A. J. Calman, priest at St. Benedict's Priory, Colwich. (1845.)

Calmar, John James, formerly a barrister.

Camm, John Brooke M., M.A. Brasenose College, Oxford, late Rector of Monkton Wyld, Dorset; and formerly of the 12th Royal Lancers. (1891.)

Camm, Reginald Percy J., M.A. Keble College, Oxford, son of the above, late curate of St. Agnes, Kennington Park, London, S.E. Now a Benedictine Monk at St. Thomas's Abbey, Erdington, Birmingham, author. (1892.)

Camm, Robert, B.A. of Worcester College, Oxford, uncle of the Rev. Dom Bede Camm. (1891.)

Camoys, The Lady, daughter of Robert Russell Carew, of Carpenders Park, Herts; wife of the sixth Baron Camoys. (1897.)

Campbell, The late Archibald D. L., of Lochnell, Argyllshire.

Campbell, The late A. D. R., M.A., formerly curate of Ashley, Newmarket. (1844.)

Campbell, The late Rev. Donald C. V., son of James Archibald Campbell, of Inverane; a Jesuit Priest.

Campbell, Sir Gilbert Edward, Bart., of Carrick-Buoy Hall, Ballyshannon, Co. Donegal, Ireland, Knight Commander of the Orders of Isabella the Catholic and Charles III. of Spain, of the Holy Sepulchre, and formerly captain of the 92nd Highlanders.

Campbell, Miss, of Edinburgh; now a nun at St. Vincent's Hospital, Dublin. (1889.)

Campbell, Miss, formerly Associate of the Clewer Sisterhood. (1865.)

Campbell, Miss, of Craigie, Ayrshire, N.B. (1898.)

Campbell, Mrs. (*née* Carr), of Durham.

Campbell, Mrs. Minton, wife of the late member for North Staffordshire. (1878.)

Campbell, Robert, advocate, and J.P. for Ayrshire, Scotland.

Campbell, Mrs. R., his wife, and family.

Campbell, Robert, M.A. of Cambridge University, late Chaplain to the Protestant Bishop of Aberdeen, and Canon of Perth Cathedral.

Campion, Mrs., of Bristol.

Cample, Arthur, of Plymouth.

Cannon, Mrs., wife of General Cannon, of Folkestone.

Cannon, The Misses, her daughters.

Canterbury, The Viscountess, daughter of the Hon. Frederick Walpole, M.P., and sister of the Earl of Orford. (1897.)

Capel, Cecil, of Spilsby, Lincolnshire. (1898.)

Capes, The late John More, M.A. of Oxford University.

Capes, Miss, his sister.

Capes, Frederick Proctor.

Carden, Captain Warner W.

Carew, Mr., of the War Office.

Carey-Elwes, V. D. H., of Billing Hall, Northamptonshire. (1874.)

Carey-Elwes, Mrs., his wife. (1874.)

Carey-Elwes, Captain Windsor, late of the Scots Guards. (1874.)

Carlisle, Mrs., wife of Captain Carlisle.

Carmichael, Miss Mary, musical composer.

Carmichael, Montgomery, author and Vice-Consul at Leghorn, brother of the above.

Carmichael, Mrs., wife of the above.

Carnegie, John, solicitor.

Carnsew, Miss, sister-in-law of the Very Rev. Benjamin Morgan Cowie, B.D., Dean of Manchester.

Carr, A. R., of Leeds.

Carr, J. W., of Leeds.

Carrington, Miss, daughter of an Anglican clergyman.

Carritt, John Price, of Shoreham. (1887.)

Carroll, J. J., son of Dr. Carroll.

Carson, William Robert, of Trinity College, Dublin, grandson of the late Protestant Bishop of Kilmore, and nephew of the Rev. Dr. Joseph Carson, Vice-Provost of Trinity College, Dublin; a priest at St. Joseph's, Derby. (1893.)

Carter, Miss Annie, of Leicester.

Carter, James, a priest, Monsignor, at St. Francis of Assisi, Midhurst, Chamberlain to His Holiness the late Pope Pius IX.

Carter, Joseph F., of Kimbolton.

Carter, Thomas, of Leicester.

Carthew, Miss, daughter of Admiral Carthew.

Cartnell, Robert E., of Clapham, London, S.W.

Case, Captain F. (1851.)

Case, Mrs., wife of Major Case, of Canterbury. (1882.)

Case-Walker, Captain, of Beckford Hall, Gloucestershire.

Case-Walker, Mrs., his wife.

Cassell, Henry, of Rome. (1879.)

Cassell, The late Mrs., his mother. (1879.)

Cassell, W. St. John.

Casson, Captain, of the 5th West York Militia.

Casson, Mrs., his wife.

Casson, William, son of the late Rev. R. B. Casson, M.A., of Haynes Vicarage, Bedford. (1893.)

Castle, H. C. P., B.A. Magdalen College, Oxford. (1894.)

Castle-Stuart, The late Earl of (Edward). (1834.)

Caswall, The late Rev. Edward, M.A. Brasenose College, Oxford, formerly curate at Stratford-under-the-Castle; a priest of the Brompton Oratory, London, S.W., author of *Hymns and Poems*. (1845.)

Catlin, Miss, daughter of the late Rector of Broadway.

Cato, Thomas E., M.A. Oriel College, Oxford, late Vicar of Wye, Kent. (1891.)

Cator, Henry William: a priest of the Brompton Oratory, London, S.W.

Cator, William Ralph, of Chippenham, nephew of the above. (1898.)

Cavanagh, Mrs., of Shuirowe, Birr, Kings County. (1884.)

Cave, Charles, of Ditcham Park, Petersfield, Hants. (1892.)

Cave, Henry, brother of the Hon. Sir Lewis William Cave, Judge of the Queen's Bench Division. (1881.)

Cave-Browne-Cave, The late Ambrose, M.A. of Oxford University, late Rector of Stretton-en-le-Field, son of the late Sir John Robert Cave-Browne-Cave, Bart. (1888.)

Cave-Browne-Cave, The late Rev. Verney, M.A. Exeter College, Oxford, brother of the above; a priest, at St. Peter's, Leamington. (1874.)

Cavendish, Charles W. M.A. Trinity College, Oxford, formerly Rector of Little Casterton, member of the Camden Society. (1850.)

Cavendish, The late Mrs. C. W., wife of the above. (1850.)

Chabot, Edwin, late churchwarden of St. James's, Hatcham.

Challis, The late H. W., M.A. and Scholar of Merton College, Oxford.

Chambers, The late Dr. Frederick, L.S.A.L., J.P., of Vicarage Crescent, Margate, for many years member of the Town Council of Margate, and thrice Mayor, he was mainly instrumental in improving the sanitary condition of that town.

Chambers, J., B.A. Worcester College, Oxford.

Chambers, Miss, formerly Mother-Eldress of the Devonport Sisters, under the late Miss Sellon; now a nun.

Chambers, Miss M., of Stamford.

Chambers, Thomas King, M.A. Christ Church, Oxford, M.D., F.R.C.S. of London, Honorary Physician to H.R.H. the Prince of Wales, Senior Consulting Physician of St. Mary's Hospital, London, author of *Some Effects of the Climate of Italy*, *Ecstasy*, *Somnambulism*, etc.

Chandler, J., B.A. of All Souls College, Oxford.

Chandless, Miss, daughter of the Q.C.; now a nun.

Chapman, Mrs. Charles Capel, daughter of the late Sir W. Crofton, Bart., of Longford House, Co. Sligo, Ireland. (1880.)

Chapman, John, M.A. of Christ Church, Oxford, late Curate of St. Pancras, London, son of the Archdeacon of Ely. Now a Benedictine Monk and Sub-Prior of St. Thomas's Abbey, Erdington, Birmingham. (1890.)

Chapman, Horace Edward, M.A. Downing College, Cambridge, late Rector of Donhead St. Andrew, near Salisbury, and brother-in-law of the Rev. Philip Fletcher, M.A., Master of the Guild of Ransom. (1894.)

Chapman, Mrs., wife of the above. (1894.)

Chapman, Miss, their daughter. (1894.)

Chapman, John, a priest, till lately Professor of Moral Philosophy at Ushaw College, now at St. Catherine, Penrith, Cumberland.

Chapman, J. H., M.A. Pembroke College, Oxford, F.S.A., formerly an Anglican clergyman; now a barrister.

Chapman, Mrs., wife of the above.

Charnley, Thomas, of Fleetwood.

Charnock, Miss L., of Fleetwood.

Chase, J., of Fleetwood.

Chattaway, Arthur L., a priest at St. Joseph's, Nechells, Birmingham.

Chatterley, Mrs., of London.

Chatterley, Miss, her daughter.

Chatterton, The late Lady, authoress.

Chatto, The late William, M.A. Emmanuel College, Cambridge, built the Catholic Church at Mary Church, near Torquay, Devonshire.

Cheeney, Alfred Denton, of Finchley. (1875.)

Chelsea, The Viscountess, daughter of Lord Alington, and wife of Viscount Chelsea, eldest son of Earl Cadogan, Lord-Lieutenant of Ireland. (1891.)

Cheries, Miss, of London.

Chese, J., of Fleetwood.

Chesshire, Miss Laura, daughter of an Anglican clergyman.

Chestor, Miss Elizabeth, of Shepherd's Bush, London, W. (1891.)

Chetwode, Miss Janet Wilmot, daughter of Edmund and Lady Janet Wilmot Chetwode, of Woodbrook, Queen's County, Ireland.

Chetwode, Miss Wilmot, her sister.

Chichester, Captain, late of the Dragoon Guards.

Child, George, of Whetstone. (1870.)

Child, Mrs. Kate, of Streatham, London, S.W.

Chirol, Mrs., wife of the Rev. Thomas A. A. Chirol, M.A., second master of St. Chad's College, Denstone, Derbyshire.

Chisholm, The late Mrs. Caroline (the emigrant's friend), wife of Major Archibald Chisholm.

Chisholm, Miss, sister of Mrs. Gray, wife of the late E. Dwyer Gray, formerly M.P. and Lord Mayor of Dublin.

Chisholm, The late Dr. S., R.A., Deputy Inspector-General of Army Hospitals.

Chittenden, Dr.

Cholmondeley, The late Rev. C. C., B.A. Balliol College, Oxford, son of the late Rector of Moreton Say, Salop, nephew of the late Right Rev. Reginald Heber, D.D., Bishop of Calcutta, and of Richard Heber, the celebrated bibliographer and scholar; a priest, and Canon of Shrewsbury. (1850.)

Cholmondeley, Reginald, nephew of Sir Tatton Sykes, Bart.

Christian, Miss Julia, daughter of the Rev. W. B. Christian, of Milntown, Ramsay, Isle of Man, now a nun.

Christie, The late Rev. Albany J., M.A. and Fellow Oriel College, Oxford, First Class in Classics, Second in Mathematics; a Jesuit Priest, author of several religious dramas. (1845.)

Christie, Henry James, B.A. Christ Church, Oxford; a priest at the Brompton Oratory, London, S.W.

Christie, Mrs., of Stanley Crescent, Notting Hill, London, W.

Christie, Miss Julia.

Christmas, Miss G. Veronica.

Christmas, W. A. Osborne, nephew of W. Christmas, formerly M.P. and D.L. of Whitfield, Co. Waterford, Ireland; father of the above, and Private Chamberlain to H.H. Pope Leo XIII.; now resident in Rome.

Christmas, Mrs., his wife.

Church, Stephen, of Londonderry, Ireland.

Churchill, Miss, daughter of Major-General Churchill.

Church-Lean, Mrs. Ross (Florence Marryat), author of several novels, and daughter of the late Captain Marryat, R.N., the novelist.

Clare, The late Countess of. (1842.)

Clark, Miss H., of Norwich.

Clark, The late Rev. Joseph George, M.A. of Magdalen College, Oxford; a Passionist Priest. (1864.)

Clark, Mrs., of Plymouth.

Clarke, Albert George, M.A. of Durham University, late Curate of Middleton, Leeds, and formerly of St. Mary's, York; a priest at St. Joseph's, Queen's Road, Aldershot. (1889.)

Clarke, Charles Henry, B.A. Sidney-Sussex College, Cambridge, formerly lieutenant in the 8th Middlesex R. V.; a priest, and Assistant Chaplain at North Hyde Schools, Middlesex. (1886.)

Clarke, Dr. C. H.

Clarke, Mrs., his wife.

Clarke, C. H., of Bath.

Clarke, Danvers, M.A. of Exeter College, Oxford, late Vicar of Iping, Sussex, and Rural Dean, at one time Professor at the Catholic University College, Kensington, London, W. (1851.)

Clarke, David, solicitor.

Clarke, John, B.A. Trinity College, Dublin, late a clergyman at East London, South Africa, formerly of the Missionary College, Dorchester. (1897.)

Clarke, Mrs. Lane, of Guernsey.

Clarke, Miss Lane, her daughter.

Clarke, Mrs., of Bristol.

Clarke, Mrs. (*née* Dearden), wife of P. J. Clarke, of Newcastle-on-Tyne. (1889.)

Clarke, Mrs., wife of the Rev. Prebendary Clarke, of Taunton. (1877.)

Clarke, Richard J., M.A. of Trinity and Fellow of St. John's College, Oxford; a Jesuit Priest, late Rector of Wimbledon College, London, S.W., now Master of Campion Hall, Oxford; author. (1868.)

Clarke, Mrs., wife of the Rev. John Clarke, of East London, South Africa. (1897.)

Clarke, Robert F., M.R.C.S.; a priest, D.D. of Rome, and late of St. John of Jerusalem, Great Ormond Street, London, W.C.; now chaplain to a Convent at Chiswick, London, W., author.

Clarke, W. H., of Spilsby, Lincolnshire. (1898.)

Clarke, William Robert, B.A. Christ's College, Cambridge, late Curate of Bray, near Maidenhead; son of the late Archdeacon of Liverpool. (1898.)

Clarkson, The Misses, of Fleetwood.

Clavering, Mrs., of Callaly.

Clayton, Miss C., a Carmelite Nun.

Clayton, Mrs. H., of Ingatestone.

Clegg, Albert, of Highbury, London, N. (1886.)

Clegg, Miss, a Sister of Mercy.

Clements, Cyril, nephew of the Rev. Gilbert Vincent Bull.

Clements, H. J., of New College, Oxford.

Clerk, The late George E., grandson of the late Right Hon. Sir George Douglas Clerk.

Clerke, Miss A. M.

Cleveland, William Cayley Henry. (1891.)

Clevelands, Mrs. W. C. H. (1891.)

Cliffe, A., son of Colonel Cliffe.

Cliffe, A. J., D.L., of Bellevue, Wexford, Ireland. (1845.)

Cliffe, Captain.

Cliffe, Colonel.

Cliffe, The Misses, his daughters.

Clifford, Miss Catherine, daughter of Captain Robert Clifford, of Cara Cottage, Co. Cavan, Ireland. (1872.)

Clifford, Frederick Charles Alfred, M.A. Trinity College, Cambridge, late Curate of Elveden, Suffolk.

Clifford, Lady, wife of the late Major-General Sir Henry Clifford, V.C.

Clifford, Mrs. (*née* Catherine Bath, of Bryn-y-mor, Swansea), wife of Walter Clifford, second son of the late Sir Charles Clifford, Bart., of Hatherton Hall, Cannock. (1883.)

Clifford, Mrs., of Carne, Co. Cavan, Ireland.

Clifton, Harry, civil engineer under the Government of India. (1887.)

Clifton, Colonel Talbot, of Lytham, Lancashire, brother of the late Lord Donington, and formerly M.P. for North Lancashire.

Clint, J., of Liverpool.

Clutterbuck, Miss, sister-in-law of the Rev. Sir J. C. Barrow, Bart. (1860.)

Clutton, Henry J., a priest at St. Mary Magdalene's, Brighton.

Clutton, Henry, architect.

Coates, Mrs., of Reigate.

Cobb, Miss M., of Bath.

Cobbold, H. Chevallier, a Suffolk squire. (1880.)

Cobbold, Mrs., his wife. (1880.)

Cochrane, Lady Catherine Elizabeth, daughter of the tenth Earl of Dundonald.

Cochrane, Mrs. H. F., of Avenue Road, Grantham, Lincolnshire.

Cocks, John J. T. Somers, M.A. Exeter College, Oxford, late Rector of Sheviock, Cornwall. (1856.)

Codd, Mrs., wife of the Rev. Canon Codd, M.A., Vicar of Beaminster, Dorset, and Rural Dean. (1888.)

Codd, The late Mrs., wife of the Rev. Edward Thornton Codd, M.A., Vicar of Bishop's Tachbrook, Warwickshire. (1877.)

Coddrington, William, of Wroughton House, Swindon.

Coddrington, Mrs., his wife.

Codrington, Lady.

Codrington, The Hon. Mrs., daughter of the late Right Hon. W. H. Smith, M.P., and family.

Codrington, Humphrey, of New College, Oxford.

Coe, Frank, B.A. of St. Edmund's Hall, Oxford; of Brooklyn House, Roath, Cardiff. (1885.)

Coffin, A. E., M.A. of Magdalen College, Oxford, late Curate of East Farleigh, brother of the late Right Rev. Dr. R. A. Coffin, Lord Bishop of Southwark. (1845.)

Coffin, The late Rt. Rev. R. A., M.A. of Christ Church, Oxford, late Vicar of St. Mary Magdalen's, Oxford. A Redemptorist Priest, for some time Provincial of the Order in England, till lately Lord Bishop of Southwark, ascetical writer. (1845.)

Coghlan, The late Rev. Thomas Lloyd, M.A. of Trinity College, Dublin, late Senior Rector of Mourne Abbey, Cork, Ireland; a priest.

Coghlan, The late Mrs. T. L., his wife.

Coghlan, Thomas Lloyd, son of the above, late curate at Stonehouse. A priest, and formerly army chaplain at Sandgate.

Coghlan, Miss Lloyd, his sister.

Coghlan, Mrs., of Woolwich.

Coghlan, W. Hay, late judge of the High Court of Bombay.

Coke, Lady Katherine, daughter of the second Earl of Wilton, wife of the Hon. Henry Coke, son of the Earl of Leicester.

Colby, Frederick Clarence Copleston, of King's College, London, and Durham University, late Curate of St. Peter's, Fulham, London, S.W. (1899.)

Coleman, H. J., now a Carmelite Priest at Rome.

Coleman, J., B.A. of Worcester College, Oxford.

Coley, Francis, son of the Rev. James Coley, M.A., Vicar of West Hampstead, London. (1893.)

Coleridge, The late Rev. Henry James, M.A. and Fellow of Oriel College, Oxford, First-Class in Classics, Scholar of Trinity College, late Incumbent of a district church, near Ottery St. Mary, Devonshire, brother of the late Lord Coleridge, Lord Chief Justice of England, and brother-in-law of the late Right Rev. Dr. John F. Mackarness, Bishop of Oxford. A Jesuit Priest, and ascetical writer. (1852.)

Coleridge, Miss, cousin of the above.

Coleridge, Miss E, her sister, a nun.

Collard, Captain, of Walthamstow.

Collard, Mrs., his wife.

Collett, D. J. T., formerly a Baptist minister.

Collier, Mrs., of Cardiff.

Collins, H., M.A. of Durham University, late curate of St. George's-in-the-East, London. A priest of the Cistercian Order, and formerly Chaplain to the Convent of Our Lady of Dolours, Wimborne, Dorset.

Collins, James, of Oxford.

Collins, John, M.A. of Oxford University, late Curate at Birkenhead.

Collins, Miss Decima, daughter of the late Captain Collins, R.N.

Collis, The late Very Rev. William, a priest, Canon of Northampton, at St. George the Martyr, Shefford, Bedfordshire.

Collyns, H. A., B.A. of Christ Church, Oxford.

Colthurst, Colonel David La Touche, now of Bournemouth, formerly M.P. for Co. Cork, son of the late Sir Nicholas Conway Colthurst, Bart.; served with the 17th Regiment in the Crimean campaign, including the siege of Sebastopol and the assault on the Redan.

Colthurst, Mrs. (*née* Douglas Drek), wife of the above.

Colthurst, Robert, brother of the above.

Colthurst, Robert Trivett, of Midford. (1878.)

Comberbach, The late Rev. Charles; a priest at St. Ann's, Chertsey.

Comberbach, The late Robert, brother of the above, and family.

Comyn, Mr., of Plymouth.

Comyn, Mrs., his wife.

Conder, Réné F. R., B.A., Non-Collegiate Student of Oxford, late Curate of St. George's, Botolph Lane, London, E.C.; now Librarian to the Marquis of Bute. (1887.)

Conder, Mrs., his wife. (1887.)

Congreve, Mrs., of Plymouth.

Connolly, Mrs., of an Anglican sisterhood.

Conroy, Miss E., of Oxford.

Consett, W. W. B., of Braiwith Hall, Yorkshire, married to Harriet, daughter of Lord Charles Kerr, son of the sixth Marquis of Lothian.

Consett, Mrs., wife of the above, and her ten children.

Considine, H., D.L. of Derk.

Conway, Miss, daughter of an Anglican clergyman.

Conyers, Miss, daughter of an Anglican clergyman, and till lately Superioress of St. Agnes's Home, Torquay.

Cook, Miss C., a nun.

Cook, Miss F., a Carmelite Nun.

Cook, John, of Cottles, Wilts. (1882.)

Cook, J. A., barrister.

Cook, Miss Mary, a nun.

Cook, Miss, of St. James's Square, Notting Hill, London, W.

Cook, The late Rev. William W. A priest (Oblate of St. Charles) at St. Charles' College, St. Charles' Square, London, W.

Cooke, W. A., M.A. of Worcester College, Oxford, late Incumbent of St. Mary's, Cuddington, Worcester Park, London, S.W. (1894.)

Cooke, Mrs. C. A., wife of the above. (1894.)

Cookesley, Dr. J.

Cookson, James, of Fleetwood.

Coombes, A., B.A., Oriel College, Oxford.

Coombes, H., M.A. and Fellow of St. John's College, Oxford, late Curate of St. Saviours', Leeds. (1845.)

Coombes, James, of Trafford Park.

Coombs, Captain Arthur V. L., M.A. Oriel College, Oxford, of the Dorset Militia, Private Chamberlain to the late and present Popes.

Coope, H. G., M.A. Christ Church, Oxford, late curate at Bucknell.

Cooper, C. D., B.A. of University College, Oxford. (1890.)

Cooper, Charles Paston, eldest son of Sir Astley Paston Cooper, of Hemel Hempstead, lately married to Princess Dolgourouki.

Cooper, John, surgeon.

Cooper, Mrs., his wife.

Cooper, Mrs., wife of Colonel Moore Cooper.

Cooper, Mrs. Moss, sister of the late John Walter, M.P., proprietor of *The Times*.

Cooper, Thomas, journalist and author.

Cooper, William, surgeon.

Cooper, Mrs. W., his wife.

Coore, G. B. M., M.A., Scholar of Corpus Christi College, Oxford, barrister, and Secretary of Duchy of Lancaster Office.

Cope, Sir Anthony, thirteenth Bart., of Bramshill Park, Hants.

Cope, Lady, wife of the above, and widow of the late Rev. Henry Tudway, an Anglican clergyman.

Cope, Miss, daughter of the late Sir William Cope, Bart.

Cope, J. Canby Biddle, M.A. Worcester College, Oxford; received the title of Marquis from His Holiness Pope Leo XIII., author. (1882.)

Copeland, The late Dr., of Cheltenham.

Copeland, Mrs., his wife.

Coplestone, C. H. L., of Castelnau, Barnes, London, S.W. (1891.)

Corbett, The late Rev. Joseph, D.D., a priest, and Chaplain to the Forces at Aldershot.

Corbett, Vincent, M.A. Trinity College, Cambridge, Second Secretary to the British Legation, Athens.

Corbett, The late Hon. Mrs. Vincent, fourth daughter of Lord Alington, and wife of the above. (1891.)

Corbyn, Henry Fisher, M.A. Jesus College, Cambridge, late Senior Church of England Chaplain to the Forces in India. (1881.)

Corcoran, Mrs., of Liverpool.

Corine, Thomas, of Liverpool.

Corke, Benjamin S., solicitor, of Cheltenham, late of Brigg. (1896.)

Cormack, E. M., of Liverpool.

Cormack, M. M., of Cheltenham.

Corrance, Henry Clemence, B.A. Christ Church, Oxford, late Rector of West Bergholt, Essex. (1898.)

Costelloe, Mrs., wife of B. F. C. Costelloe, M.A., member of the London County Council and of the London School Board.

Costelloe, Mrs. Wallace, of Borrisokane, Parsonstown, Co. Tipperary. (1888.)

Cottenham, The Countess of, wife of the third Earl. (1895.)

Cotton, Miss, daughter of the late Provost of Worcester College, Oxford, and neice of the late Rev. Dr. Pusey.

Cotton, Lady, wife of the late Admiral Cotton. (1898.)

Cotton, Major Walter, R.A., of Rangoon, India. (1891.)

Cottrell, Herbert, of Birmingham.

Cottrell, Mrs., his mother.

Cottrell, The Misses, of Blackheath.

Counsellor, Dr.

Courtauld, George, junr., M.A. Trinity College, Cambridge.

Courtayne, H. de Villiers, of Killarney, Ireland.

Courtnay, Admiral George.

Courtney, Miss, sister of the Protestant Bishop of Jamaica.

Courtney, Miss, daughter of the tenth Earl of Devon, a nun. (1868.)

Courtney, Thomas, M.A.

Cousens, E., of Plymouth,

Coventry, The late Lady Alexina, daughter of the late Earl Fife, K.T. (1879.)

Coventry, Alphonsus M., a Servite Priest and Prior of Our Lady of Seven Dolours, Bognor, Sussex.

Coventry, John, M.A. Magdalen Hall, Oxford, late Rector of Tywardreath, grandson of the sixth Earl of Coventry.

Coventry, Mrs. J., wife of the above.

Coward, W. Scott, of Trinity Hall, Cambridge, one of her Majesty's Inspectors of Schools.

Cowell, The late Rev. Henry; a Jesuit Priest at St. Joseph's, Bedford Leigh, Manchester. (1864.)

Cowell, Miss. M., of Sunderland.

Cowell, Ralph, of Fleetwood.

Cowley, The late Rev. Alban; a Passionist Priest at St. Joseph's Retreat, Highgate, London, N.

Cox, Charles, B.A. Exeter College, Oxford, formerly an Anglican clergyman.

Cox, Captain, of the 1st Royal Surrey Militia.

Coxon, Mrs., wife of M. A. Coxon, of the Bombay Civil Service, and daughter of the late Sir G. Anderson, Governor of Ceylon.

Coxon, Miss Attwell, of Hong-Kong.

Cracroft-Amcotts, Mrs., wife of Colonel Weston Cracroft-Amcotts, of Walcott Hall, Northampton.

Craig, J. Young.

Craig, Mrs. J. Young, and her three sons.

Craig, W. Young, formerly M.P. for North Staffordshire. (1891.)

Craigie, Mrs. ("John Oliver Hobbs"), the novelist. (1892.)

Crapper, Miss M. M., of Oxford.

Craven, The late Augustus, formerly Private Secretary to the late Lord Palmerston, *Attaché* at Leghorn, Paris, Brussels, and *Chargé d'affaires* at Darmstadt, translated Lord Bulwer and Mr. Evelyn Ashley's *Life of Lord Palmerston* into French, and at the request of Her Majesty Queen Victoria made an abridged translation into the same language of the *Life of the Prince Consort*.

Crawford, Francis Marion, M.A. Trinity College, Cambridge, son of Thomas Crawford, the sculptor. At one time editor of the *Indian Herald*, novelist and author of *Ave Roma Immortalis*. (1894.)

Crawford, The late Mervyn, M.A., M.D., LL.D., Trinity College, Cambridge. (1850.)

Crawford, Mrs., his wife, and family. (1850.)

Crawford, Mrs. Virginia Mary, the essayist. (1889.)

Crawley, The late Rev. E. L., M.A. Christ Church, Oxford, late Curate of St. Saviour's, Leeds; a priest. (1845.)

Crawley, F. R., of Cheltenham.

Crawley, Herbert, of South Tottenham, London, N.

Crawsday, Mrs. William, of Glamorganshire. (1896.)

Crewe, The late Hon. Miss, sister of the third Lord Crewe. (1842.)

Crichton-Stuart, Patrick J., great-grandson of the first Marquis of Bute.

Crispin, Admiral.

Crispin, Mrs., his wife.

Crispin, Miss Alberta, her daughter, and godchild of Her Majesty Queen Victoria.

Crispin, Miss Victoria, her sister.

Crispin, General.

Croak, James, of Bolton.

Crofton, Morgan W., B.A. Trinity College, Dublin, F.R.S., Fellow of the Royal University of Ireland, late Professor of Natural Philosophy at Queen's College, Galway, now Professor of Mathematics, etc., at the Catholic University College, Dublin.

Croker, Lieutenant Arthur Charles, late of the 77th Regiment, son of the late Colonel Croker and cousin of the Earl of Listowel. (1858.)

Crommelin, A. C. D., of Blackheath, London, S.E.

Crommelin, A. L. Y. D., M.A., Trinity College, Camb.

Cross, A., of Plymouth.

Cross, Henry M'Intosh, B.A. and late Scholar of Pembroke College, Oxford ; formerly Curate of Lenton, Northampton, Curate-in-Charge of Arkley, Barnet, Chaplain and Form-Master at Eastbourne College; now Vice-President of St. Hugh's, St. Edmund's College, Ware. (1896.)

Crosse, Herbert L., solicitor, of Wigmore Street, London, W. (1880.)

Crowe, Mrs., wife of Captain Crowe, of Folkestone.

Crown, Sir R.

Crowther, The late Rev. T. A., D.D., a priest, formerly Military Chaplain in China and India, till lately of St. Winefride, Welshpool, Montgomeryshire, and Chaplain at St. Joseph's College, Dumfries, N.B.

Croxton, Miss, daughter of Captain Croxton, of Landels, Carmarthenshire, late of Oswestry.

Cruickshank, Miss, of Taunton.

Cruickshanks, J. C., of Rugby.

Cubitt, Thomas, of Merton College, Oxford, and of Eden Hall, Edenbridge, Kent. (1893.)

Cuffe, Captain, of Connaught.

Cuffe, J. O., of Missenden.

Culley, Matthew, M.A. Magdalen College, Oxford, late an Anglican clergyman; a priest.

Cullin, Mrs. J. R., of Warwick Gardens, Kensington, London, W.

Culverwell, T. J., of Bristol.

Culverwell, W., of Shepton Mallet.

Cumberland, James Bentinck. (1894.)

Cumberlege, The late Rev. Arthur B., B.A. Trinity College, Cambridge; a priest.

Cumbes, Mrs., of Canonbury, London.
Cump, Alfred, of Plymouth.
Cunliffe, H. J. St. B., M.A. Exeter College, Oxford.
Cunningham, J. C., late an Anglican clergyman.
Cunningham, R. B. D., J.P., of Hensol, N.B.
Cunynghame, Miss, formerly of Wantage Sisterhood, now a nun. (1880.)
Curling, Mrs., wife of Admiral Curling.
Curran, Mrs., wife of James Curran, a Quaker, of Dublin.
Currie, Andrew, the sculptor.
Currie, The late W. Bertram, the banker, brother of Lord Currie, British Ambassador at Rome.
Currie, Mrs. Bertram.
Currie, Hon. Mrs. Wodehouse, daughter of Lord Lyveden.
Currie, Mrs., late of the Convent of Mercy, Great Ormond Street, London, W.C. (1888.)
Currie, Miss Florence, her daughter; a nun. (1888.)
Curtis, The late Sir Lucius, Bart., of Gatecombe, Hants. (1848.)
Curtis, The late Lady, wife of the above. (1848.)
Curtis, Miss, a nun.
Curtis, Robert L., J.P., ex-mayor of West Ham, London. E.
Curtis, Miss, his daughter.

DAGGER, Miss Margaret, of Fleetwood.

Dagger, Miss Mary, her sister.

Dagger, William, her brother.

D'Albanie, Lady Alice, daughter of the sixteenth Earl of Erroll, and wife of the late Count d'Albanie, who claimed to be a descendant of Prince Charles Edward Stuart.

D'Albiac, Sir Charles.

D'Albiac, Lady, his wife.

Dale, J. D. Hilarius, M.A. Oriel College, Oxford, late Curate of Frome Selwood; a priest, and for some time in charge of St. John's, Brentford, W., author of *Ceremonial According to the Roman Rite*, etc. (1846.)

Dale, S., of Torquay, and family.

Dalgairns, The late Rev. John B., M.A. Exeter College, Oxford, an eminent writer in the *Contemporary Review* and elsewhere; a priest of the Brompton Oratory, London, S.W. (1844.)

Dallington, Mrs., of Ipswich.

Dalrymple, Mrs., of London.

Dalrymple, Sir Walter Hamilton, Bart., of the Lodge, North Berwick, N.B.

Dalston, Edwin, of Liverpool.

Dalton, Mrs. Mabel S. C. M., wife of an Essex clergyman, and her four children.

Daly, Hon. Mrs. Robert.

Daly, Mrs. Dominic, wife of former Governor of Borneo. (1878.)

Daly, Mrs., of South Kensington. (1878.)

Dalziel, Mrs., wife of Captain Dalziel.

Daniel, Edward Osman, late of Swansea, now of London (1868.)

Daniell, E. M., a priest at St. Mary's, East Finchley, London, W.

Daniell, Maxwell, of Hatfield. (1882.)

Daniell, Robert, of New Forest, Co. Westmeath, Ireland.

Danvers, Miss, of Chislehurst.

d'Arcis, Comte (François Louis de Ruvigny), now of Bath, second son of the late Marquis de Ruvigny, descendant of the celebrated Marquis de Ruvigny, the leader of the French Protestants in the reign of Louis XIV. (1889.)

D'Arcy, Mrs., wife of Colonel D'Arcy, late Governor of the Falkland Islands.

Darley, Henry Warren.

Darley, Mrs. Henry Warren, his wife.

Darlington, Joseph, M.A. Brasenose College, Oxford, late Rector of Thornden, Eye, Suffolk, son of Ralph Darlington, Town Clerk of Darlington. A Jesuit Priest of the Irish province, Fellow of the Royal Irish University, and Professor of the Catholic University College, Dublin. (1878.)

Darnell, The late Rev. Nicholas, M.A. and Fellow of New College, Oxford, formerly an Anglican curate, son of the late Rector of Stanhope. A priest at St. John of Beverley, Haydon Bridge, Northumberland. (1852.)

Darnell, Captain W. N., of the 84th Regiment.

Darnell, Mrs., his wife.

Darnley, Mrs. Charles, sister of the Rev. H. Gates, of St. Dominic's Priory, Newcastle-on-Tyne.

Dashwood, Captain, of Torquay.

Dashwood, C. F., of St. Michael's Torre, Devon.

Dashwood, Mrs., his wife.

Dashwood, The Misses, daughters of Admiral Dashwood.

Daunt, Mrs. O'Neil, of Kilcastle, Cork. (1846.)

Davenport, Joseph Lancelot, M.A. Jesus College, Cambridge.

Davey, H., of the War Office.

Davey, Mrs., of Chaucer Road, Acton, London, W. (1895.)

Davey, The Misses, her three daughters, all nuns. (1895.)

Davidson, Captain, of Folkestone.

Davidson, Mrs., his wife.

Davidson, J., of Folkestone.

Davie, George, M.A. Exeter College, Oxford, Head Master of Kensington Collegiate School.

Davie, The late Hon. Theodore, Chief Justice and ex-Premier of British Columbia.

Davies, Adolphus Jacob, of Liverpool.

Davies, Miss, a nun.

Davies, Miss Julia, of Malta.

Davies, Miss Lloyd, of Carmarthen.

Davies-Cooke, Aubrey G. K., son of the late Major Davies-Cooke, R.A. (1884.)

Davies-Cooke, Mrs. J. R., mother of the above. (1882.)

Davies-Cooke, Miss Kathleen, her daughter. (1884.)

D'Avigliano, The Duchess of (*née* Lady Emily Pelham-Clinton), second daughter of the sixth Duke of Newcastle, and wife of the Duke d'Avigliano, youngest son of the late Prince Philip Doria Pamphili-Landi. (1879.)

Davis, Francis, of Holywood, Belfast, a well-known North of Ireland poet, under the pseudonym of "The Belfast Man".

Davis, Frederick, of Malta.

Davis, George, of Liverpool.

Davis, G. E. B., B.A. of London University.

Davis, G. H. Leighton, of Ardmulchan House, Navan, son of the late Rev. Dr. Davis, Secretary of the Religious Tract Society.

Davis, John, of Liverpool.

Davis, J. H., of Clifton.

Davis, Miss Margaret, of Oxford.

Davis, T., M.A. Cambridge University, late Curate of St. John's, Torquay. (1891.)

Davis, Mrs., his wife. (1891.)

Davison, The late Hon. Mrs., daughter of the second Lord Graves, and wife of Major-General Davison.

Davoust, Baroness (*née* Amy Phipps), daughter of the Rector of Selsea, Chichester.

Davy, G. J., M.A. Exeter College, Oxford, formerly an Anglican clergyman.

Dawe, G. E., a non-collegiate student of Oxford, now a Carmelite Priest.

Dawe, The late Rev. J., B.A. St. Mary's Hall, Oxford, a priest.

Dawe, J., of Plymouth.

Dawes, Miss Emily, of Saffron Hill, London.

Dawson, C. A., M.A. Balliol College, Oxford. (1880.)

Dawson, Charles, M.A. Pembroke College, Oxford.

Dawson, Charles B., M.A. Exeter College, Oxford, late Curate of All Hallows, Southwark, London, S.E.; a Jesuit Priest at Manresa, Roehampton, London, S.W. (1891.)

Dawson, Miss Effie, daughter of the late Colonel Dawson, of the 90th Regiment.

Dawson, Miss, her sister.

Dawson, Miss Lina, her sister.

Dawson, Ernest, of Queen's College, Oxford.

Dawson, Miss Massey, granddaughter of Lord Sinclair.

Dawson, Mrs., daughter of Admiral Michael Seymour, and wife of the late Colonel Dawson, of the 90th Regiment.

Dawson, The late William V., M.A. St. Mary's Hall, Oxford, formerly incumbent in the Diocese of Ripon.

Day, Mrs. Shirley, of Bournemouth, and children.

Dayman, Alfred J., B.A. of Exeter College, Oxford, late curate at Wasperton.

Dayman, Mrs. A. J., wife of the Rev. A. J. Dayman, M.A., Rector of Shillingstone, son of the late Rev. Charles Dayman, Vicar of Great Tew, Oxford.

Dayman, The late Mrs., wife of the late Rev. Charles Dayman, Vicar of Great Tew, Oxford, and formerly Curate of St. James's, Dover.

Dayman, Miss Flavia, her daughter.

Dayman, The late Miss Helen Montjoy, her daughter.

Deacon, Mrs., great-granddaughter of the late Most Rev. Lord Decies, Archbishop of Tuam.

Deacon, Thomas, of Grantham.

de Ainslie, The late Colonel, of the 1st Dragoon Guards.

Dean, Miss, of Bouverie Road, Folkestone.

Deane, Edward B., D.C.L. and Fellow of All Souls' College, Oxford, late Rector of Lewknor. (1855.)

Deane, Mrs., his wife. (1855.)

Deane, Mrs., of Torquay.

Deane, Mrs., of Carmarthen.

Deane, Thomas Robert, barrister.

Dearie, J., of Plymouth.

De Bary, R., of Weston Hall, Warwickshire.

De Betham, The late Rev. Frederick, solicitor, a Jesuit Priest at St. Edmund's, Bury St. Edmunds. (1838.)

de Burgh, Hubert, of Trinity College, Dublin, late Curate of Lawshall. A priest, till lately in North America, now at St. Edward the Confessor's, Newhall, Burton-on-Trent. (1857.)

de Burgh, R. L., M.A. late Vicar of West Drayton, Middlesex. (1881.)

de Burgh, Mrs., his wife. (1881.)

De Castro, J. C., of Woodend.

De Castro, Mrs., his wife.

de Charmoz de Bressan, Baroness, niece of the late Rear-Admiral Sir Richard O'Conor, K.C.B.

de Corson, Baroness, relative of His Eminence the late Cardinal Manning.

de Cosson, Baron C. A., F.R.G.S. of Pycroft, Chertsey. (1877.)

de Cosson, Baroness Elizabeth, of Chertsey. (1868.)

de Damas de Hautefort, Countess (née Young).

Dees, The late James, J.P., of Riversdale, Bellingham, Northumberland.

de Fauconpret, Countess, great-granddaughter of the late Rev. John Wesley, founder of the sect which bears his name.

de Gernon, Mrs. (née Braham), of Athcarne Castle, niece of Frances, Countess Waldegrave.

de Gramont, The Dowager Duchess, daughter of W. A. Mackinnon, late M.P.

de la Bedoyère, Mildred, Marquise, youngest daughter of the first Lord Greville.

de la Felde, Count, M.A. of Oxford University, and late Vicar of Tortington, Chichester. (1854.)

de la Haye, Mrs., sister of the Dowager Lady Inchiquin.

Delane, Mrs., of Rotherham.

Delane, Miss, her daughter.

Delaney, Mrs. P., of Newtown, Queen's County, Ireland.

de la Torre Diaz, Countess (née Wilcox).

Delf, H., of Norwich.

Dell, Robert E., B.A. University College, Oxford, son of Rev. Robert Dell, M.A., sometime Fellow of Corpus Christi College, Cambridge; late Organising Secretary of the Committee of Church Defence and Church Instruction; now editor of *The Weekly Register*. (1897.)

della Marmora, The late Countess (née Matthew).

de Ligne, The late Augusta Princess Edward, daughter of the late Sir David Cunynghame, Bart., and wife of the late Prince Edward de Ligne, formerly President of the Belgian Senate.

De Lisle, The late Ambrose, of Garendon Park, and Grâce Dieu Manor, Leicestershire.

De Lisle, Mrs., wife of the above, and daughter of Sir Richard Sutton, second Bart.

de Lubersac, Viscountess (Augusta), daughter of the Rev. Percival Fyre, M.A., Rector of St. Winnow, Cornwall, formerly Rector of Holy Trinity, Brompton, London, S.W.

de Mattos, Richard, undergraduate of St. Andrews University, a Carthusian Monk.

de Moleyns, Hon. Mrs., wife of the late Hon. Colonel de Moleyns.

Denbigh, The late Earl of (Rudolph William Basil Feilding), Count of the Holy Roman Empire, Knight Grand Cross of the Order of Pius. (1850.)

Denham, Miss Jessie, of Ravenscourt Park, London, W. (1888).

Denny, Harmar C., B.A. St. John's College, Oxford, a Jesuit Priest at St. Francis Xavier's, New York, U.S.A.

Dent, Frederick, a priest at St. John's, Rhymney, Monmouthshire.

de Paravicini, Baroness, wife of Baron de Paravicini, M.A. and Fellow of Balliol College, Oxford.

Dering, E. H., author of *The Lady of Raven's Coombe*, *Freville Chase*, etc.

Dering, Mrs. Emma Cordelia, wife of Evelyn J. Heneage Dering.

Dering, Lieutenant Heneage, of the Coldstream Guards. (1859.)

Des Champs, Madame, of Babbacombe Cliffe, Torquay, adopted daughter of Lady Mount Temple.

de Sforza Cæsarini, Duchess (*née* Caroline Shirley).

de Trafford, The late Lady.

de Trafford, Lady Adelaide, youngest daughter of the second Earl Cathcart, G.C.B.

Devas, C., M.A. Balliol College, Oxford.

de Vere, Aubrey, the poet, son of Sir Aubrey, second baronet. (1851.)

de Vere, Lady, wife of the late Sir Vere Edmond de Vere, Bart. (1851.)

de Vere, The late Sir Vere Edmond, third bart. (1851.)

de Vere, Sir Stephen Edward, Bart., of Currah Chase, Limerick, some time M.P. for Limerick. (1851.)

Deverell, William, of Cottles, Wilts. (1867.)

Deverill, Captain, a Jesuit lay-brother.

de Villefranche, Baroness.

Devitt, Dr.

Devitt, Miss, his daughter.

Devon, The late Edward Baldwin, twelfth Earl of, of Christ Church, Oxford, J.P. and D.L. for Devonshire; for sometime Captain, 1st Devon Yeomanry Cavalry; and formerly M.P. for Exeter and East Devon. (1870.)

Dewar, David Erskine, M.A., B.C.L. and Fellow of New College, Oxford, and late Rector of Friesthorpe. A priest at Our Lady of the Rosary, Staines. (1878.)

Dewar, The late Mrs. D. E., his wife. (1878.)

Dewar, The Misses, their two daughters. (1878.)

de Watteville de Loins, Countess, daughter of the late Rear-Admiral Sir Richard O'Conor, K.C.B., and sister of Lady O'Connell and of the Baroness de Charmoz de Bressan.

Dewhurst, H. W., M.A., late Curate of St. Barnabas, Southwark, London, S.E. (1852.)

Dick, J., of Dalkeith.

Dick, Miss Louisa P., daughter of the late George Stuart Dick, of Edith Lodge, St. Lawrence, Thanet, and granddaughter of the late General G. Dick, of the Bengal Army.

Dick, Mrs., of Dalkeith.

Dick, Miss, her daughter.

Dick, William Douglas, M.A. Exeter College, Oxford, and D.L., for Forfarshire.

Dickins, Mrs., wife of the Rev. Herbert Dickins, M.A., Chaplain to the Warwick County Asylum, son of the Rev. Dr. Dickins, Vicar of Emscote, Warwick. (1890.)

Dickinson, F., of Plymouth.

Dickson, The late Lieutenant Hughes.

Digby, The late Kenelm H., B.A. Trinity College, Cambridge, son of the late Very Rev. W. Digby, Dean of Clonfert, and grand-nephew of the first

Baron Digby; author of *The Broadstone of Honour*, etc. (1824.)

Dill, Mrs., wife of the Rev. Dr. Dill of Clonmel, Ireland.

Dill, Miss Evelyn, her daughter, now a nun in England.

Dillon, Hon. Mr., late of the Home Office.

di Salvo, Marchioness (née Claxton).

Dix, C. M., M.A., and unattached student of Oxford University, now assistant-master at the Oratory School, Edgbaston, Birmingham. (1878.)

Dixon, Rev. C. H., M.A., formerly curate at Fewston. (1850.)

Dixon, J., of Liverpool.

Dixon, Joshua, M.A. Brasenose College, Oxford, formerly an Anglican clergyman; now a Missionary Priest in Texas.

Dixon, Miss, daughter of General Dixon, a nun.

Dixon, Richard, of Liverpool.

Dixon, Robert, of Liverpool.

Dobson, W. E., J.P., of The Park, Nottingham.

Dobson, Mrs. W E , his wife.

Dobson, Miss, her daughter.

Dodsworth, The late W., B.D. Trinity College, Cambridge, late Vicar of Christ Church, St. Pancras, London, N.W. (1847.)

Doe, J. H., M.A. Trinity College, Cambridge, late Vicar of Eaton Bray, near Dunstable. (1890.)

Dolling, The late Miss, niece of the late Admiral Brooking.

Dolman, Mrs. M., wife of Marmaduke Dolman, barrister, and daughter of Major Wand, late of Chester Court and Manston Hall, Yorkshire.

Domvile, The late Sir Charles Compton William, Bart., of Templeague and Santry House, Co. Dublin.

Donaldson, Alexander Melbourne, M.A., late Curate of Farmborough, Bath. (1877.)

Donaldson, Archibald, nephew of Professor Donaldson.

Donaldson, The late James Kennedy M.A. of Edinburgh University.

Donington, The late Lord (Charles Frederick Abney-Hastings), of Donington Park, Derby, and of Loudoun Castle, Galston, N.B., father of the present Earl of Loudoun. (1890.)

Donovan, Mrs. C. J., of Great Marlow, wife of a Government Engineer.

Dorat, Mrs., wife of Colonel Dorat.

Dorey, John, of Cottles, Wilts. (1861.)

Dorman, Miss. A. L. P.

Dormer, The late Hon. Mrs. J. B.

Dormer, Mrs. Miles, her sister.

Dougham, Mrs., of Orrel Park, Aintree.

Douglas, Lord Archibald Edward, son of the seventh Marquis of Queensberry; a priest at St. George's Cathedral, Southwark, London, S.E.

Douglas, Sir Charles Eurwicke, K.C.M.G., M.A. St. John's College, Cambridge, at one time Private Secretary to the late Viscount Goderich, King-of-Arms of the Order of St. Michael and St. George, formerly M.P. for Warwick and Banbury, author of *Long Resistance and Ultimate Conversion.*

Douglas, Lady, his wife.

Douglas, The late Rev. Edward, M.A. Christ Church, Oxford, cousin of the late Marquis of Queensberry, a Redemptorist Priest, and Rector of St. Alfonso's, Rome. (1842.)

Douglas, The late Lady Elizabeth, daughter of the seventh Marquis of Queensberry.

Douglas, Lady Elizabeth, daughter of the second Earl Cathcart, and wife of General Sir John Douglas, G.C.B.

Douglas, The late Rev J., B.A. Christ Church, Oxford, formerly an Anglican clergyman; a priest.

Douglas, Mrs. J. D., of Benares.

Douglas, J. H., of Leith, N.B.

Douglas-Hamilton, The late Lord Charles George Archibald, son of the twelfth Duke of Hamilton and Brandon, premier peer of Scotland, formerly Lieutenant 11th Hussars, A.D.C. to Lord Napier of Magdala during the Abyssinian War. (1885.)

Douglass, Edward B., D.D., of Rome, late curate at Emscote; a priest, Canon and Rural Dean at St. Barnabas Cathedral, Nottingham. (1868.)

Douglass, The Misses, his sisters. (1868.)

Dove, J. D., B.A. Exeter College, Oxford.

Dove, The late T. D., M.A. Emmanuel College, Cambridge, late Curate of St. Mary Magdalen's, Munster Square, London, W.

Dover, George, M.A. Exeter College, Oxford; a priest at St. Thomas of Canterbury, Longhorsley, Morpeth. (1872.)

Downer, H., of Limerick.

Downes, James Francis ; a priest at St. Patrick's, Bradford.

Downie, Mrs., of Havant, Hants, and family.

Doyle, Mrs. Catherine, of Liverpool.

Doyle, Mrs. C. J., of Edinburgh.

Draffen, Mrs. Katherine A. J., only daughter of Edwin Rowley, Gawthorpe Hall, near Wakefield, and wife of George Algernon Draffen, son of Colonel W. Pitt-Draffen, late of R.M.A. (1883.)

Drane, The late Rev. Augusta Theodosia, Prioress of the Dominican Convent, Stone: author of *Christian Schools and Scholars*, etc.

Drew, The late Rev. Joseph W. Wright, M.A. St Alban's Hall, Oxford, member of the Royal Asiatic Society. A priest, and late of St. Edward the Confessor's, Romford, Essex. (1864.)

Drew, Francis D. Bickerstaffe, B.A. of Oxford University, a priest, Monsignor, and for seven years Chaplain to the Forces at Plymouth, now at Malta. (1879.)

Drinkwater, The late Rev. Thomas A., a priest at Our Lady of Mount Carmel and St. Joseph's, Battersea, London, S.W., and Chaplain to the late Countess Tasker.

Driver, T. W. H., of Cheltenham.

Drudge, J., of Liverpool.

Drummond, Charles, late member of the English Church Union, of Llantarnum, Wales. (1886.)

Drummond, Lister, B.L., son of Maurice and the Hon. Mrs. Drummond, barrister and secretary of the

Guild of Our Lady of Ransom for the Conversion of England. (1883.)

Drummond, Miss M., his sister. (1896.)

Drummond, Hon. Mrs. Maurice, eldest daughter of the second Lord Ribblesdale, stepdaughter of the first Earl Russell. (1896.)

Drummond, Richard Hay, of Hawthornden, son of second Sir Francis Walter Drummond, Bart., and descendant of the poet.

Du Boulay, Miss, of Torquay, daughter of an Anglican clergyman, a nun.

Duff, Groves, M.D. Edinburgh University, formerly a member of the Bengal Medical Service, son of the late Rev. Dr. Duff, of Calcutta. (1880.)

Duff, Mr., his wife, and family. (1880.)

Duffus, Harris, of Cambridge University.

Dugmore, Captain, late of the 64th Regiment.

Dugmore, Hon. Mrs., his wife, and second daughter of the second Lord Brougham.

Duke, The late Dr., M.A. of Oxford University, F.R.C.P., M.R.C.S., was Assistant Surgeon of the International Ambulance during the Franco-Prussian War. (1846.)

Duke, The late Rev. Herbert C., his son, a priest at St. Anne's, Keighley.

Duke, Mrs., sister of the late Duchess of Argyll.

Duncan, Lady.

Duncan, Miss, her daughter.

Dundas, Hon. Blanche, sixth daughter of the second Viscount Melville. (1889.)

Dundas, The late Lady Margaret Matilda, third daughter of the first Earl of Zetland, a Benedictine nun of the Perpetual Adoration at St. Scholastica's Priory, Atherstone, Warwickshire.

Dundas, Miss, daughter of Lady Dundas.

Dundas, Miss Mary, of Carron Hall, Stirlingshire, a nun. (1882.)

Dunlop, A. C., B.A. Magdalen College, Oxford; late President of the Chamber of Commerce, Southampton. (1879.)

Dunlop, Captain, son of Admiral Dunlop, C.B.

Dunlop, Mrs., wife of Admiral Dunlop, C.B.

Dunn, Major F., late of the Royal Canadian Rifles.

Dunn, Mrs., wife of George Dunn, of Harley Street, Cavendish Square, London, W., mother of Monsignor Dunn.

Dunn, J. C., B.A. New College, Oxford, Inspector of Secular Education in the Archdiocese of Westminster.

Dunn, Miss Maude, relative of Major F. Dunn.

Dunn, Philip Vincent, her brother.

Dunraven, The late Earl of. (1855.)

Durant, George Charles, of Hampstead, London, N.W.

Durell, J. P., M.A. University College, Oxford, late an Anglican clergyman, formerly tutor at the Catholic University College, Kensington, London, W.

Durell, John Tindall, M.A. St. Peter's College, Cambridge, formerly an Anglican clergyman.

Durnford, Miss Emma, daughter of the Rev. Prebendary Durnford. (1898.)

Durnford, Miss Esther Mary, her sister. (1895.)

Duthie, Charles J., M.A. Trinity College, Oxford, late Curate of St. Paul's, Knightsbridge, London, and Chaplain to the Earl of Kinnoull. A priest at Our Lady Star of the Sea, North Berwick, N.B. (1888.)

Dykes, The late Rev. Thomas, M.A. Clare College, Cambridge, late Curate of Holy Trinity, Hull. A Jesuit Priest at St. Wilfrid's, Preston, Lancashire. (1850.)

Dyson, The late Rev. Owen, a Dominican Priest, formerly an architect.

AGER, F, of Tuam, Ireland.

Eaglesim, The late Rev T. P. A., M.A. Worcester College, Oxford, and late Curate of St. Paul's, Oxford. A priest of the Birmingham Oratory. (1877.)

Earle, John Charles, M.A. Oriel College, Oxford, late curate at Ongar, author of poems, etc. (1851.)

Earle, Miss, daughter of the Rev. Henry J. Earle, M.A., Rector of High Ongar, Essex.

Earnshaw, John, a priest at St. Patrick's, Bradford.

Earnshaw, Mrs. W., his mother.

Earnshaw, The Misses, her daughters.

East, C. W., of St. Peter's Park, London, W. (1863.)

Eaton, Charles O., M.A. Trinity College, Cambridge, D.L., of Tolethorpe Hall, Stamford. (1860.)

Eaton, Mrs. C. O., his wife. (1860.)
Eaton, John Richard, M.A. of Cambridge University, barrister. (1860.)
Eaton, Mrs. J. R., his wife. (1860.)
Eckett, S. Barton, of Birmingham, journalist.
Eden, Lady. (1898.)
Eden, The Hon. Ashley, son of the fourth Lord Auckland. (1898.)
Eden, William Martin, a priest, and Professor at the English College, Lisbon.
Eden, Major W. T., of the Bombay Staff Corps.
Edgar, Mrs. Austin, of Kreithood, N.B.
Edgar, The Misses, her daughters.
Edgar, Miss Caroline E., authoress.
Edgcomb, Thomas.
Edgcome, The late Rev. Richard, a priest.
Edgcome, William, a Jesuit Priest at St. Mary's, Bristol. (1866.)
Edger, Miss C. O., a Benedictine Nun.
Edmonds, George Columba, a Benedictine Priest at Fort-Augustus, N.B.
Edmonstoune, Cranstoun, The late Charles, of Corehouse, Lanark, N.B.
Edmunds, Miss, of Rome.
Edmunds, W. Martin, M.A. Trinity College, Cambridge, formerly M.P. (1869.)
Edwards, Albert, of the Madras Railway. (1891.)
Edwards, A. C., barrister.
Edwards, Miss Christina, of Liverpool.
Edwards, Frederick T. A., a priest at Brighton.

Edwards, Hiram, of Liverpool.
Edwards, J. B., of the Bank of England.
Edwards, Martin, of Liverpool.
Edwards, Martin, Coroner of the Newport District of Monmouthshire. (1888.)
Edwards, Miss, of Bath.
Egan, M. A., of Oxford
Egan, M. J., of Liverpool.
Egerton, John, M.A. Keble College, Oxford, late Rector of Odd Rode. (1894.)
Egerton, Reginald Arthur, of West Cromwell Road, Kensington, London, S.W.
Egerton, Mrs. R. A., his wife.
Eland, Mrs., wife of the late Rev. H. G. Eland, M.A., Vicar of Bedminster, Somerset. (1884.)
Elden, Mrs., sister of Mrs. Alfred Scott Gatty.
Eliot, Henry A., M.A. Merton College, Oxford.
Ellerby, Captain, R.A.
Elliott, R., of Plymouth.
Ellis, F. C., M.A. Queen's College, Oxford.
Ellis, J., M.A. St. John's College, Oxford.
Ellis, Mrs. Mary, of Acton Vale, London, W.
Elmes, Sidney W., of South Kensington, London.
Elmes, Mrs., wife of the above.
Elwell, Mrs., wife of an Anglican clergyman.
Embry, J. H., of St. Edmund's Hall, Oxford. (1885.)
Emery, Charles Frederick, Treasurer of the Guild of Our Lady of Ransom. (1878.)
Emly, The late Lord (William Monsell), P.C., M.A. Oriel College, Oxford, Lord-Lieutenant of Co.

Limerick, sometime Postmaster-General during the Right Hon. W. E. Gladstone's Administration.

Encombe, Viscount, of Magdalen College, Oxford, eldest son of the Earl of Eldon. (1897.)

Engledon, Charles, of Heston Hall, Co. Carlow, Ireland.

Enson, The late Captain, of the Royal Navy. (1845.)

Errington, G. H. F., of Queen's College, Oxford. (1894.)

Erskine, The late George B., M.A. Merton College, Oxford; of Dryburgh Abbey, formerly an Anglican clergyman.

Eskrigge, John B., formerly Curate of the Church of the Annunciation, Brighton; a priest (Oblate of St. Charles) at St. Francis of Assisi, Notting Hill, London, W. (1881.)

Estcourt, The late Rev. Edgar, M.A. Exeter College, Oxford, late curate at Cirencester; a priest, and Canon of the Cathedral of Birmingham. (1845.)

Euan-Smith, Lady, wife of Colonel Sir Charles Euan-Smith, K.C.B., British Minister to Colombia. (1897.)

Eustace, John, a Quaker.

Eustace, Mrs. J., his wife.

Evans, Miss, of Huddersfield. (1889.)

Evans, Charles, of Bristol.

Evans, Miss Francisca, of Newport, Monmouthshire; a nun at Bayeux, France. (1887.)

Evans, H., of Birmingham.

Evans, Miss Mary, of Manchester. (1883.)

Evans, William, M.A. Brasenose College, Oxford; late an Anglican clergyman at Roath, Cardiff. (1898.)
Everett, M., of Plymouth.
Evetts, Benjamin, of Manchester. (1894.)
Ewart, Dr.
Eye, W., M.A. of Oxford University, late Curate of St. George's-in-the-East, London, E.
Eyston, Mrs., wife of Charles Eyston, of Buckland, Farringdon, Beds. (1887.)
Eyston, Mrs., wife of Edward Eyston, Manor House, Bampton, Oxford. (1887.)

ABER, The late Frederick W., D.D., M.A. and Fellow of University College, Oxford, and late Rector of Elton; Superior of the Brompton Oratory, London, S.W.; poet and ascetical writer. (1845.)
Fagge, John Frederick, M.A. University College, Oxford, and late Rector of Aston Cantlow, brother of the late Rev. Sir J. Fagge, Bart., M.A. (1877.)
Fagge, Mrs., his wife, and family. (1877.)
Fagge, Miss Mary, her daughter. (1877.)
Fairfax, Mrs. Cholmeley, of Brandsby Hall, Yorkshire.
Fairhall, Miss, of Kilburn Orphanage. (1895.)
Fairlie, Francis, son of the late Colonel Fairlie, of Coodham, N.B.
Fairlie, James Ogilvie, M.A. Christ Church, Oxford, of Myres Castle, Fife; Chamberlain to H.H. Pope Leo. XIII.

Fairlie, Mrs., wife of the above, sister of T. Buchanan, M.P.

Falcon, Lieutenant C. Gordon, of the Royal Engineers. (1888.)

Fane, Miss, daughter of the Rev. Prebendary Fane; now Marchesa Luzzali.

Farman, Samuel, M.A. of Cambridge University, late Vicar of St. John's District Church, Colchester. (1880.)

Farmer, The late Dr. Cottenham, of Hexham, Northumberland.

Farmer, Dr.

Farmer, Mrs., his wife.

Farmer, Henry; a Jesuit Priest at St. Joseph and St. Francis Xavier's, Richmond, Yorkshire.

Farmer, Mr., late organist of St. Bartholomew's, Brighton. (1879.)

Farren, William, the celebrated actor.

Farren, Mrs. W., his wife, and family.

Fawkes, Alfred, M.A. Balliol College, Oxford, late Curate of St. Bartholomew's, Brighton; a priest at St. Mary Magdalen's, Brighton. (1876.)

Fayers, George F. D., of St. John's Wood, London, N.W.

Featherstone, Lady.

Fegen, The late Frederick J., R.N., C.B., son of the late Captain Richard Fegen, R.N., a barrister and formerly Naval Counsel to Admiral H.R.H., the Duke of Edinburgh, K.G. (1877.)

Feilding, The late Viscountess, daughter of David and Lady Emma Pennant, of Downing. (1850.)

Felgate, The late William, M.A. Trinity College, Cambridge, formerly an Anglican clergyman. (1847.)

Fell, Miss, of Rotherham.

Fellowes, The late Mrs. T. A., of Donington Priory.

Fellowes, The Misses, her daughters.

Fellows, Reginald Bruce, M.A. Trinity College, Cambridge; Assistant-Auditor of the Local Government Board. (1893.)

Fenn, Edward F., a priest at St. Catherine of Sienna's, Horse Fair, Birmingham. (1844.)

Fenn, Thomas W., a priest at St. Joseph's, Tewkesbury.

Fennings, Dr. Allen, L.R.C.P., M.R.C.S., L.S.A., member of the British Medical Association, of Notting Hill, London, W., late house-surgeon at Charing Cross Hospital.

Fennings, Mrs., his wife, and family.

Fenwick, V. J., M.A. Caius College, Cambridge.

Ferguson, Surgeon-General Charles, of the Medical Staff Corps.

Ferguson, Captain E. F. T., late of the Indian Navy.

Ferguson, Mr., late of St. Mary's (Episcopal) Cathedral, Edinburgh. (1898.)

Ferguson, Mrs., his wife. (1898.)

Fernandez, Miss Elizabeth Anne, of Midford. (1880.)

Ferrario, Mrs. Flora, sister of George Pauling, of The Lodge, Effingham, Surrey.

Ferrers, Hugh N., M.A. King's College, Cambridge; barrister at Singapore.

Fetherstone, Robert, J.P. for Co. Limerick, Ireland.

Ffrench, Miss, of Monevaye Castle, Co. Galway, Ireland.
Fickling, Duncan, late of Bournemouth, Hants. (1893.)
Fickling, Hugh, a priest at St. George's Cathedral, Southwark, London, S.E.
Field, The late Henry, the pianist. (1835.)
Field, The late James Philip, journalist and manager of the *Sydney Nation*. (1859.)
Fielder, Miss, daughter of General Fielder; now a nurse in the Jubilee Institution, Dublin.
Fieldwick, Robert Wulstan, of Cromer House, Putney, London, S.W.
Fincham, Dr. George, M.A. St. John's College, Oxford.
Fincham, Mrs., his wife.
Finlason, W. F., barrister.
Finlason, Mrs. W. F., his wife.
Firebrace, The late James, attorney.
Firebrace, The late Samuel, LL.D., Judge at Demerara, and his three sons.
Firebrace, The Misses, his two daughters.
Firth, Mrs., of Rotherham.
Fish, Mrs., wife of the Rev. J. Leonard Fish, M.A., Rector of St. Gabriel's, Fenchurch, with St. Margaret Pattens, London, E.C., and family. (1880.)
Fitzgerald, Miss Geraldine, sister of R. W. Penrose Fitzgerald, of Corkbegg Castle, Co. Cork, Ireland.
Fitzgerald, Gerald C. Purcell, M.A. of Trinity College, Cambridge.
Fitzgerald, The late Field-Marshal Sir J. Forster, G.C.M.G.

Fitzgerald, Miss, daughter of Dr. Fitzgerald.

Fitzgerald, The late Hon. Mrs. Percy, daughter of the tenth Viscount Massereene and Ferrard.

Fitzgerald, Mrs., wife of the Rev. John Fitzgerald, M.A., Vicar of Camden Town, London.

Fitzgibbon, Augustus, son of the Hon. Gerald and Lady Louisa Fitzgibbon.

Fitzgibbon, Charles, his brother.

Fitzgibbon, John, his brother.

Fitzgibbon, Louis, his brother.

Fitzgibbon, Valentine, his brother.

Fitzgibbon, Lady Louisa, daughter of the third Earl of Clare and wife of the Hon. Gerald Fitzgibbon.

Fitzgibbon, Miss Florence, her daughter.

Fitzpatrick, Richard, brother of Lord Castletown.

Flamstead, The late Colonel.

Flamstead, Mrs., his wife.

Flesher, J. H., M.A. of Christ College, Cambridge.

Fletcher, Miss Constance, grandniece of the late Rev. Dr. Pusey. (1896.)

Fletcher, Miss Margaret, daughter of the Rev. C. J. Fletcher, late Rector of Carfax, Oxford. (1898.)

Fletcher, Miss Philippa, her sister. (1898.)

Fletcher, Philip, M.A. Exeter College, Oxford, late Curate of St. Bartholomew's, Brighton, brother of Sir Henry Fletcher, fourth Bart., M.P.; a priest at Caterham, Surrey, Master and Founder of the Guild of Our Lady of Ransom for the Conversion of England. (1878.)

Flint, Miss, sister of Captain Flint, R.A., for many years an Anglican nun at Clewer. (1889.)

Flint, Miss Constance, her sister. (1885.)

Flockhart, J. F., B.A. Jesus College, Cambridge.

Flowers, George French, Mus. Doc. of Oxford University.

Floyd, J. Arthur, of Bury St. Edmunds, grandson of a Wesleyan minister. (1897.)

Floyer, T. Burnes, M.A., formerly an Anglican clergyman, and J.P. for Staffordshire.

Foley, Lady. (1850.)

Foley, The late Henry, solicitor, a Jesuit lay brother, author of *Records of the English Province of the Society of Jesus.* (1846.)

Foljambe, Mrs. Savile, relative of the late Selina, Lady Milton. (1850.)

Foljambe, Miss, her daughter. (1850.)

Foote, The late Lady Elizabeth, daughter of the fifth Marquis of Queensberry.

Forbes, Dr.

Forbes, The late Miss Christina, of Invernan, Aberdeenshire, N.B.

Forbes, Miss, daughter of the Rev. W. Forbes, M.A., late Rector of Manchester, Jamaica. (1878.)

Forbes, Miss R., her sister. (1878.)

Forbes, Reginald, grandson of Sir William Forbes, sixth Bart. of Pitsligo.

Forbes-Robertson, Miss, sister of the well-known actor.

Forbes-Robertson, Miss Marie Desirée, her sister; authoress.

Ford, G., M.A., late Curate of St. Mary's, Soho, London, W.

Ford, James, J.P., of Wraxall Court, Somerset.

Ford, Miss Mary Dominica, a nun, and Foundress of St. Margaret's Home.

Forman, Dr. (1860.)

Formby, The late Rev. Henry, M.A. Brasenose College, Oxford, late Rector of Riversdean, Wales; a priest, and Professor at St. Bede's College, Manchester. (1846.)

Forster, C. J. P., M.A. Oriel College, Oxford, late Curate at Stoke Abbas.

Forster, Mrs. C. J. P., his wife.

Forster, Mrs., wife of General Forster, late Secretary to H.R.H., The Duke of Cambridge.

Forster, Mrs., wife of Dr. Thomas Forster.

Fortescue, The late Edward Bowles Knottesford, M.A. Wadham College, Oxford, late Provost of St. Ninian's, Perth, N.B., brother-in-law of the late Most Rev. Dr. Tait, Archbishop of Canterbury; author of various works. (1875.)

Fortescue, Mrs., wife of the above and granddaughter of the late Lady Caroline Barham.

Fosberry, Miss Florence, of Limerick. (1875.)

Fosberry, Miss, niece of the above. (1880.)

Foster, Mrs. A.

Foster, Lady, wife of Sir Charles Foster, Bart.

Foster, Charles G., M.A. Magdalen Hall, Oxford, late Curate of St. Martin's, Scarborough; a priest at St. James's, Spanish Place, London, W.

Foster, Edward, son of Dr. Thomas Foster.

Foster, Harvey, M.A. St. Peter's College, Cambridge; now of the Indian Civil Service.

Foster, Thomas, LL.D., Trinity College, Cambridge.

Foster, William, solicitor, of Alnwick, Northumberland.

Fothergill, Joseph, of Wickham Park, Newcastle-on-Tyne.

Fothergill, William, M.A., late Curate of St. Paul's, Knightsbridge, London, W.

Fountaine, Miss, daughter of Andrew Fountaine, of Narford Hall, Norfolk.

Fowell, A. Wellesly, formerly an Anglican clergyman at Great Yarmouth.

Fowell, Mrs. A. W., his wife, and family.

Fowler, Miss Amy C., daughter of the Rev. F. W. Fowler, M.A., Chaplain of the Bath Union Workhouse; for some time matron of the late Father Damien's Hospital. (1882.)

Fowler, The late Dr., M.R.C.S., F.S.A., of Ormond Terrace, Cheltenham. (1859.)

Fowler, Mrs., his wife. (1880.)

Fowler, Mrs., wife of the late Colonial Secretary of Trinidad.

Fowler, Reginald, son of the late Dr. Fowler, a priest at St. Joseph's, Guildford, Surrey. (1859.)

Fowler, The Misses, his sisters. (1859.)

Fowler, Mrs., sister of George Pauling, of The Lodge, Effingham, Surrey.

Fownes, The late Rev. John Edward Curtis, M.A. Pembroke College, Oxford, late Curate of St. Mary Woolnoth, London, E.C.; a Jesuit. (1890.)

Fox, The late Dr. Charles James.

Fox, Mrs., his wife, grandniece of Madame Guyon.

Fox, Dr. Francis.

Fox, Mrs. J. A., youngest daughter of the late Count W. F. Wratislaw, of Rugby.

Fox, Laurence C. Prideaux; a priest (Oblate of Mary Immaculate) formerly at the Church of the English Martyrs, Tower Hill, London, E.C., now in the United States.

Fox, Miss, daughter of Dr. Fox, of Falmouth, a Quaker, now a nun.

Fox, Miss Sophia, her sister.

France, Miss Ellen, who built the Catholic Church at Leamington.

Francillon, Robert Edward, LL.M. Trinity Hall, Cambridge; Senior in Law Tripos.

Franklin, Lady Edith, daughter of Earl Howe. (1894.)

Franks, Miss Mary Anne, of Midford. (1855.)

Fraser, Mr., of Rome. (1884.)

Fraser, Mrs., his wife. (1884.)

Frazer, John, a priest, and till lately at St. Joseph's, Bury, Lancashire.

Frazer, Major. (1852.)

Frazer, Miss, formerly an Anglican nun.

Freeland, John; a priest at St. Etheldreda's, Ely, Cambridge. (1878.)

Freeman, W. G., M.A., late an Anglican clergyman, of Plymouth, Devonshire.

Freeman, Mrs. W. G., his wife.

Fremantle, Miss Cecilia, daughter of Vice-Admiral T. F. Fremantle.

Fremantle, Miss Emma, her sister.

Freme, Lieutenant-Colonel.

Freme, Miss, his daughter.

Fricker, Mark Anthony; a priest, Canon at St. Mary's, Rathmines, Dublin.

Frisbie, Captain.

Fritzhorley, Mrs. (née Williams), of Hendon. (1880.)

Froude, Edmund, nephew of the historian.

Froude, Hurrell, brother of the above.

Froude, Mrs. William, sister-in-law of the historian.

Froude, Miss, her daughter.

Frye, Lieutenant Arthur Henry, late of the Madras Army.

Fuller, Miss Annie Eleanor, daughter of Mrs. G. A. Fuller. (1886.)

Fuller, Miss Emma Blagden, her sister. (1883.)

Fuller, Mrs., wife of G. A. Fuller, Postal Surveyor of the North Midland District of England. (1882.)

Fuller, Miss Mary Constance, her daughter. (1885.)

Fuller, Harry Albert, M.A. Trinity College, Dublin, late Vicar of Llanfair, Kilgeden, Abergavenny, Wales. (1898.)

Fuller, Mrs., wife of the late Captain Fuller, the sculptor.

Fullerton, Alexander G., of Bollintoy Castle, Antrim, late Treasurer of the Association for the Propagation of the Faith. (1846.)

Fullerton, The late Lady Georgina, sister of the late Earl Granville, K.G., authoress of *Grantley Manor*, etc. (1846.)

Fulton, Major-General, of the Bengal Army.

ABB, Baker, barrister, of Abergavenny.

Gabb, Charles Augustine Baker, son of a Monmouthshire Anglican rector.

Gabb, The late John Baker, his brother.

Gabb, Powell Baker, his brother.

Gage, Lady. (1851.)

Gainsborough, The second Earl of (Charles George Noel), Knight of the Order of Christ, Lord Lieutenant and Custos Rotulorum of Rutlandshire. (1851.)

Gainsborough, The late Countess of, wife of the second Earl, and daughter of the sixteenth Earl of Erroll. (1851.)

Gainsford, W. D., barrister and J.P., of Skendleby Hall, Spilsby, Lincolnshire.

Gainsford, Miss, his sister.

Gainsford, The Misses, his four daughters.

Gaisford, The late Major, of Offington, eldest son of the late Dean of Christ Church, Oxford.

Gaisford, Lady Alice Mary, youngest daughter of the seventh Marquis of Lothian.

Gaisford, Thomas, J.P., husband of the foregoing.

Gale, Thomas, late organist of St. Agatha's (Protestant) Church, Finsbury, London, formerly assistant-organist at Christ Church, Clapham, London, now at the Redemptorist Church, Clapham. (1890.)

Galton, Mrs. J. L., wife of the Rev. J. L. Galton, M.A., Rector of St. Sidwell's, Exeter.

Galton, Miss, of Glengariffe, Bournemouth.

Galton, Theodore, M.A. Trinity College, Cambridge, of Hadzor, Worcestershire.

Gandy, Charles E., of Truro Theological College, late Curate of St. James's, Plymouth, and of St. Michael's, Edinburgh, N.B.; a priest, and secretary to the Right Rev. Dr. William Vaughan, Bishop of Plymouth. (1888.)

Gape, Major, of St. Michaels' Manor, St. Albans. (1874.)

Gardiner, The late Rev. Leonard; a Dominican Priest and Chaplain of the Convent of St. Rose, Stroud, Gloucestershire.

Gardiner, Mrs., wife of Captain Gardiner.

Garnett, A. W., B.A. Balliol College, Oxford.

Garnett, The late Rev. E. Peel, M.A. Brasenose College, Oxford, late Curate of Holy Trinity, Oxford; a priest of the Brompton Oratory, London, S.W. (1871.)

Garnett, Lieutenant H. Percy, of the 2nd Regiment.

Garnett, Mrs., daughter of Colonel F. H. Constance.

Garnett, Major T. W., late of the 85th Regiment.

Garratt, William Frederick H., M.A., formerly an Anglican Missionary in India, author of *The History of the Holy House*, etc. (1884.)

Garrett, Gerald, of London.

Garside, The late Rev. Charles Brierley, M.A. Brasenose College, Oxford, late Curate of All Saints', Margaret

Street, London, W.; a priest and author of *Sacrifice of the Eucharist, Helpers of the Holy Souls, Discourses on Some Parables of the New Testament, The Prophet of Carmel*, etc. (1850.)

Garside, Miss, his sister. (1850.)

Gates, Charles Leopold.

Gates, Miss Evelyn Adelaide, his sister.

Gates, Mrs. Emma Cordelia, her mother.

Gates, Sebastian B., a Dominican Priest at St. Dominic's Priory, Newcastle-on-Tyne, her son.

Gatty, Charles Scott, F.S.A., son of the Vicar of Ecclesfield.

Gauntlett, H., of Kensington Square Mansions, late of the Charity Commission.

Gauntlett, Mrs., wife of the above.

Gauntlett, Vincent, their son.

Gavin, The late Mrs., wife of the late Major Gavin, formerly M.P. for Limerick, daughter of Montiford Westropp, of Mellon House, Co. Limerick.

Gavin, Mrs. E. D., of Hornsey, London, N. (1895.)

Gawthorn, W. Rees, formerly secretary to H. E. the late Cardinal Wiseman, Archbishop of Westminster, and to the Most Rev. Dr. English, late Archbishop of Trinidad, founder of several Catholic schools in the West Indies. (1849.)

Gawthorn, Mrs. W. Rees, his wife. (1849.)

Gawthorn, Miss Rees, their daughter. (1849.)

Gayton, Miss, of Brighton, now a Carmelite Nun.

Geary, Gabriel, a Benedictine Monk at Downside, Bath. (1877.)

George, Charles Joseph, of Midford. (1881.)
George, Miss Agnes Florence, his sister. (1881.)
George, Miss Elizabeth Mary, his sister. (1881.)
George, Miss Henrietta Mary, his sister. (1881.)
Gerard, Colonel, of Rocksoles, N.B.
Gerrard, Mrs. (née Goodench), of Eyark, Ruthin, North Wales. (1887.)
Giannini, Edward, late Rector of Llandawke, South Wales. (1894.)
Gibson, Mrs. M., of London. (1887.)
Gibson, Hon. William, B.A. Merton College, Oxford, J.P. for Co. Meath and Co. Dublin, eldest son of Lord Ashbourne, Lord Chancellor of Ireland. (1892.)
Gibson, Hon. Mrs. W., wife of the above (née Marianne de Montbrison) and sister to the Comtesse Edmond de Pourtalès, of an ancient French Calvinist family. (1896.)
Gifford, Hon. Mrs. Edgar, formerly Mrs. Thomas Booth. (1874.)
Gilbert, Henry, of Colchester. (1894.)
Gilbert, James, of New Peckham, author.
Gilbert, John, of Granville Road, Acton, W., and Old Broad Street, London, E.C. (1894.)
Giles, C., son of Felix Giles of Rosslyn Grove, Hampstead, a priest and Secretary to the Bishop of Shrewsbury. (1863.)
Giles, Felix, of Rosslyn Grove, Hampstead, London, N.W. (1863.)
Giles, Mrs., his wife, and her three sons. (1863.)

Giles, Miss, her daughter, a nun. (1863.)
Gill, Miss Mary, a nun at the Convent of the Sacred Heart, Wandsworth, London, S.W. (1891.)
Gilliat-Smith, F. E., of Bruges. (1883.)
Gilliat-Smith, Mrs., his mother. (1880.)
Gilliat-Smith, Mrs. F. E., formerly a novice of the East Grinstead Sisterhood. (1883.)
Gisborne, Mrs. H. F., of Derby, sister to Lady Evans.
Gladstone, The late Hugh, grandson of Sir Thomas Gladstone, Bart., formerly of St. Edmund's College, Ware.
Gladstone, The late Miss Lucy, sister of the late Right Hon. W. E. Gladstone.
Glasson, W. J. Wharton, M.A. and Bursar of St. John's College, Oxford. (1888.)
Glasson, Mrs. W. J. W., his wife. (1888.)
Glenie, The late Rev. John Melville, M.A. St Mary's Hall, Oxford, late Perpetual Curate of Mark; a priest and canon. (1845.)
Glynes, Miss Jessie, of Hampstead, London.
Godard, The late John, celebrated in early photography.
Goddard, I., a priest, Monsignor, late of St. Mary's, Chislehurst, and formerly Chaplain to Her Imperial Majesty the Empress Eugénie.
Godley, Richard James Dyne, M.A. Emmanuel College, Cambridge, late Curate of St. John's, Bathwick, Bath, Somersetshire. (1883.)
Godsell, Miss Rosa, of Llantarnam. (1888.)
Goldstone, William, M.A., late Curate of St. Michael's, Wakefield.

Goldstone, Mrs. W., his wife.

Goldsmid, Nathaniel A., M.A. Exeter College, Oxford. (1850.)

Goldsmid, Mrs. N. A., his wife. (1850.)

Göltz, Dr., M.A. Christ College, Cambridge, late Rector of Christ Church, Southwark, London, S.E. (1850.)

Good, The late Captain, of the Royal Navy. (1849.)

Goodfellow, Colonel C. A., V.C., of the Royal Engineers.

Goodrich, J., a priest of the Pious Society of Missions at Monte Video, South America.

Goodrich, Lionel, barrister, now a priest at the Sacred Heart, Hampton Wick.

Goodwin, Thomas Gordon, Christ Church, Oxford, a priest, till lately Assistant Priest at the Sacred Heart, Brighton, and Priest-in-Charge of St. Philip Neri's, Uckfield, Sussex, author.

Goolden, D. H., solicitor.

Goolden, Mrs. D. H., his wife.

Gordon, The late Rev. A. B., M.A. of Cambridge University, formerly an Anglican clergyman; a priest.

Gordon, Miss A. M., of Abergeldie.

Gordon, Lady Duff. (1847.)

Gordon, F. J., B.A. St. Peter's College, Cambridge.

Gordon, G. R., of Ellon Castle, Aberdeenshire, N.B.

Gordon, J., B.A. Trinity College, Cambridge.

Gordon, J., M.A. Brasenose College, Oxford, late Curate of Christ Church, St. Pancras, London, N.W. (1847.)

Gordon, Miss, of Prince's Gate, Kensington, London, W.

Gordon, R., M.A. Oriel College, Oxford, late an Anglican clergyman.

Gordon, W., B.A. Trinity College, Cambridge.

Gore, Colonel Pollock.

Gormanston, Viscountess (*née* Connellan), wife of Viscount Gormanston, G.C.M.G., Governor of Tasmania. (1880.)

Gosselin, Sir Martin le Marchant, K.C.M.G., M.A. Christ Church, Oxford, late *attaché* to the English Embassy at St. Petersburg, then First Secretary at the Embassy in Paris; now Minister-Plenipotentiary at Paris. (1878.)

Gough, George, of Clensmore House, Woodbridge. (1858.)

Gough, Miss, of Rathronan, Clonmel, granddaughter of the late Very Rev. Dean of Derry and grandniece of the late Lord Gough. (1880.)

Gough, Major Percy, her brother. (1880.)

Gould, Henry J., of Calcutta.

Grace, Mrs. (*née* Thistlewaite), of Gracefield.

Graffin, Mrs. C. J., of Carlton Vale, Maida Vale, London.

Graham, Charles, now Bishop of Cisamus, Coadjutor and Vicar-General to the Right Rev. Dr. William Vaughan, Bishop of Plymouth, uncle to H. E. Cardinal Vaughan, Archbishop of Westminster. (1856.)

Graham, The late Colonel W. H., of the Royal Engineers, brother to the Bishop. (1856.)

Graham, Mrs. Douglas Cunningham.

Graham, Miss E. Cunningham.
Graham, Miss Isabel, of Boulogne. (1874.)
Graham, Mrs., of Wimbourne.
Grahame, Rev. Francis, B.A., late an Anglican clergyman.
Granard, The late Earl of (George Arthur Hastings Forbes), K.P., Knight and President in Great Britain and Ireland of the Order of Malta, Knight Grand Cross of the Order of St. Gregory the Great, Lieutenant-Colonel commanding 9th Battalion P.C.O. Rifle Brigade, one of the Senate of the Royal University of Ireland and President of the Catholic Union of Ireland. (1869.)
Granard, The Countess of, wife of the above.
Grant, Ignatius, of St. John's College, Oxford, a Jesuit Priest at St. Ignatius', Stamford Hill. (1842.)
Grant, The late James, the celebrated novelist.
Grant, Mrs., wife of the above.
Grant, James, son of the above.
Grant, Roderick, son of the above, a priest at Holy Trinity, Brook Green, Hammersmith, London, W.
Grant, Miss, the actress.
Grant, Mrs., wife of an Anglican clergyman.
Grant, Miss, sister of Sir Alexander Grant, Bart., Vice-Chancellor of Edinburgh University.
Grant, William, late M.O.C.R., ex-member of the English Church Union and of the A.P.U.C. (1881.)
Grantham, Thomas Henry, M.A., late Curate of Slinfold, Sussex.

Grantham, Mrs. T. H., his wife.
Gray, Lewis, Aberdeen.
Gray, The late Edward Dwyer, M.P. for Co. Carlow, Lord Mayor of Dublin (1879-80), son of the late Sir John Gray, M.P., proprietor of *Freeman's Journal*. (1876.)
Gray, The late Baroness, of Gray.
Gray, The late Miss Lucia, of Luneau, St. Brieux, France. (1828.)
Gray, Miss, of St. Asaph, North Wales. (1878.)
Gream, Miss, daughter of the Anglican Rector of Rotherfield.
Gream, Miss Hilda, daughter of the Rev. Nevill Gream, M.A., one of Her Majesty's Inspectors of Schools.
Greathead, Mrs., wife of the Rev. Stevenson Greathead, an Anglican clergyman.
Green, Andrew, M.A. Trinity College, Cambridge, late Curate of St. Paul's, Oxford.
Green, Mrs. A., his wife.
Green, Mrs. Charles Martin, of Newcastle-on-Tyne.
Green, Eric F., a priest at the Guardian Angels, London, E. (1887.)
Green, Miss E., his sister. (1888.)
Green, Everard, F.S.A., Rouge Dragon, College of Arms.
Green, James, of Leeds.
Green, James Spurgeon, M.A. Christ College, Cambridge, forty years Vicar of Brundell, Wilton, Norfolk. (1898.)
Green, J. Philip, Judge at Bombay, India.

Green, Mrs. (*née* Biddulph), of Co. Tipperary, Ireland.

Green, Robert Isidore, a Benedictine Monk at Our Lady of Mount Carmel, Redditch.

Green, Mrs. T., of Leeds.

Greene, The late Rev. C. V., B.A. Keble College, Oxford; a priest (Oblate of St. Charles). (1880.)

Greene, Joseph James, M.A. St. Peter's College, Cambridge, late Curate-in-charge of St. Bartholomew's, Brighton; a priest (Oblate of St. Charles), at Our Lady of the Holy Souls, Kensal New Town, London, W. (1875.)

Greenwood, Miss Dora, of Bruges.

Greenwood, Miss, of Oxford.

Greig, Captain P. H., of the Bombay Staff Corps.

Gregson, Canon, B.A. Durham University, formerly Curate in Colombo, Norfolk and Bethnal Green, late Vicar of Townsville, North Queensland, Australia. (1897.)

Gretton, George, of Swindon Hall, Gloucestershire.

Gretton, Mrs. G., his wife.

Grey, Miss E., now a nun at the Convent of the Sacred Heart, Dundrum, Co. Dublin. (1878.)

Grey, Francis W., son of Admiral the Hon. G. Grey, and nephew of Earl Grey. (1885.)

Grey, Professor Frederick, now of Montreal, Canada, nephew of Earl Grey. (1886.)

Grey, The late Lady, daughter of Admiral Sir R. Spenser, wife of the late Sir George Grey, of New Zealand. (1851.)

Grimshaw, Miss, of Dublin,

Grimshaw, Reginald, son of O'Donnell Grimshaw, of Belfast, and cousin to Dr. Thomas Grimshaw, C.B., Registrar-General for Ireland. (1893.)

Grimshawe, Samuel, J.P., of Erwood Hall, Lancashire.

Grimshawe, Mrs. S., his wife, and family.

Grinfield, Thomas, son of the Rev. T. Grinfield, M.A., an Anglican clergyman.

Grindle, E. S., "Presbyter Anglicanus," M.A. and late Scholar of Queen's College, Oxford, formerly Curate of St. Paul's, Brighton; Master of Grindle's Hall, Oxford. (1876.)

Grisewood, Harman, of Daylesford House, M.A. Christ Church, Oxford, late an Anglican clergyman. (1871.)

Grisewood, Mrs. H., his mother. (1871.)

Grissell, Hartwell de la Garde, M.A. Brasenose College, Oxford, F.S.A., Chamberlain to His Holiness Pope Leo XIII. (1868.)

Grouse, The late Frederick Salmon, C.I.E., M.A. Queen's College, Oxford; of the Bengal Civil Service.

Gruggen, F. W. E., solicitor.

Gruggen, Mrs., wife of the Vicar of Pocklington.

Gulson, Miss, niece of the late Josiah Spode, J.P. of Rugeley. (1886.)

Gunning, Miss, of Cambridge. (1895.)

Gurdon, A. B., now a priest at Hampton Wick.

Gurdon, P., B.A. University College, Oxford, formerly an Anglican clergyman; now a Carthusian Monk.

Gurvey, Miss S. A., of Liverpool.

Guy, Lady, wife of the late Sir Philip Guy, Bart.

ACK, W. Gilford, of Exeter. (1891.)
Hackins, Miss Alice, of Liverpool.
Haigh, The late Rev. Daniel, priest, built the Catholic Church of St. Thomas and St. Edmund of Canterbury, Erdington, Birmingham. (1850.)
Haines, The late Mrs. Harriet, of Barnet.
Hales, George, of Cottles, Wilts. (1859).
Hales, Lieutenant, of the Royal London Militia.
Halesworth, Mrs., of Taunton.
Haliburton, The late Major John F.
Haliburton, Mrs., his wife.
Haliburton, Miss, her daughter.
Halkett, Mrs. Craigie, of Cramond, Midlothian, N.B.
Hall, Charles, of Liverpool, son of the late Rev. Charles Hall, M.A., of Wadebridge, Cornwall. (1850.)
Hall, Mrs. C., his wife. (1850.)
Hall, The late James, Scholar of Balliol College, Oxford.
Hall, Admiral Robert, late Secretary to the Admiralty.
Hall-Hall, Miss Marion.
Hallé, The late Sir Charles, LL.D., Principal of the Royal Manchester College of Music, husband of Madame Norma-Neruda, the celebrated violinist.
Hallet, Mrs., of Samos Road, Anerley, London, S.E.
Hallett, Mrs. V., of Steventon, Whitchurch, Hants. (1892.)
Hamel de Manin, Countess.

Hamer, Mrs. J., daughter of the late C. Blake Allnatt, of Shrewsbury, barrister.

Hamilton, The late Duchess of (Princess Mary of Baden), daughter of H.S.H., Prince Charles Louis Frederick, late reigning Grand Duke of Baden. (1855.)

Hamilton, C., formerly an Anglican clergyman, at Exeter.

Hamilton, Frank, of London. (1894.)

Hamilton, Miss M., niece of the sixteenth Lord Dillon, daughter of W. J. Hamilton, M.P.

Hamilton, Mrs., wife of the late Captain J. F. C. Hamilton, R.N.

Hamilton, Robert R., journalist and author.

Hamilton, Thomas S., of the Bombay Civil Service. (1833.)

Hamilton, Mrs. T. S., his wife and family. (1883.)

Hammond, J., M.A., late Curate of St. George's-in-the-East, London, E.

Hammond, Miss, granddaughter of the late Most Rev. Lord Decies, Protestant Archbishop of Tuam.

Hands, Colonel W., of the Madras Staff Corps.

Hanmer, A. J., M.A., of Tiverton, late an Anglican clergyman.

Hanson, Eric D., non-collegiate student of Oxford University, a Jesuit.

Hardcastle, Lieutenant John Herschel, of the Royal Artillery. (1894.)

Harden, Miss, daughter of the late Colonel Harden.

Harding, Egerton, J.P., son of Egerton W. Harding, J.P., of Old Springs, Market Drayton. (1882.)

Harding, E. B., B.A. Exeter College, Oxford, nephew of the late Rev. Dr. Pusey; now organist at the Birmingham Oratory.

Harding, W. Egerton, J.P., of Old Springs, Market Drayton. (1879.)

Harding, Miss, of St. Mary Church, Torquay.

Hardwick, Mr., solicitor.

Hardwick, Mrs., daughter of R. Basset, of Cardiff.

Hardwicke, Dr. William Wright, of Osborne House, Rotherham.

Hardwicke, Mrs. W. W., his wife.

Hardy, Henry J., M.A. St. Alban's Hall, Oxford, late Curate of St. Peter's, Vauxhall, London; a priest, late of St. Mary and St. Thomas of Canterbury's, Harrow, now at Boxmoor, Herts. (1875.)

Hare, Mrs., sister-in-law of the Venerable Archdeacon Hare, and daughter of Sir J. D. Paul, Bart.

Hare, T. Leman, of The Firs, Streatham, London, S.W.

Hargitt, Mrs., wife of Dr. Hargitt, of Leicester. (1885.)

Harkin, Miss May, daughter of Colonel Harkin, of Tenby. (1892.)

Harper, Miss Frances, of London.

Harper, The late Rev. George, M.A. Pembroke College, Oxford, late an Anglican clergyman, brother of a former Protestant Bishop in Australia; a Jesuit Priest. (1850.)

Harper, Herbert E., proprietor of *Harper's Gazette*.

Harper, Mrs., wife of the above, and family.

Harper, The late Philip, surgeon.

Harper, Mrs., formerly Mrs. St. John Eckel.

Harper, Samuel B., M.A. Trinity College, Cambridge, formerly of St. Ninian's, Perth, N.B. (1851.)

Harper, Mrs. S. B., his wife. (1851.)

Harper, The late Rev. Thomas Norton, M.A. Queen's College, Oxford, late Incumbent of St. Peter's, Buckingham Palace Gate, London, S.W.; a Jesuit Priest, and Professor at Stonyhurst College, Blackburn. (1851.)

Harper, William, M.A. Pembroke College, Oxford, formerly an Anglican clergyman.

Harris, Walter B., lately married to Lady Mary Savile, eldest daughter of the Earl of Mexborough.

Harris, The late Rev. James; a Jesuit Priest at the Church of St. Francis Xavier's, Liverpool. (1848.)

Harris, Dr.

Harris, Mrs., his wife.

Harris, Lady.

Harris, Major. (1880.)

Harris, Mrs., of St. Helier's, Jersey.

Harris, Miss, author of *From Oxford to Rome*.

Harris, Mrs. Mary, of Forest Gate, London, E. (1888.)

Harrison, Bernard, the artist, son of Frederic Harrison, leader of the English Positivists. (1895.)

Harrison, The late Rev. Herbert, formerly captain of Westminster School, afterwards a Priest of the Brompton Oratory, London, S.W.

Harrison, H. L., B.A. Christ Church, Oxford, of the Bengal Civil Service.

Harrison, Mrs. F. M. D., of Uxbridge Road, London, W.

Harrison, Mrs., wife of the late Dr. Harrison, of Ambleside, Westmoreland.

Harrison, Captain W., of the Royal Artillery.

Harrod, Henry D., B.A. New College, Oxford, son of the late H. Harrod, F.S.A., of Aylsham, Norfolk. (1879.)

Hart, C.A. Burleigh, M.A., late Curate of Carrington, Lincolnshire. (1885.)

Hart, William Henry, F.S.A., solicitor.

Hartland, The late Henry Albert, the artist, of Mallow, Ireland.

Hartley, Edward, of Spinney Oak, Addleston, Surrey.

Hartley, Miss, of Bayswater, London.

Harvey, Thomas, non-collegiate student of Oxford, cousin of the Right Rev. Dr. Alexander, Protestant Bishop of Derry. (1887.)

Harvey, Miss, of Stockton.

Harvey, W. Beevor, cousin of Sir Charles Harvey, Bart. (1887.)

Hatchell, Mrs., daughter of the late Sir Robert Graham, Bart., wife of the late Captain Hatchell, of the 69th Bengal N.I.

Hathaway, Frederick, M.A., Fellow and formerly tutor of Worcester College, Oxford, late Curate of St. Mary Magdalen's, Oxford; a Jesuit Priest in America. (1851.)

Haward, Mrs., wife of Dr. Haward, and daughter of the Very Rev. Dean of Lichfield.

Hawker, The late Robert Stephen, M.A. Magdalen Hall, Oxford, late Rector of Morwenstow, Cornwall, poet and author. (1875.)

Hawker, Mrs. R. S., his wife. (1875.)

Hawkes, Richard H., of Bristol.

Hawkins, Mrs., of Orlando Road, Clapham Common, London, S.W.

Hawthorn, Miss Alice M., of West Croydon.

Hay, Miss Charlotte, daughter of Lord James Hay of Seaton, son of the seventh Marquis of Tweeddale.

Haycock, Captain.

Haye, Davie, of the Middle Temple, London.

Hayne, Miss, daughter of an Anglican clergyman.

Hayward, F. M., a priest at St. Henry's, Derwent, Sheffield.

Haywarden, Miss Frances. (1849.)

Headlam, G. E., Bible Clerk of All Souls' College, Oxford. (1897.)

Headlam, The late John, M.A. Pembroke College, Cambridge, late an Anglican clergyman.

Healey, Miss Florence.

Heathcote, Mrs., wife of the late Rev. W. B. Heathcote, M.A. and Fellow of New College, Oxford, and Precentor of Salisbury Cathedral.

Heathcote, Sir William Percival, Bart., of Merdon, Bournemouth, and of Hursley Park, Hants.

Hedley, Miss Fanny. (1866.)

Hedley, Miss Hannah, her sister, a nun. (1866.)

Hemery, Miss Mary C. de Villiers, of Barnet, Herts. (1881.)

Hemry, Henri Frederick, formerly organist at St. Andrew's, Newcastle-on-Tyne, St. Cuthbert's, North Shields, and of St. Bede's, South Shields, for a considerable time Professor of Music at Ushaw College, author of the *Crown of Jesus*, music, etc.

Henderson, E. B., M.A. and late Scholar of Pembroke College, Cambridge; barrister, of Leeds.

Henderson, F., a priest of the Pious Society of Missions in Piedmont, Italy.

Henderson, William, of Torquay.

Heneage, Hon. Mrs. (1845.)

Henn, J., M.A., late Curate of St. James's, Bristol.

Henry, Miss Marguerite, niece of the late Sir Thomas Henry, chief magistrate for London.

Henson, T. W., of Barnet, Herts.

Hepburne, Mrs. Cosmo, relative of the Rev. H. Hepburne, S.J.

Hepburne, Miss C. Gordon, her daughter.

Hepburne, Henry, a Jesuit Priest at St. Mary's, Horseferry Road, Westminster, London, S.W.

Hepburne, J. S., relative of the above.

Herbert, George, solicitor.

Herbert, The late J. R., the artist and Royal Academician, his best work being the decoration of the Peers' Robing Room, in the adornment of which he spent eighteen years.

Herbert, Lady Mary, sister of the Earl of Pembroke, now Baroness Mary von Hügel. (1873.)

Herbert, Hon. Mrs., of Llanarth, daughter of Lord Llanover.

Herbert, Mrs., wife of G. Herbert, barrister.

Herbert, W. J. A., of Bournemouth. (1896.)

Herbert, of Lea, The Lady, mother of the Earl of Pembroke and of Countess de Grey; authoress. (1862.)

Hesketh, Miss, daughter of the late Sir Thomas Hesketh, Bart.

Hetherington, Mrs., of Portsmouth.

Hewitt, The late Hon. Mrs., wife of the Hon. James W. Hewitt, eldest son of Lord Lifford.

Hewson, J., formerly a member of the Cowley Brotherhood, now a Jesuit Priest of the English Province.

Heys, The late Rev. Mother M. Magdalene, Prioress of Syon Abbey, daughter of the late Rev. J. Heys of Staffordshire. (1858.)

Heysham, Henry Nunez, late of Aylesford.

Heywood, The late Lady, wife of the late Sir Percival Heywood, Bart.

Hibbert, Colonel, of the Royal Canadian Rifles.

Hibbert, The late Captain Washington, of Billing Hall. (1849.)

Hibgame, Frederick Thurlow, fourth son of the late Lieutenant-Colonel E. F. Hibgame, H.E.I.C.S., of Norwich. (1877.)

Hickman, Major, of St Leonards.

Hickman, Mrs., his wife.

Hickman, The Misses, her daughters.

Hickman, Major J. M., of the Royal Army Medical Corps, London.

Hicks, John; a priest of the Order of Marists at Notre Dame de France, Leicester Place, London, W.C.

Hicks, Miss, of Tooting Graveney, London, S.W.

Higgins, The late Captain Henry.

Higgins, The late Lady Hilda, daughter of the tenth Earl of Winchelsea.

Higgins, The late Matthew, the "Jacob Omnium" of the *Times*.

Higginson, N. H., B.A. of Exeter College, Oxford.

Hill, Benjamin, B.A. St. John's College, Cambridge; a Passionist Priest, at Valparaiso, Chili, South America. (1866.)

Hill, George, of Rathmines, Dublin. (1893.)

Hill, G. H., M.A. Trinity College, Cambridge, late Rector of Saltford. (1846.)

Hill, Miss Georgina Dora, of Thomastown, Co. Kilkenny, grandniece of the late Rev. James C. Connolly, M.A., Chaplain of Woolwich Dockyard. (1874.)

Hill, J., M.A., formerly an Anglican clergyman.

Hill, Percival G., brother of the Rev. Benjamin Hill, C.P. (1889.)

Hill, W. J., M.A. Trinity College, Cambridge.

Hilliard, Miss, grandniece of Dr. Ferguson, formerly Physician to Her Majesty Queen Victoria; a Sister of Mercy.

Hilliard, Miss Cecilia, her sister, now a nun in Baltimore, U.S.A.

Hinson, Miss Margaret, daughter of the late Anglican Rector of Horton.

Hirst, Joseph, J.P., of Yorkshire.

Hirst, W., of Selwyn College, Cambridge; now a Dominican.

Hitchcock, J., son of the Rev. H. W. Hitchcock, M.A., Vicar of St. John's, Torquay, Devonshire. (1893.)

Hitchcock, Miss, sister of the Rev. H. W. Hitchcock, M.A., Vicar of St. John's, Torquay, Devonshire. (1893.)

Hoare, Edward, of London University, son of the Rev. J. W. D. Hoare, B.A., late Vicar of St. Philip's, Sydenham, London, S.E.; a priest of the Order of Charity, at Wadhurst, Sussex. (1881.)

Hoare, Francis Buchanan.

Hoare, Francis O'Donoghue, of London University, son of the Rev. J. W. D. Hoare, B.A., late Vicar of St. Philip's, Sydenham, London, S.E.; a priest (Oblate of St. Charles) and Professor at St. Charles' College, Bayswater, London, W. (1881.)

Hoare, J. W. D., B.A. Trinity College, Dublin, son of an Irish clergyman, and late Vicar of St. Philip's, Sydenham, London, S.E. (1881.)

Hobbs, Miss, of Bristol.

Hodge, Miss Elizabeth, of Liverpool.

Hodgson, Miss, late of the Anglican Sisters who accompanied the Cowley Fathers to India.

Hodson, C. E., M.A. Trinity Hall, Cambridge, late Anglican Chaplain to Sir George Nares' Arctic Expedition.

Hodson, Mrs., of Brighton.

Hoey, Mrs. Cashel, *née* Johnson, authoress of *The Life of Madame de la Rochefoucault*, etc.

Holcome, Miss Josephine.

Holden, Henry, solicitor.

Hole, Mrs. Charles, of North View, Bideford. (1886.)

Holiday, Mrs. Elizabeth, of London.

Hollamby, The late Mrs. Jane, of Tunbridge Wells, Kent.

Holland, The late Lord (Henry Edward Fox). (1850.)

Holland, The late Lady, his wife. (1850.)

Holland, The late Mrs. F. J., wife of the Rev. Canon Holland, M.A., of Canterbury Cathedral. (1889.)

Holland, S. Taprell, of Otterspool, Aldenham, near Watford, Honorary Treasurer of the Benevolent Society for the Relief of the Aged and Infirm Poor.

Holmes, Miss Annie Emma, now a nun, and Canoness of St. Augustine's Convent, Bruges, Belgium.

Holmes, Joseph, of Liverpool.

Holmes, Miss Mary, authoress of *Hints on Music*, etc.

Holmes, Colonel Richard, late of the 39th Regiment.

Holms, Douglas, son of John Holms, formerly M.P. for Hackney. (1890.)

Holt, Arthur, son of Colonel Holt.

Honywood, Sir John, Bart., of Evington, Ashford, Kent; also his two sons and two daughters. (1895.)

Hood, The late Rev. Edward, solicitor; a Jesuit Priest at All Saints', Wardour Castle, Tisbury, Salisbury. (1845.)

Hooke-Robinson, Mrs. Noel, of Ovington Square, London, S.W. (1866.)

Hooper, Dr., B.A. Caius College, Cambridge, and M.B. of London University.

Hope, Miss Ada.

Hope, The late Rev. Douglas, M.A. Christ Church, Oxford, great-grandson of the second Earl of Hopetoun, late Curate of St. John the Divine, Kennington, London, S.E.; a priest, and Director of St. Vincent's Home for Boys, Harrow Road, London, W. (1877.)

Hope, Mrs. D. Boyce, of Dumfriesshire, N.B. (1868.)

Hope, Mrs., daughter of General de Rapp, of Paris. (1858.)

Hope, Mrs., of The Hermitage, Torquay, Devonshire.

Hope, John, grandson of General de Rapp, of Paris. (1858.)

Hope, Miss R. E., daughter of Mrs. D. Boyce Hope, of Dumfriesshire. (1868.)

Hope-Johnstone, Lady.

Hope-Johnstone, Miss, her daughter.

Hope-Scott, The late J. R., M.A. and Fellow of Merton College, Oxford, Q.C., D.C.L., grandson of the second Earl of Hopetoun. (1851.)

Hopkins, The late Rev. Gerald M., M.A. Balliol College, Oxford, Fellow of the Royal University of Ireland; a Jesuit Priest, and Professor of Classics at the University College, Dublin. (1866.)

Hopkins, Thomas, of Llantarnam. (1885.)

Hopkins, Mrs., his wife. (1885.)

Horn, Miss Flora, daughter of the former Recorder of Hereford; now a nun.

Hornby, Edward Owen, M.A. St. John's College, Cambridge; of The Nook, Fareham, Hants. (1869.)

Hornby, Mrs., his wife. (1868.)

Horne, E., M.A. St. John's College, Cambridge, late Vicar of St. Lawrence's, Southampton.

Horne, Mrs., his wife.

Horne, The Misses, her daughters, both nuns.

Horne, Percy Ethelbert, a Benedictine Monk at St. Gregory's, Downside. (1874.)

Horsfield, Miss Mary, of Colchester. (1894.)

Hostage, John, of Chester.

Hostage, Mrs., his wife.

Hoste, Wyndham H. Nelson, barrister, M.A. Christ Church, Oxford, brother of the late Rear-Admiral and Baronet.

Houghton, Colonel. (1889.)

Houghton, Mrs., his wife. (1889.)

Houghton, John, M.A. Trinity College, Cambridge, formerly an Anglican clergyman.

Houghton, Matthew P., B.A. Caius College, Cambridge. (1854.)

Houldsworth, The late Mrs. Henry, of Carrick House, Ayr, N.B. (1872.)

Household, Miss, formerly Associate of East Grinstead Sisterhood, now a nun at Mill Hill. (1868.)

Housworth, Miss Maud, of Ludington. (1868.)

Howard, Lady Anne Jane, daughter of the fourth Earl of Wicklow.

Howard, Esme William, son of the late Henry Howard of Greystoke; formerly *attaché* at the British Embassy at Rome. (1898.)

Howard of Glossop, The late Clara, Lady, daughter of the late John Greenwood of Swarcliffe Hall,

Ripley, Yorkshire, and wife of the second Lord Howard of Glossop, cousin to the Duke of Norfolk, K.G., E.M. (1882.)

Howard of Glossop, Hyacinthe, Lady, second wife of the second Lord Howard of Glossop.

Howard-Hodges, Miss, now Mother Fidelis and Superioress of the Convent of St. Philomena, Rome. (1875.)

Howard-Hodges, Miss Edith, youngest sister of the above. (1897.)

Howarth, Arthur W., a priest at Our Lady of Good Counsel, Eastwood, Nottingham.

Howden, The late Lord, G.C.B., better known as General J. Caradoc.

Howell, J. S., of Chiswick, London, W. (1892.)

Howell, Mrs., wife of the above. (1892.)

Howell, Russell, M.A. of Christ Church, Oxford, late Vicar of St. Veep, Cornwall.

Howell, Mrs. Russell, his wife.

Howitt, The late Mrs. Mary, the celebrated authoress, wife of the late William Howitt, author of *History of Priestcraft*, etc. (1883.)

Howitt, Miss, her daughter. (1883.)

Huddlestone, John Gilbert, of Keble College, Oxford. (1895.)

Hughes, Miss Ada, of Liverpool.

Hughes, Miss Catherine, daughter of W. J. Hughes, of Glancothy, Carnarvonshire; now a Dominican Nun. (1879.)

Hughes, The late Rev. Henry Bailey, son of the late Rev. Howel Hughes, Rector of Trefriew, Carnarvonshire, and great-grandson of the late General Sir Edmund Reilly Cope, Bart.; a priest in Carnarvonshire, Wales.

Hughes, S. J., son of T. Hughes of Reigate.

Hugo, Miss Charlotte, niece of the Most Rev. Dr. Temple, Archbishop of Canterbury; now a nun in New York.

Humphrey, William, M.A. of Aberdeen University, late Incumbent of St. Mary Magdalen's, Dundee, and Chaplain to the Bishop of Brechin ; a Jesuit Priest at St. Beuno's College, St. Asaph, author of *Divine Teacher*, *Written Word*, *Other Gospels*, *Mary Magnifying God*, etc. (1868.)

Hunnybun, W. M., M.A. Caius College, Cambridge, late Vicar of Bickernoller, at one time Professor at the Catholic University College, Kensington, London, W.; now Secretary of the Catholic School Committee.

Hunnybun, Mrs. W. M., his wife.

Hunt, Mrs. (*née* Davidson), of Tulloch.

Hunt, Dr. Lewis Gibson, M.A. of Acadia College, Nova Scotia, M.D. of McGill College, Montreal, L.R.C.P. of Edinburgh, L.F.P.S. of Glasgow, now of Sheffield.

Hunter, Assistant-Commissary, of Dublin.

Hunter, The late Rev. Evans Haynes, M.A. Trinity College, Cambridge, formerly an Anglican clergyman ; a priest.

Hunter, The late Sylvester, formerly a barrister, of Trinity College, Cambridge ; a Jesuit Priest, formerly Rector of St. Beuno's College, Wales, author of *Outlines of Dogmatic Theology*, etc. (1857.)

Hunter, The late Miss, a Benedictine Nun, his sister. (1860.)

Hunter, Rev. Thomas William, M.A. Hertford College, Oxford, late Rector of Callander, N.B.; now Secretary of the Westminster Diocesan Education Fund for Poor Children. (1897.)

Hunter-Blair, Lieutenant-Colonel, of the Scots Fusilier Guards, second son of the late Sir David Hunter-Blair, third Bart. (1869.)

Hunter-Blair, Sir David Oswald, fifth Bart., M.A. Magdalen College, Oxford; of Dunskey, Wigtonshire; late Captain of Royal Ayrshire Militia; son of the late Sir Edward Hunter-Blair, Bart.; a Benedictine Priest at St. Benedict's Abbey, Fort Augustus, N.B. (1875.)

Hunter-Blair, Mrs., wife of John Hunter-Blair, son of the third Baronet.

Huntingtower, The late Lord, eldest son of the seventh Earl of Dysart.

Huntley, D. G., of Aldershot. (1879.)

Hunwick, Miss May Frances.

Huson, William Bernard, late of the Cowley Brotherhood; a Jesuit Priest and Professor at St. Beuno's College, North Wales.

Hutcheon, John, banker, of Aberdeen.

Hutchins, E. J., M.A. Trinity College, Cambridge; for sometime M.P.

Hutchinson, John, barrister.

Hutchinson, Mrs., foundress of St. Catherine's Convent, Edinburgh.

Hutchison, F. B., a Benedictine Monk at Our Lady Star of the Sea and St. Michael, Workington, Cumberland.

Hutchison, The late Rev. William Antony, M.A. Trinity College, Cambridge; a priest of the Brompton Oratory, London. (1845.)

Hutchison, Miss, daughter of the Rector of Checkley.

Hutchison, William J. M., S.C.L. St. Mary's Hall, Oxford, late Curate of St. Endellion, Cornwall, Private Chamberlain to the late and present Popes. (1851.)

Hutchison, Mrs. W. J. M., his wife. (1851.)

Hutton, Mrs. Arthur.

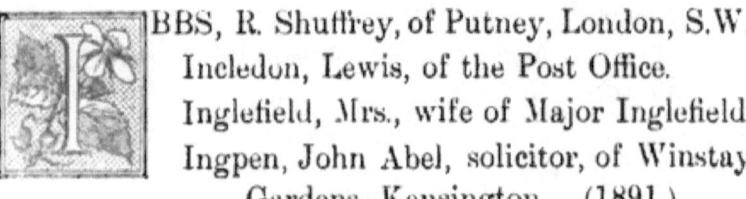BBS, R. Shuffrey, of Putney, London, S.W.

Incledon, Lewis, of the Post Office.

Inglefield, Mrs., wife of Major Inglefield.

Ingpen, John Abel, solicitor, of Winstay Gardens, Kensington. (1891.)

Innes, Lieutenant. (1852.)

Innes, Mrs., his wife. (1852.)

Irvine, Mrs. D'Arcy, wife of Captain D'Arcy Irvine, R.N.

Irving, Mrs. Edward, of Singapore and Bruges. (1893.)

Irwin, The late Mrs., wife of the late P. D. Irwin, of Ferndale Road, Clapham, S.W. (1860.)

JACKSON, Lieutenant Arthur, of the 6th Regiment.

Jackson, Captain, son of the Protestant Bishop of Antigua.

Jackson, Edmund, late Curate of St. Peter's, Barnsley, (1899.)

Jackson, Miss, daughter of the Rev. Canon Jackson, M.A., an Anglican clergyman; now a nun.

Jackson, Captain H. M., Colonial Secretary, Gibraltar.

Jackson, R. C., of South Lodge, Limerick.

Jackson, the Hon. Mrs., mother of the Countesse di Azevedo. (1897.)

James, H., barrister.

James, The late Rev. Henry, M.A. Worcester College, Oxford, formerly Vicar of St. Andrew's, Wells Street, London, W., a Jesuit Priest. (1851.)

James, Miss Julia, daughter of the late Edwin James, formerly M.P. for Marylebone; a nun at Hammersmith, W.

James, Miss Margaret E., of Tenby, authoress.

Jarrett, Colonel. (1848.)

Jarrett, Mrs., his wife. (1848.)

Jarvis, George, surgeon.

Jarvis, Stephen Eyre; a priest of the Order of Charity at St. Etheldreda's, Ely Place, Holborn Circus, London, E.C.

Jarvis, Mrs., his mother.

Jarvis, Miss, her daughter.

Jee, The late Deputy-Inspector-General Joseph, C.B., V.C., of Queniborough Hall, near Leicester; Honorary Surgeon to Her Majesty Queen Victoria.

Jeffcoat, James, of Gloucester; a Jesuit Priest of the Irish Province. (1882.)

Jeffrey, Miss C. M., of Worthing. (1889.)

Jeffries, wife of Colonel Jeffries.

Jenkins, The late Frederick, of Aberdare, Abergavenny, Wales. (1879.)

Jenkins, Thomas, received at Rome. (1885.)

Jerrard, J. H., D.C.L. and Fellow of Caius College, Cambridge, late an Anglican clergyman and Principal of Bristol College, Fellow and Examiner of the London University. (1851.)

Jerrard, Mrs. J. H., his wife. (1851.)

Jerrard, Miss, her daughter. (1851.)

Jocelyn, Miss Edith Eva, of Midford Castle. (1855.)

Johns, Thomas Raymond; a Dominican Priest in California.

Johnson, Arthur, of Stoke Newington. (1888.)

Johnson, Arthur, B.A. Keble College, Oxford.

Johnson, G. F., son of the late British Consul at Antwerp, Belgium.

Johnson, Mrs., mother of G. F. Johnson.

Johnson, Lionel P., B.A. New College, Oxford; author and journalist. (1892.)

Johnson, Mrs., of Cross, wife of George G. Johnson, formerly M.P. for Exeter, and daughter of the late Sir Theodore Brinckman, Bart.

Johnson, Miss, of Oxford. (1892.)

Johnson, Mrs. R. (*née* Hanson), wife of Robert Johnson, of Brook Green, Hammersmith, London, W. (1869.)

Johnston, Harold, of Trinity College, Oxford. (1894.)

Johnston, Miss Ada, daughter of William Johnston, M.P. for South Belfast. (1898.)

Johnstone, The late J., of Alva, late Secretary of the Superior Council of the Brotherhood of St. Vincent de Paul, and President of the Catholic Caledonian Society of Edinburgh.

Johnstone, J. S., M.A. Pembroke College, Oxford. (1863.)

Johnstone, Major, of Folkestone.

Johnstone, The Misses, his daughters.

Jolley, Gwilt, the artist. (1890.)

Jolley, Mrs. G., his wife. (1896.)

Jolliffe, Arthur, son of Cleaves Jolliffe.

Jolliffe, Mrs. Cleaves, his mother.

Jones, Arthur Barclay, Choir-master of the Brompton Oratory, and Professor at the Guildhall School of Music. (1889.)

Jones, Miss Bertha Parry, daughter of Dr. Jones of Ruthin, North Wales. (1893.)

Jones, B. W., solicitor.

Jones, Charles, of the Custom House. (1876.)

Jones, Mrs. Coventry, granddaughter of the late Earl of Coventry, and sister of the Rev. John Coventry, M.A., an Anglican clergyman.

Jones, The Misses, her daughters.

Jones, Frederick F., B.A. Pembroke College, Cambridge, late Curate of Kemerton, Gloucestershire; a Jesuit Priest at Our Lady Immaculate and St. Joseph's, Prescot. (1871.)

Jones, Griffiths Coventry, relative of the Rev. John Coventry, M.A.

Jones, Henry Francis John, of Humpheston Hall, Salop, M.A. of Oxford University, late an Anglican clergyman.

Jones, John, of Chester.

Jones, John Hugh, of Jesus College, Oxford; a priest at St. Helen's, Carnarvon, North Wales. (1865.)

Jones, The late Rev. Joseph, late a Wesleyan minister; a priest.

Jones, Miss Mary, a Carmelite Nun.

Jones, Mrs. Owen, wife of the author of *The Grammar of Ornament*.

Jones, Richard, architect, of Ryde, Isle of Wight,

Jones, Mrs. R., his wife.

Jones, T. Suffield, B.A. New Inn Hall, Oxford.

Joyce, G. H, B.A. Oxford University, late an Anglican clergyman, son of the Vicar of Harrow-on-the-Hill, Middlesex; now a Jesuit. (1894.)

Joyce, P. S. R., of London. (1898.)

Joyce, Sydney, M.A. Christ Church, Oxford.

Judge, J. R., barrister. (1846.)

KARSLAKE, Charles J., brother of the late Sir John Karslake, Q.C., M.P., sometime Attorney-General in the late Lord Beaconsfield's Government. A Jesuit Priest at St. Walburge's, Worcester. (1862.)

Karslake, Henry J., his brother; a priest in Dartmouth, formerly Inspector of Schools in the archdiocese of Westminster. (1862.)

Kavanagh, Mrs. C. A., of Craigie House, Co. Carlow, Ireland.

Kearney, Count.

Kearney, Countess.

Kearney, Countess Alice, her daughter.

Keatinge, Baroness, daughter of the Right Hon. Richard Keatinge, Irish Judge of Probate.

Keble, L. H., solicitor, of London.

Keith, Captain Blake, of the 39th Regiment.

Kelke, W. H., M.A. Brasenose College, Oxford, late Curate of Bedford Leigh; now a barrister.

Kelly, Miss Ida, daughter of Mrs. H. C. Millage, of Paris.

Kelly, Mrs. J. P. H., sister of the Rev. Gilbert Vincent Bull.

Kempe, Frederick Shakersley, of Richmond, Surrey.

Kempe, Reginald C., M.A. Magdalen College, Oxford, formerly an Anglican clergyman.

Kempthorne, Miss, of Wimbledon, S.W.

Kenmare, The late Countess of, daughter of the late Sir Robert Wilmot, Bart., mother of the present Earl of Kenmare, K.P., P.C., formerly Lord Chamberlain. (1852.)

Kenmare, The Countess of, daughter of the late Rev. Lord Charles Thynne, M.A., son of the second Marquis of Bath; wife of the present Earl of Kenmare. (1852.)

Kennard, Charles H., M.A. University College, Oxford, formerly Curate of Newland, Malvern; a priest, Canon, and till lately at the Holy Name, Cannington, Bridgwater, now Chaplain to the Catholic undergraduates of Oxford. (1868.)

Kennedy, The late Lord Gilbert, brother of the second Marquis of Ailsa. (1850.)

Kennedy, Lieutenant J. F. Shaw, late of the 79th Highlanders, son of John Shaw Kennedy, of Kirkmichael, Maybole, N.B. (1880.)

Kennedy, The late Lord Nigel, brother of the second Marquis of Ailsa. (1850.)

Kennedy, Miss Louise, of London.

Keon, Mrs., daughter of Major Hawkes, and wife of the late Hon. Miles Gerald Keon, Colonial Secretary at Bermuda.

Kenny, Courtney Birmingham, landed proprietor in Co. Mayo, Ireland.

Kent, Mrs. Charles, authoress of *Evelyn Kent*, and other novels.

Kent, The late Lieutenant W., R.N., only son of the late Captain Kent, R.N., and father of Charles Kent, the poet and journalist.

Kenyon, John George, M.A., S.C.L. Christ Church, Oxford, grandson of the second Lord Kenyon, formerly a Papal Zouave, Private Chamberlain to His Holiness Pope Leo XIII.

Kerby, Miss Louisa, daughter of the Recorder of Mayfield.

Kerr, Miss A., now a nun at the Convent of the Sacred Heart, Dundrum, Co. Dublin. (1880.)

Kerr, Lady Amabel, daughter of the sixth Earl Cowper, and wife of Admiral Lord Walter Talbot Kerr. (1871.)

Kerr, Lady Cecil, youngest daughter of the sixth Marquis of Lothian, a nun. (1852.)

Kerr, The late Lord Henry Francis, M.A. St. John's College, Cambridge, late Rector of Dittisham, J.P. for Devonshire, second son of the sixth Marquis of Lothian. (1852.)

Kerr, Lady Henry Francis, his wife, daughter of the late Sir A. Hope, G.C.B. (1852.)

Kerr, The late Rev. Henry Schomberg, son of the above, Commander in the Royal Navy; a Jesuit Priest, and Army Chaplain at Cyprus. (1852.)

Kerr, Miss K., now a nun at the Convent of the Sacred Heart, Dundrum, Co. Dublin. (1880.)

Kerr, Major-General Lord Ralph Drury, C.B., late Colonel of the 10th Hussars, third son of the seventh Marquis of Lothian. (1853.)

Kerr, Vice-Admiral Lord Walter Talbot, K.C.B., served in the Baltic during the Russian War, late Commander of the Medway Steam Reserve, Secretary to the Admiralty, late Commander of the Channel Squadron, now Lord Commissioner of the Admiralty, fourth son of the seventh Marquis of Lothian. (1852.)

Kerr, William, son of the late Lord Henry Francis Kerr, M.A., a Jesuit Priest at the Church of the Sacred Heart, Wimbledon, London, S.W. (1852.)

Kerrick, T., of Harlestone House, Norfolk.

Kerrick, Mrs. T., his wife.

Kershaw, The late Rev. John, a Unitarian; a priest, Monsignor, Rural Dean, Canon of Salford and Priest-in-charge of All Saints', Barton-on-Irwell, Manchester. (1837.)

Kiernan, Francis, surgeon.

Kiernan, Miss, of South Kensington, London.

Kilmaine, The Dowager Lady. (1875.)

King, Edwin, of Christ Church, Oxford. (1894.)

King, Mrs. Elizabeth Augustine, wife of the late Dr. Richard King, the polar traveller.

King, Miss Elizabeth, daughter of Richard King, of the Ordnance Department; now editing the *Angelus Magazine*.

King, Francis, relative of the Anglican Bishop of Lincoln; now Curator of the Catholic Biblical Museum, Chelsea, London. (1890.)

King, Miss Isabelle Lichfield, now a Sister of Mercy.

King, Mrs. Hamilton, of Hale End, Essex, authoress of the *Disciples*, etc. (1890.)

King, The late Mrs. John, aunt of the Rev. Owen King, of Courtfield, Ross, Herefordshire. (1886.)

King, Henry F., of Kilburn, London.

King, Holland, late of Brighton, now of South Kensington, London.

King, Mrs., wife of the above.

King, Miss Martha, daughter of Richard King, of the Ordnance Department.

King, Owen C. H., King's College, London, late Curate of Llantarnam, Newport, Monmouthshire, a priest in charge at Courtfield, Ross, Herefordshire. (1885.)

King, Thomas, M.A. Jesus College, Cambridge, Her Majesty's Chief Inspector of Schools, Bath. (1883.)

King, T. A., M.A. Exeter College, Oxford, formerly an Anglican clergyman, then a solicitor. (1844.)

Kingdon, The late Rev. George R., Scholar and M.A. of Trinity College, Cambridge; a Jesuit Priest at Beaumont College, Old Windsor. (1847.)

King-Salter, Captain Edward Philip.

Kingsford, The late Mrs. Annie, M.D. of Paris, wife of the Rev. Algernon G. Kingsford, M.A., Vicar of Atcham, Shropshire; Founder of the Hermetic Society for the Study of Religious Philosophy, and President in 1883 of the Theosophical Society, authoress of *Beatrice, The Perfect Way, Rosamunda, La Rage et M. Pasteur, Roi ou Tyran,* etc. (1870.)

Kirby, Miss Agnes Anne Maltby, of Midford. (1881.)

Kirk, Francis Johnston, B.A. Trinity College, Dublin, late Curate of Gorey, in the diocese of Ferns, Ireland; a priest (Oblate of St. Charles) at

St. Mary of the Angels, Bayswater, London, W. (1854.)

Kirk, Joseph Robinson, B.A. Trinity College, Dublin, brother of the above. (1850.)

Kirwan, The late John F. S., of Moyne, Co. Galway, High Sheriff of Co. Longford; nephew of the late Lord Netterville. (1852.)

Kirwan, Lady Victoria, daughter of the second Marquis of Hastings; wife of the foregoing.

Kitson, Samuel, of Leeds, a well-known sculptor now in the United States. (1890.)

Knight, Alfred, a priest of the Order of Charity at St. Mary's, Newport, Monmouthshire.

Knight, Lieutenant William Osmund, of the 2nd West India Regiment; a Benedictine Monk and Sub-Prior of St. Gregory's Monastery and College, Downside, Bath.

Knill, The late Sir Stuart, Bart., K.S.G., of Crosslets in the Grove, Blackheath, London, S.E., was Lord Mayor of London 1892-93.

Knott, G. R., late member of the Council of the Anglican Guild of All Souls, and Churchwarden of St. Columba's, Haggerston, London, N. (1891.)

Knowles, Mrs., of Bruges. (1895.)

Knowles, Richard B., son of Sheridan Knowles, late editor of the *Nineteenth Century*. (1849.)

Knox, Mrs. Anna S. (*née* Longridge), wife of Dr. Charles F. Knox, of Trinidad, and sister-in-law of the Hon. Charles Leotaud, member of the Legislative Council of Trinidad. (1875.)

Knox, The late Rev. Thomas Francis, B.A. Trinity College, Cambridge, First Class Classical Tripos and Chancellor's Medalist, D.D. of Rome, son of the late Hon. John Henry Knox, M.P., and of Lady Mabella Josephine Needham, daughter of the first Earl of Kilmorey; and grandson of the first Earl of Ranfurly. A priest of the Brompton Oratory, London, S.W., author. (1845.)

Küttner, Samuel W. formerly chaplain to the Protestant Bishop of Jerusalem.

Kyle, Henry Greville, B.A. Merton College, Oxford. (1890.)

Kynaston, J., M.A. Trinity College, Cambridge, formerly an Anglican clergyman; now a solicitor. (1853.)

Kynaston, Mrs., his wife, and daughter of the late John Peel, M.P. for Tamworth. (1853.)

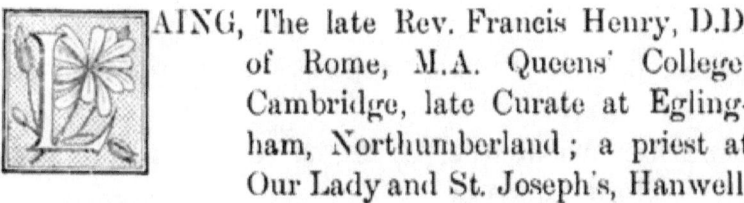LAING, The late Rev. Francis Henry, D.D. of Rome, M.A. Queens' College, Cambridge, late Curate at Eglingham, Northumberland; a priest at Our Lady and St. Joseph's, Hanwell, Middlesex. (1846.)

Laing, The late Robert, formerly Town Clerk of Jedburgh.

Laing, The late William, M.A., late an Anglican clergyman, brother of the late Rev. F. H. Laing, D.D. (1889.)

Laing-Meason, The late A., M.A. of Oxford University, formerly an Anglican clergyman. (1839.)

Laing-Meason, The late Major, late of the 8th Hussars. (1839.)

Laing-Meason, The late Hon. Mrs. (1839.)

Laing-Meason, Miss K. (1887.)

Laing-Meason, The late Lieutenant Malcolm, late of the 10th Hussars, journalist and author. (1839.)

Lamb, Mrs., wife of Francis Lamb, barrister.

Lamb, Miss, her daughter.

Lamb, Frank, B.A., Corpus Christi College, Cambridge.

Lamb, S. B., solicitor, of London.

Lamb, Mrs., his wife.

Lambart, Alfred, grandson of the late Earl of Cavan.

Lambe, The late Rev. David, a priest.

Lambe, Richard Wentworth, D.L., of Durham.

Lambert, Lady.

Lambert, Miss, daughter of Sir G. Lambert, Bart.

Lamotte, Digby H. R. N., M.A. Trinity College, Oxford. (1896.)

Lamprell, The Misses, daughters of Captain T. G. Lamprell.

Lancaster-Woodburne, G. B., M.A. Queen's College, Oxford, barrister.

Lander, W. W., the banker.

Lane, Cecil Bruce.

Lane, Mrs. Charles Leveson.

Lane, Henry Murray, Chester Herald in Her Majesty's College of Arms.

Lane, The late Mrs. H. M., his wife.

Lane, Mrs., wife of Major Lane, of Uske. (1882.)

Lane-Fox, George, M.A. Christ Church, Oxford, Vice-Chancellor of the Primrose League. (1867.)

Lane-Fox, the late Mrs., daughter of General Slade and wife of the above. (1867.)

Lane-Fox, Miss, his sister. (1893.)

Langdon, Charles Baskerville, M.A. University College, Oxford, late Curate of Plympton St. Mary's, Plymouth; a priest in charge of the Catholic Church at Launceston, Cornwall. (1883.)

Langdon, Mrs., of Boulogne.

Langrishe, Mrs. Helen, of Knocktoper Abbey, Co. Kilkenny, daughter of the Right Hon. Fitzwilliam Hume-Dick, of Humewood, Co. Wicklow, and wife of Hercules Robert Langrishe, only son of Sir James Langrishe, Bart. (1894.)

Langston, Miss, foundress of an Anglican sisterhood.

Langston, Mrs., of Rochester. (1899.)

Laprimaudaye, C. J., M.A. St. John's College, Oxford, late Rector of Lavington. (1850.)

Laprimaudaye, Mrs. C. J., his wife. (1850.)

Lascelles, Francis, M.A. Trinity College, Cambridge, formerly curate at Merevale; now a barrister.

Lascelles, Miss M. A., daughter of Rowley Lascelles, J.P., of Pencraig, Boneath, Cardiganshire.

Lassetter, Frederick. (1890.)

Lassetter, Leslie B., B.A. Magdalen College, Oxford, late Curate of St. Germain's, Roath, Cardiff; a Redemptorist Priest at St. Mary's, Kinnoull, Perth, Scotland. (1889.)

Latham, The late Mrs., wife of Mr. Justice Latham, of Bombay, daughter of the late Rev. G. E. Hutchinson, M.A., Canon of Chichester, and niece of the Right Rev. Dr. Moberley, Bishop of Salisbury.

Latham, Frank, of Cival Lodge, East Sheen, Surrey.

Latham, Mrs., wife of the above.

La Touche, Charles, of Marlay.

La Touche, Miss Elizabeth Louisa, of Bellevue, Delgany, Co. Wicklow, Ireland. (1891.)

La Touche, Miss Fanny, her sister. (1860.)

Laughlin, T. R. N., proprietor and editor of the *Port of Spain Gazette*, Trinidad, West Indies.

Laughton, Herbert Richard, son of Dr. Laughton, of Herne Bay; a priest at St. James's, Manchester Square, London, W. (1885.)

Lavie, Miss Flora, of London.

Law, The late Lieutenant Augustus Henry, R.N., a Jesuit Missionary of the Zambesi Mission, South Africa. (1852.)

Law, The Hon. Mrs. Charles.

Law, Mrs. Edmund, of London.

Law, Mrs. Elizabeth, a nun.

Law, Miss Helen Ann, now a Sister of Mercy.

Law, The late Captain J. G., of the Royal Navy. (1852.)

Law, The late Hon. William Towry, M.A., late Vicar of Harborne, and Chancellor of the Diocese of Bath and Wells, fifth son of the first Lord Ellenborough. (1851.)

Law, The Hon. Mrs., wife of the above. (1851.)

Lawrence, Captain.

Lawrie, The late Richard, formerly Revising Barrister for Northumberland. (1889.)

Lawson, H. G., M.A. Wadham College, Oxford.

Laylor, Miss Laura, of Dublin.

Layton, Miss, of Taunton.

Layton, C. Temple, late of The Croft, Mitcham, Surrey, (1882.)

Layton, Mrs., wife of the above, and her three children. (1882.)

Lean, Arthur Stuckey, M.A. Trinity College, Oxford.

Lean, Mrs., of London.

Leathley, Mrs. W. H., wife of the barrister, and authoress of popular tales for the young.

Le Courteur, Colonel, of Jersey.

Lee, Ambrose de Lisle, Bluemantle Pursuivant of Arms, son of the Rev. Dr. F. G. Lee, Vicar of All Saints', Lambeth, S.E. (1881.)

Lee, Mrs. Austin, daughter of the late Most Rev. Dr. Trench, Archbishop of Dublin, and wife of the first Secretary to the British Embassy, Paris. (1899.)

Lee, Mrs. Caroline, daughter of Sir J. Cottrell, Bart.

Lee, The late Mrs., cousin of Cardinal Newman and wife of the Rev. Dr. F. G. Lee, Vicar of All Saints', Lambeth, London, S.E. (1881.)

Leeming, The late Mrs. W., of Alder Hey, West Derby, Liverpool.

Lees, Miss Alice, granddaughter of the late Rev. Sir Harcourt Lees, Bart., formerly an Anglican sister at Clewer Convent, near Windsor.

Lees, John Cathcart, brother of the late Rev. Sir Harcourt Lees, Bart., of Dublin.

Leeson, A., late an Anglican clergyman.

Leeson, Miss Frances M. G.

Legge, Edward, nephew of the Earl of Dartmouth. (1878.)

Leigh, Henry, of Liverpool.

Leigh, J., of Brasenose College, Oxford.

Leigh, William, D.C.L., J.P., of Woodchester Park, Gloucestershire. (1844.)

Le Mesurier, Alfred, of Oriel College, Oxford.

Le Mesurier, Henry, his brother.

Le Mesurier, Mrs., their mother.

Le Mesurier, The Misses, her daughters.

Lennox, The late Lord Alexander Gordon, fourth son of the fifth Duke of Richmond and Gordon. (1878.)

Lennox, Lady Sussex.

Leslie, Archibald, of Edinburgh.

Leslie, Mrs., his wife.

Leslie, Mrs., of London.

Leslie, The Misses, both nuns.

Leslie, Mrs. Charles A., wife of Charles A. Leslie, eldest son of Charles A. Leslie, of Balquhain, N.B.

Leslie, Charles, of Glasgow.

Leslie, Mrs. Charles J., his wife.

Leslie, Mrs. Cuthbert (*née* Drummond), wife of Cuthbert Leslie, of Hassop Hall, Hassop, Derbyshire. (1897.)

Leslie, L., late an Anglican clergyman. (1889.)

Leslie, William Eric; a Jesuit Priest at the Church of the Immaculate Conception, Farm Street, London, W.

Lessetter, A., formerly an Anglican clergyman.

Letherby, Mrs., of London.

Lever, Miss Helena, of Lancaster.

Lever, Miss Julia, her sister.

Levett, Lawrence L., a priest in Shrewsbury.

Levick, Ernest E., a priest at St. Anne's Cathedral, Leeds. (1878.)

Lewis, The late David, M.A. and Fellow of Jesus College, Oxford, late Curate of St. Mary the Virgin, Oxford; translator of the works of St. Teresa. (1846.)

Lewis, The late Hon. Mrs. David, wife of the above, and daughter of the first Lord Methuen. (1846.)

Lewis, F. W., of Cardiff.

Lewis, Mrs. H., wife of Henry Lewis of New Bond Street, London, W. (1881.)

Lewis, Henry Owen, formerly M.P. for Carlow.

Lewis, Mrs. H. O., his wife.

Lewis, Mrs. (formerly Mrs. Spedding), of Whitehaven.

Lewthwaite, William Henry, M A. Trinity College, Cambridge, late Vicar of Clifford; a priest of the Order of Charity.

Leyland, The late Francis Alexander, of Halifax, son of the late Robert Leyland, a distinguished Yorkshire naturalist.

Leys, Mr., son of a Scottish minister.

Liebert, E., of London.

Liebert, Mrs., wife of the above.

Liebert, Miss, their daughter.

Liechtenstein, The late Princess Mary (*née* Fox), daughter adoptive of the late Lord Holland; authoress.

Lilly, William S., LL.M. and Honorary Fellow of St. Peter's College, Cambridge, Secretary of the Catholic Union of Great Britain, author.

Lindsay, The late Hon. Colin, ex-President of the English Church Union, author of *De Ecclesia et Cathedra*, etc., son of the seventh Earl of Crawford and Balcarres.

Lindsay, The late Lady Frances, wife of the above, and daughter and co-heiress of the fourth Earl of Wicklow.

Lister, John, M.A. Brasenose College, Oxford, son of the late Dr. Lister of Sandown, Isle of Wight; a well-known archaeologist and Vice-President of the Bradford Historical and Antiquarian Society.

Little, The late Sydney Hamilton, M.A. Exeter College, Oxford, late Curate of St. Peter's, Bournemouth, and Metropolitan Organising Secretary of the Additional Curates' Society, brother to the Rev. Canon Knox-Little; till lately British Consul at Cadiz, and for some time editor of the *Catholic Times*. (1886.)

Little, Mrs. S. H., wife of the above. (1886.)

Littleboy, W. H., late Curate of Sheston.

Littledale, Mrs., of Bournemouth.

Livingstone, E. D., late clergyman of the Episcopal Church, Beauly, N.B.

Livius, Thomas S., M.A. Oriel College, Oxford, late Curate of St. Kea, Cornwall; a Redemptorist Priest at St. Mary's, Clapham, London, S.W. (1862.)

Lloyd, A., B.A. Exeter College, Oxford, late Curate of All Hallows, Southwark, London, S.E. (1891.)

Lloyd, The late H. W., M.A. and Scholar of Jesus College, Oxford, formerly Curate of Kevidiog. (1846.)

Lloyd, J. J. Hinde, B.A. Wadham College, Oxford.

Lloyd, Mrs., of Cardiff.

Lloyd, Mrs., daughter of the late Sir John Craven Carden, the third Bart., and mother of Lady Rossmore.

Lloyd, Mrs., of Cardiff.

Lloyd, The Misses, of Torquay.

Lloyd, The late Rev. Trevor, M.A. Magdalen Hall, Oxford; a Jesuit Priest.

Lloyd, T. E. A., B.A. of Magdalene College, Cambridge.

Lloyd, T. J. E. A., of Magdalen Hall, Oxford.

Lloyd-Davies, Miss, relative of Sir M. D. Mowbray Lloyd, Bart., D.L. for Cardiganshire.

Locke, Mrs., wife of Major Locke, son of General and Lady Matilda Locke.

Lockhart, The late Rev. William, B.A. Exeter College, Oxford; a priest and Procurator-General of the Rosminian Order, Rector of St. Etheldreda's, Holborn, London, E.C., author of *The Old Religion*, etc. (1844.)

Lockhart, Mrs., mother of the above. (1844.)

Lockhart, Miss, her daughter. (1844.)

Lockyer, Miss, daughter of Captain Lockyer, R.N.

Loisette, Professor, the well-known Lecturer on Memory. (1886.)

Londonderry, The late Elizabeth, fourth Marchioness of, daughter of the third Earl of Roden.

Long, Maurice St. Clair, B.A. Merton College, Oxford.

Longman, John, of London. (1849.)

Longman, William, of London.

Longridge, Captain Cecil, formerly of Jersey. (1882.)

Longueville, Thomas, Christ Church, Oxford; and of Llanforda, Oswestry. (1877.)

Longueville, Mrs., wife of the above. (1877.)

Lord, Frederick Bayley, M.A. St. John's College, Oxford, late Rector of Farnborough, near Bath, Somersetshire. (1877.)

Lord, Mrs., wife of the above, and family. (1877.)

Lorie, Charles, a priest of the Pious Society of Missions, in Chili, South America.

Lothian, The late Cecil Chetwynd, fourth Marchioness of, and only daughter of the second Earl Talbot. (1850.)

Louis, Sir Charles, Bart., of Monaco.

Louth, The Lady. (1888.)

Lovell, Charles, of London.

Lovell, Stuart, his brother.

Lovell, William, his brother.

Lovell, William, M.A. Exeter College, Oxford, late Curate at Wantage.

Lovell, Mrs., niece of Sir Henry Bishop.

Lowe, William, formerly British Consul at Mentone, France. (1896.)

Lowrie, Mrs., wife of the late Captain Lowrie, for many years Governor of York Castle and President of the North and East Riding District Branch of the English Church Union. (1887.)

Lowrie, Miss Anne S., her daughter. (1888.)

Lowrie, Sydney, her son. (1888.)

Lucas, Edward, of Herongate, near Brentwood, Essex.

Lucas, The late Edward, brother of Frederick Lucas, for many years Secretary of the Catholic Academia. (1853.)

Lucas, The late Frederick, B.A. of London University, sometime M.P. for Meath, and first editor of the *Tablet*. (1850.)

Lucas, Mrs. F., wife of the above, a Quaker. (1850.)

Lucas, The late Mrs., mother of the late Frederick Lucas, B.A. (1850.)

Lucas, Miss Margaret, of Liverpool.

Lucas, Mrs., wife of Captain Lucas.

Luck, The late Rev. F. Augustine, a Benedictine Monk.

Luck, The late Rt. Rev. J. E., a Benedictine Monk and afterwards Bishop of Auckland, New Zealand.

Luck, Thomas, a priest, Canon, Rural Dean and Rector of St. Mary's, East Hendred, Stevenson, Berks.

Ludlow, Sir Henry, M.A. and late Fellow of St. John's College, Cambridge, late Chief Justice of Trinidad, B.W.I.

Lumley, The late E., the publisher. (1843.)

Lumsden, H. G., of Clova and Auchindoir, Aberdeenshire.

Lyall, William H., M.A. St. Mary's Hall, Oxford, late Rector of St. Dionis', Backchurch, London, E.C., now member of Council of the Association for the Propagation of the Faith. (1880.)

Lyall, Mrs., wife of the above. (1880.)

Lyle, John Stevenson, B.A. Trinity College, Dublin, formerly an Anglican clergyman; now a priest at Hawick, N.B.

Lynch, Mrs., wife of Charles J. Lynch, J.P. of Petersburg, Galway, Ireland.

Lyons, The late Viscount, uncle to the fifteenth Duke of Norfolk, K.G., and for many years British Ambassador at Paris. (1887.)

Lyons, Miss, daughter of Captain Lyons, R.N.

MABLEY, Miss C. M., of Brighton.

MacCartan, Mrs., wife of John J. MacCartan, of Thomastown, Co. Kilkenny, Ireland. (1861.)

MacCree, Mrs., of Kilburn, London. (1896.)

Macdonald, Sir Archibald Keppel, Bart., of East Sheen, Surrey, and of Woolmer, Liphook, Hants.

MacDonald, Mrs. George, of Glasgow. (1853.)

Macdonald, Hamilton, B.A. of Cambridge University, late Chaplain to H.M.S. *Vernon*. (1898.

MacDonnell, Colonel Alexander, of Belfast. (1870.)

MacDougall, Charles E., son of the Hon. Justice MacDougall.

MacDougall, Mrs., wife of the above, and daughter of the late Colonel J. Jackson, of the Madras Army.

Macfarlane, Sir Donald Horne, late M.P. for Carlow and Argyleshire, son of the late Allan Macfarlane, J.P. for Caithness.

Mack, Mrs., of Paston Hall, Norfolk.

Mackay, Miss Elizabeth Marie Margaret Herd, of St. Andrews, N.B.; daughter of a clergyman of the Church of Scotland.

Mackenzie, Major.

Mackenzie, Lieutenant John, R.N.; son of Captain Mackenzie.

Mackenzie, Mrs., wife of the above.

Mackenzie, Kennett, of Bruges, Belgium. (1890.)

Mackenzie, Mrs., wife of the above, and two children. (1890.)

Mackenzie, L. M., B.A. Exeter College, Oxford.

Mackinnon, Campbell, B.A. Queen's College, Oxford, late incumbent of Port Royal, Jamaica, formerly Consular Chaplain at Lima. (1879.)

Mackinnon, Mrs., wife of above, and family. (1878.)

Mackintosh, Miss, of Edinburgh.

Maclean, Miss, daughter of the late Sir Louis Monro Maclean, Bart.

Maclean, Miss Louisa, her sister.

Maclean, Charles Donald, Mus. Doc.; Madras Civil Service (ret.). (1899.)

Macleod, Rev. C., late Curate of St. Germain's, Roath, Cardiff. (1886.)

MacLeod, John G., M.A. Exeter College, Oxford; a Jesuit Priest at Manresa House, Roehampton, S.W.; brother of the Countess of Caithness. (1854.)

Macmullen, The late Rev. Richard Gell, M.A. and Fellow of Corpus Christi College, Oxford, and late Vicar of St. Mary Magdalen's, Oxford. A priest, and Canon of Westminster. (1846.)

Macmullen, The late Major-General, brother of the above. (1855.)

Macpherson, W. A. Gordon, M.A. of Edinburgh University, now Principal of the High School, Neuilly, Paris.

Madan, James R., M.A. Queen's College, Oxford, formerly Principal of the Protestant College at Warminster; a priest and private Chaplain at Trafalgar House, Salisbury. (1872.)

Maggee, Miss, of South Kensington, London. (1884.)

Maggee, Miss N., her sister. (1884.)

Maguire, Mrs., wife of Major Maguire, of Cheltenham.

Maguth, Miss Rossita, only daughter of Rev. Dr. Maguth, member of the Senate of Cambridge University.

Mahoney, Mrs. Ann, of Colchester. (1893.)

Maidstone, Viscountess, daughter of Sir George S. Jenkinson, Bart., and widow of the only son of the tenth Earl of Winchelsea.

Maillard, Thomas, B.A.

Mainwaring, Mrs., of Kensington.

Maitland, Miss Frances, of Kenmure Castle, New Galloway, N.B.

Maitland, Miss Helen Stuart, daughter of Stuart Cairne Maitland, of Dundrennen and Compstone. (1877.)

Maitland, Miss, daughter of the Rev. J. Maitland, J.P. and D.L. for Kirkcudbright, and granddaughter of the Hon. Mrs. Bellamy Gordon, of Kenmure.

Maitland, Captain W., of the Bengal Staff Corps.

Maister, Reginald, late of Llanthony Abbey, Wales. (1885.)

Major, Charles, of Upper Osbaldistone Road, Stoke Newington. (1888.)

Major, Mrs., wife of the above and nine children. (1888.)

Major, Miss, daughter of the late Rev. Seymour Major, Curate of St. Paul's, Lorrimore Square, Walworth, S.E. (1869.)

Malcolm, Mrs. John, of Aberdeen.

Malleson, The late Colonel George Bruce, C.S.I., of the Bengal Staff Corps, author of *History of the Indian Mutiny*, etc.

Mallet, Miss, daughter of Hugh Mallet, of Ash House, North Devon.

Mallock, Miss, sister of the essayist and niece of James Anthony Froude, the historian.

Malpass, The late Rev. Thomas, a priest.

Manbey, William John, solicitor.

Mangles, A. S., B.A. Magdalen College, Oxford. (1894.)

Mann, Mrs., of Rotherham.

Manners, Admiral Russell Henry, F.R.S., of the Duke of Rutland's family.

Manners, Mrs., wife of the above.

Manners, Miss, her daughter.

Manning, Captain Charles F. S. Downes, of Balliol College, Oxford, and of the Royal Fusiliers, formerly Lieutenant in the Royal Dragoon Guards, son of the late Charles J. Manning, the late Cardinal's brother. (1857.)

Manning, The late Charles J., elder brother of the late Cardinal. (1857.)

Manning, The late Mrs., wife of the above, and daughter of the late Rev. Sir Augustus Brydges Henniker, Bart., M.A. (1857.)

Manning, The late Venerable Henry Edward, M.A. Balliol College, Oxford, and Fellow of Merton, formerly Rector of Lavington and Archdeacon of Chichester; afterwards Cardinal Priest, and Archbishop of Westminster. (1851.)

Manning, The late Rev. W. H., nephew of the Cardinal, a priest, Monsignor, and Rector of St. Charles' College, Bayswater. (1857.)

Mansel, Miss Winifred, sister of Mrs. Algar Thorold, daughter-in-law of Dr. Thorold, Bishop of Winchester; now a Sister of Charity of St. Vincent de Paul.

Mapei, Mrs. Emma, wife of a physician.

Maphson, J., late Curate of St. Mary's, Soho, London, W.

Maples, The late Rev. Frederick G., B.A. St. John's College, Cambridge, formerly Curate of St. Mary's, Soho, London, W.; a priest, and till lately at Our Lady and St. Patrick', Limehouse, London, E. (1868.)

Marras, Ernest, of London.

Marriage, J., of Birmingham, a Quaker.

Marriage, Mrs., his wife.

Marryat, Miss Augusta, of Bruges, relative of the late Captain Marryat, the novelist.

Marsh, Ernest; a priest of the Salesian Order at the Sacred Heart, West Battersea, London, S.W.

Marsh, The late William Hennessy, for seventy-eight years Vicar of Little Compton, Gloucestershire. (1885.)

Marshall, A. F., B.A. of Oxford University, formerly Anglican curate at Liverpool, author of *Comedy in Convocation*, etc.

Marshall, The late Frank, the dramatic author, husband of the late Miss Ada Cavendish, the celebrated actress.

Marshall, The late Rev. Henry J., M.A. Pembroke College, Oxford, D.D. of Rome, late Curate of Burton Agnes; a priest. (1846.)

Marshall, The late Sir James, K.C.M.G., C.M.G., M.A. of Oxford University, late Curate of St. Bartholomew's, Moor Lane, London, E.C., Hon. Treasurer of the Catholic Truth Society.

Marshall, The late T. W. M., M.A. Trinity College, Cambridge, formerly Vicar of Swallowcliffe, Wilts., late one of Her Majesty's Inspectors of Schools, Knight of St. Gregory the Great, author of *Christian Missions, My Clerical Friends, Protestant Journalism*. (1845.)

Marshall, Mrs., of Kensington.

Marshall, Miss, stepdaughter of the Rev. Baring Gould.

Martin, Miss Alice Wykeham, daughter of the Rev. R. Martin, of Leeds Castle, Kent.

Martin, Miss Barbara, daughter of Captain George Bohun Martin, R.N.

Martin, The late Rev. Edward R., a priest.

Martin, Mrs., wife of the late Major Martin.

Martin, Miss, of Mill House, Chelmsford, daughter of the Engineer to the Peninsular and Oriental Company. (1899.)

Martin, The late Geoffrey, of Galway. (1837.)

Martin, Miss Jane, sister-in-law of the late Right Rev. Dr. Attley, Bishop of Hereford. (1882.)

Martindale, Charles, of London.

Martindale, Miss Laura, cousin of Mrs. Davies-Cooke, wife of the late Major J. R. Davies-Cooke, of Rutland Gate, London, S.W. (1884.)

Martyn, Miss E., of Rugeley. (1874.)

Maskell, The late William, M.A. University College, Oxford, formerly Vicar of St. Mary's, Torquay, and Examining Chaplain to the Bishop of Exeter. (1845.)

Mason, Jacob Montagu, M.A. of Oxford University, formerly Rector of Silk Willoughby, Lincolnshire. (1879.)

Mason, Mrs., of Clapham, London, S.W. (1896.)

Mason, The Misses, her daughters. (1896.)

Massen, Dr.

Massingberd-Mundy, Charles John Henry, of South Ormsby Hall, Lincolnshire.

Masters, Mrs., wife of George W. Masters, of Duncan House, Deptford, Kent.

Mather, F. Harry V., B.A. Keble College, Oxford, son of the Rev. Canon Mather of St. Paul's, Clifton, Bristol, late Curate of St. Bartholomew's, Brighton. (1897.)

Mathias, Mrs., mother of Colonel Mathias, C.B., A.D.C., the hero of Dargai.

Mathias, Miss Florence, her daughter.

Matthews, Colonel.

Matthews, Mrs. Florence Charlotte, wife of Captain James Matthews, of the Bombay Port Trust. (1897.)

Matthews, Miss, daughter of an Anglican clergyman.

Matthews, Miss, of Dublin.

Matthews, John, of London.

Matthews, Mrs., wife of the above.

Matthews, John Hobson, of Cardiff, solicitor, Hon. Secretary and founder of St. Teilo's Historical Society.

Matthews, Miss L., daughter of Captain Matthews, of Bombay.

Maturin, Basil William, B.A. Trinity College, Dublin, late an Anglican clergyman and member of the Society of St. John the Evangelist, now a priest. (1897.)

Maude, Mrs. Arthur, of London.

Maude, The late Rev. Arthur V., B.A. of Durham University, and formerly lieutenant in the 77th Regiment, grandson of the first Viscount Hawarden ; a priest at the Brompton Oratory, London, S.W. (1855.)

Maude, W. C., of Exeter College, Oxford. (1855.)

Maurel, Madame (*née* Mackay), daughter of the late John Mackay, the banker, of Inverness, N.B.

Maurice, R. R., a priest at St. Vincent of Paul, Knutsford, Cheshire, and Chaplain to H.M. Prison.

Maw, John Henry, of Brixton, London, S.W.

Maxwell, The Hon. Mrs. Marmaduke C.

May, A. Herbert, M.A. Wadham College, Oxford, late Curate of St. Paul's, Oxford. (1891.)

May, Mrs., wife of the above. (1891.)

May, Felix, a priest at St. Patrick's, Leicester.

May, George Aloysius, of Midford, Bath. (1882.)

Maycock, G. B., of Edgbaston, Birmingham.

Maycock, Mrs. Mary Elizabeth, wife of Bernard Joseph Maycock, B.A., LL.B., solicitor, of Harborne, near Birmingham.

Mayhearne, Mrs., of Manchester.

Mayne, Captain Jasper Graham, late of the Inniskillen Fusiliers, and District Inspector of Musketry, now Chief Constable of East Suffolk. (1882.)

Mayo, Arthur, V.C., B.A. Hertford College, Oxford, at one time Midshipman in the Indian Navy, and late Curate of St. Peter's, Plymouth.

Mayo, Mrs., wife of the above.

McAvoy, Mrs., of Acton, London, W., and her three children.

McCall, Archibald S., of Magdalen College, Oxford; a priest at St. Philip's, Arundel, Sussex.

McChristie, Mrs., wife of the City Revising Barrister.

McCreath, The late Mother Mary, of the Convent of Mercy, Crispin Street, Spitalfields.

McGavin, W. P. M., of Clapham, London, S.W.

McGowan, The late General, who served during the Indian Mutiny.

McGree, Miss, daughter of a former Anglican Chaplain at Gibraltar, now a nun.

McKay, Mrs., of London.

McKenna, Mrs., granddaughter of the late Sir Joseph Barrington, Bart., and wife of W. McKenna.

McKenzie, Lewis, of Brighton.

McLaurin, Julius, late Professor of Mathematics at Stonyhurst College, son of the late W. C. A. McLaurin, late Dean of Moray and Ross.

McLaurin, The late Miss V., his sister, a Franciscan Nun.

McLaurin, The late W. C. A., late Dean of Moray and Ross.

McLaurin, The late Mrs., wife of the above.

McMurdie, Henry S., formerly an Anglican clergyman; a priest, and till lately Professor of Logic and Metaphysics at Mount St. Mary's College, Maryland, U.S.A. (1848.)

Meady, Richard, of Cloudesley Lodge, Southampton, son of an Anglican clergyman.

Meakinson, H. R., sometime Vicar of St. Andrews, Sydney, Australia.

Meason, The late Rev. A. Laing, a Jesuit Priest. (1839.)

Meason, The late Major Laing, of the 8th Hussars. (1839.)

Meason, The late Hon. Mrs. Laing. (1839.)

Meason, The late Mrs. Malcolm Laing, wife of Major Laing Meason. (1839.)

Meason, Miss Laing, her daughter, a nun. (1839.)

Meers, A., late Anglican curate at Douglas, Isle of Man.

Melhuish, Mrs., of London.

Mends, Mrs., wife of the late Captain Mends, R.N.

Meredith, W. H. Stewart, B.A. Merton College, Oxford, formerly an Anglican clergyman. (1887.)

Merewether, C. J., of Christ Church, son of the late Dean of Hereford.

Merewether, Mrs., wife of the late Dean of Hereford.

Merewether, The Misses, her daughters.

Metcalfe, John Henry, son of Captain Metcalfe, grandson of the late Rector of Kirkbride, Cumberland.

Metcalfe, Mrs., wife of the above.

Mexborough, John Charles, fourth Earl of.

Meynell, Mrs. Wilfred (née Thompson), sister to Lady Butler, painter of "The Roll Call"; authoress of *Preludes*, etc.

Meyrick, The late Rev. Thomas, M.A. and Scholar of Corpus Christi College, Oxford, formerly an Anglican clergyman; a Jesuit Priest. (1845.)

Michie, Charles, shipmaster, Aberdeen.

Middleton, Miss, formerly an Anglican Sister at All Saints', Margaret Street, London, W.

Middleton, Warren B., a priest at the Sacred Heart, Bideford, Devonshire.

Mildmay, Mrs., of Chelsea, S.W.

Miles, Mrs., wife of Francis Miles of the Admiralty. (1867.)

Milford, Lady, daughter of the fourth Earl of Wicklow, wife of Richard, Lord Milford.

Millage, Mrs. H. C., wife of an English journalist in Paris.

Millard, Christopher Sclater, M.A. Keble College, Oxford, son of the late Rev. Canon Millard, Vicar of Basingstoke, Hants; studied for some time at the Salisbury Theological College. (1897.)

Miller, J., publisher, of Edinburgh.

Miller, Mrs., of Panmure House, Forfarshire, N.B.

Mills, Mrs., wife of a Cornish Anglican clergyman.

Mills, B. R. V., of Christ Church, Oxford, son of Arthur C. Mills, at one time M.P. for Exeter.

Mills, Henry Austin, of Trinity College, Cambridge; a priest at the Birmingham Oratory.

Mills, H. E. Stuart, formerly an Anglican rector; now a priest in charge of St. Mary's, Chepstowe, Monmouthshire.

Mills, Richard, of Brasenose College, Oxford, solicitor.

Mills, Mrs., wife of the above.

Milman, Gustave, of Stoke Newington, London. (1888.)

Milne, Mrs. Gordon, wife of the late Incumbent of St. James's, Cupar Fife, N.B. (1864.)

Milne, G. L. Gordon, her son. (1864.)

Milne, J. E. Gordon, R.N., her son. (1864.)

Milne, William, of Durham; formerly a Presbyterian.

Milner, H., formerly Curate of Barnoldswick.

Milner, Wilfrid Leahy, of St. John's College, Cambridge, now at the English College, Rome. (1892.)

Milsome, William John, of Brighton. (1888.)

Minster, T., M.A. St. Catherine's College, Cambridge, late Vicar of St. Saviour's, Leeds. (1852.)

Mitchell, Captain, of Buldaire and Balfour.

Mitton, Arthur Tennant, M.A. St. Catherine's College, Cambridge, late Vicar of Stowmarket and Markyate, Dunstable. (1899.)

Mivart, Mrs. Caroline Georgina, mother of Professor Mivart. (1846.)

Mivart, Charles Lister, her son. (1846.)

Mivart, Mrs. Mary Ann, wife of the Professor. (1856.)

Mivart, Professor St. George, F.R.S., of Harrow and King's College, London, at one time Professor at Louvain University, author of many scientific works. (1844.)

Moberley, William, late Vicar of Easton, Winchester.

Moger, Miss Caroline, of Midford. (1848.)

Moger, Miss Charity, of Midford. (1848.)

Moger, Miss Maria Marina, of Midford. (1852.)

Moir, Dr., of Edinburgh.

Molesworth, Sir Paul William, Bart., M.A. Trinity College, Cambridge, late Rector of Tetcott, Devonshire. (1852.)

Molesworth, Lady, wife of the above. (1852.)

Molyneux, Miss, formerly an Anglican Sister at All Saints', Margaret Street, London, W., now a nun of the Canonesses of St. Augustine, Hoddeston.

Molyneux, Miss Rose, of Brighton.

Moncks, Miss Ellena, of Liverpool. (1892.)

Monro, Mrs., wife of the Rev. W. C. Monro, of King's College, London, and formerly Curate of St. Paul's, Knightsbridge, and her two children.

Monselle, The late Rev. Stanislaus, a Dominican Priest.

Monselle, The late Rev. Vincent, a Dominican Priest.

Montagu, Mrs., wife of Robert Montagu, grandson of the sixth Duke of Manchester.

Monteith, The late Robert, of Carstairs, M.A. Trinity College, Cambridge.

Monteith, Mrs., wife of the above.

Montgomery, The late Hon. Mrs. Alfred, second daughter of the first Lord Leconfield, mother of the Marchioness of Queensberry, and authoress of *On the Wing*, *The Eternal Years*, etc.

Montgomery, George, M.A. Trinity College, Dublin, formerly a clergyman of the Irish Church. (1845.)

Montgomery, James Wallace, M.A. (a Presbyterian), of the Castle, Garvaghy, Aughnacloy. (1891.)

Moody, Mrs. Mary, of London.

Moody, Robert Sadlier, M.A. Christ Church, Oxford, late Curate of Aston. (1855.)

Moody, Mrs., wife of the above. (1855.)

Moore, The late Rev. Algernon, of London University, a priest.

Moore, Captain, of the Royal Navy.

Moore, Captain. (1849.)

Moore, Miss, of Folkestone.

Moore, The late Charles of Mooresfort, Tipperary, sometime M.P., and father of Count Arthur Moore, M.P.

Moore, Clement Harrington, M.A. Christ Church, late Curate of St. Barnabas's, Oxford; a priest, and Domestic Prelate to H.H. Pope Leo XIII. (1872.)

Moore, George, solicitor. (1848.)

Moore, James B., a priest at Aberavon, Glamorganshire.

Moore, John E., a Jesuit Priest at Manresa, Roehampton, S.W.

Moore, R., ex-Missionary of the Society for the Propagation of the Gospel in India.

Moore, The late Rev. Roderick, formerly of the Civil Service; a priest at St. George's Cathedral, Southwark, London, S.E.

Moore, W. H., surgeon, of Woodbridge.

Moore, Mrs., wife of the above.

Mordaunt, Mr., brother-in-law of the Rector of Beckworth. (1868.)

Mordaunt, Mrs., wife of the above. (1868.)

Mordaunt, Miss, her daughter. (1868.)

Mordaunt, The late Rev. Wilfrid; a Jesuit Priest at St. Mary's, Westminster. (1865.)

Mordaunt, Miss, his sister.

Morell, J. Reynell, of the British Museum.

Moreton, Francis, eldest son of Captain the Hon. Percy Moreton, and grandson of the first Earl of Ducie.

Morgan, A., librarian of Walsall.

Morgan, Miss, of Bridgend, Glamorganshire.

Morgan, Mrs., late of Wolverhampton.

Morgan, Francis Aloysius, of Lancaster. (1857.)

Morgan, Miss Mary Illtyd, Superior of St. Michael's Home, Treforest.

Morgan, Thomas, member of the Llantaranm School Board. (1868.)

Morland, The late Rev. Henry, B.A. Hertford College, Oxford, late curate at Middle Clayton; a priest. (1855.)

Morrell, Mrs., wife of the late Rev. Baker Morrell, B.A., Curate of St. Cuthbert's, Earl's Court, London, W. (1885.)

Morris, Charles Smyth, M.A. of New College, Oxford, eldest son of Thomas Charles Morris of Brynmyrddin, and nephew of William Morris, M.P. for Carmarthen Burghs. (1883.)

Morris, David Henry Martin, fifth son of John Morris, of Duddington House, Sunbury-on-Thames.

Morris, The late Rev. John, of Trinity College, Cambridge; a Jesuit Priest, formerly Rector of St. Stanislaus, Roehampton, S.W., author of *Troubles of Our Catholic Forefathers*, etc., etc. (1846.)

Morris, The late Rev. John Brande, M.A. and Fellow of Exeter College, Oxford, formerly an Anglican clergyman; a priest of the Brompton Oratory. (1846.)

Mortimer, Samuel, of Cottles, Wilts. (1865.)

Morton, Miss Lindon, of Birmingham. (1885.)

Mossman, The late Thomas Wimberley, B.A., Hon. D.D. of the University of the Southern States of America, and Rector of East and West Torrington, Wragby, Lincolnshire. (1885.)

Moultrie, John, B.A. New College, Oxford, late Curate of Christ Church, Doncaster. (1890.)

Mowbray, W. J. L., formerly a Wesleyan.

Mowbray, Mrs., wife of the above, and family.

Moxon, C. J., member of the Institute of British Architects.

Muddiman, J. G., M.A. Exeter College, Oxford, solicitor, of St. Clement's Inn, Strand, W.C. (1897.)

Muir, Dr., of Edinburgh.

Muldary, The late Mrs. J. Mill, niece of the late Earl of Limerick.

Muller, Miss Zila Henrietta, of Plymouth. (1879.)

Mullins, Mrs., wife of Colonel Mullins. (1881.)

Mulvaney, William, J.P., of Billindaggin, Enniscorthy, Co. Waterford.

Munko, Dr.

Munro, The late Rt. Rev. Alexander; a priest, Domestic Prelate to H.H. Pope Leo XIII., Canon and Provost of the Cathedral Chapter of Glasgow. (1834.)

Munro, Philip Gun, B.A. of Magdalen Hall, Oxford, and late Curate at Ware; a priest at St. John's, Horsham, Sussex. (1852.)

Munroe, Miss, of Seymour Street, London, W.

Munroe, Mrs., of Brighton.

Munson, Miss Emma, of Colchester. (1893.)

Murphy, Mrs., widow of an Irish clergyman, now a nun at Gibraltar.

Murphy, Arthur, of Prior Park. (1844.)

Murphy, James, of Prior Park. (1844.)

Murphy, Miss Jane, of Manchester. (1857.)
Murphy, Henry, of Prior Park. (1844.)
Murphy, Miss Maria Anne, of Prior Park. (1844.)
Murray, Mrs., of Westward Ho, Devonshire.
Murray, Lady Agnes, of Polmaise.
Murray, The late Mrs., of Philiphaugh.
Murray, Mrs. James, of Edinburgh.
Murray, John, eldest son of John Murray, of Philiphaugh.
Murray, Mrs., wife of the above.
Murray, Mrs. John, of Edinburgh.
Murray, W., formerly Incumbent at Colchester.
~~Myers, Frederick, B.A., formerly Perpetual Curate of Keswick; a Jesuit Priest at Stonyhurst College, Blackburn, Lancashire.~~
Myers, Mrs., of Hyde Park Court, London, W.

NASIF, Amin, late Director of Protestant Missions in Cairo. (1881.)
Nash, Francis H., M.A., late Curate of All Saints', Oxford, and son of the late Rev. Dr. Nash. (1865.)
Nash, Mrs., wife of the above. (1865.)
Nash, Mrs. de Lacy, niece of General de Lacy.
Neave, J. A., non-collegiate student of Oxford University.
Neave, Richard, of the War Office.
Neligan, William Hayes, formerly Curate of the Anglican Church; now a priest and Vicar-General of the Bahamas Islands, author. (1860.)

Nelson, The Countess (*née* Lady Mary Agar), daughter of the second Earl of Normanton, wife of the third Earl.

Nelson, The Hon. Charles Horatio, second son of the third Earl Nelson. (1896.)

Nelson, H., late Curate of Frome Selwood, Somerset.

Nelson, The Hon. Thomas Horatio, of Keble College, Oxford, third son of the third Earl Nelson.

Nesbitt, Captain, late of the Royal Artillery.

Nethercott, Miss Maria, of Dublin, authoress. (1893.)

Neve, The late Rev. Frederick R., M.A. Oriel College, Oxford, late Vicar of Poole Keyns; a priest and Provost of Clifton. (1845.)

Nevile, Ralph H. C., Trinity College, Cambridge; of Wellingore Hall, Grantham.

Nevill, Lord William Beauchamp, fourth son of the Marquis of Abergavenny, formerly A.D.C. to the late Duke of Marlborough when Viceroy of Ireland. (1886.)

Neville, William, of Brighton. (1849.)

Neville, William Payne, M.A. Trinity College, Oxford; a priest of the Birmingham Oratory.

Nevins, Mrs. Probyn, of Kensington.

Nevins, The Misses, her daughters.

New, The late Rev. F. T., M.A. St. John's College, Oxford, late Curate of Christ Church, St. Pancras, London; a priest. (1847.)

New, Mrs., wife of the above, and cousin of the late Bishop of Lichfield (Dr. Selwyn) and to the late Lord Justice Selwyn. (1847.)

New, Mortimer, of London.
New, Colonel Selwyn, late of the Madras Army.
Newburgh, Margaret, Countess of, daughter of the first Marquis of Ailsa.
Newcastle, Henrietta Adela, Dowager Duchess of. (1879.)
Newdegate, Alfred, M.A. Christ Church, Oxford, late Vicar of Kirk Hallam, cousin of the late Charles N. Newdegate, M.P. for North Warwickshire. (1875.)
Newdegate, Mrs., wife of the above, and family. (1875.)
Newell, The late Rev. Reginald; a Dominican Priest.
Newman, His Eminence the late John Henry, B.D., M.A. and Fellow of Trinity College, Oxford, Fellow of Oriel, and formerly Vicar of St. Mary the Virgin's, Oxford. For some time Rector of the Catholic University, Dublin, Cardinal Deacon, and Superior of the Birmingham Oratory, author. (1845.)
Newnham, Captain F. G., late of the Indian Army, Bombay. (1879.)
Newnham, Mrs., wife of the above. (1879.)
Newton, Lieutenant Robert, of the Royal Navy.
Nichol, Pringle, Scholar, Exhibitioner and B.A. of Balliol College, Oxford, author of *The Life of Victor Hugo*, etc.; son of the late Professor Nichol, of Glasgow University. (1894.)
Nicholl, Captain Iltid, R.N., second son of the late Right Hon. J. Nicholl, M.P.
Nichols, Dr., of London.
Nicholson, Beckett, solicitor.

Nicholson, Miss, of Bath.

Nicholson, Miss, of Inglewood, Wimbledon, London, S.W.

Nicholson, Major William, late of the 3rd Lancashire Militia.

Nicholson, Mrs., late Lady Principal of the Convalescent Home at Hemel Hempstead. (1869.)

Nicols, The late Rev. David Charles, M.A. St. Peter's College, Cambridge, Crosse University Scholar, late Curate of All Saints', Margaret Street, London, W.; a priest, and till recently in charge of St. Helen's, Ongar, Essex.

Nightingale, Lieutenant Ernest, youngest son of Sir Charles Nightingale, seventh baronet.

Nightingale, Mrs. E., wife of the above, daughter of Thomas Nimmo, and niece of Sir Thomas Gladstone, Bart.

Nimmo, The Misses, relatives of the late Right Hon. W. E. Gladstone, both nuns.

Noble, The late Lieutenant John Edmund, of the King's Own Yorkshire Light Infantry.

Norfolk, The late Minna, Duchess of, sister to the late Viscount Lyons, English Ambassador to France, and wife to the fourteenth Duke of Norfolk. (1856.)

Norfolk, The late Duchess of (née Lady Flora Abney-Hastings), niece to the last Marquis of Hastings, and wife to the fifteenth Duke of Norfolk, K.G., E.M. (1875.)

Norman, G. B., M.A. Trinity College, Cambridge, late Curate at Weston.

Norman, Herman Cameron, B.A. Trinity College, Cambridge, now at the British Embassy at Cairo.

Norris, Henry, a priest at St. John the Baptist's, Tamworth, Staffordshire.

North, George, of Cardiff. (1886.)

North, H. G., M.A. St. John's College, Oxford, late a clergyman of the Anglican Church. (1895.)

North, William Henry John, eleventh Lord, son of the tenth Baroness North, and grandson of the third Earl of Guilford; Knight of Malta. (1879.)

North, Frederica, Lady, wife of the above. (1879.)

Northcote, Charles Gilbert, of Tregothnan Road, Clapham, London, S.W. (1898.)

Northcote, James Spencer, M.A. and Scholar of Corpus Christi College, Oxford, First Class in Classics, late Curate at Ilfracombe. A priest, and Provost of the Cathedral Chapter of Birmingham, author. (1846.)

Northcote, Mrs. Stafford, sister-in-law of the late Lord Iddesleigh.

Northcote, Miss, daughter of the late Rev. Stafford Northcote, a nun.

Norton, Brinsley, of London.

Norton, Charles, son of the Hon. G. Norton, and nephew to Lord Grantley.

Norton, Fletcher, of London.

Norton, T. N., formerly Curate at Devizes.

Nunney, Miss, of Oxford. (1889.)

Nunney, Miss E. M., her sister. (1890.)

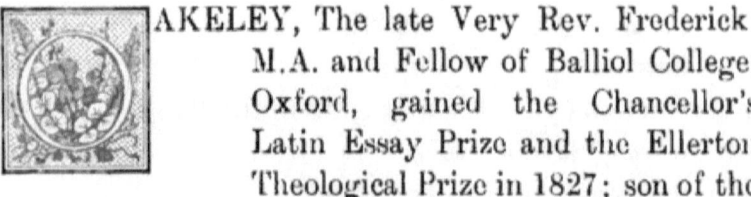AKELEY, The late Very Rev. Frederick, M.A. and Fellow of Balliol College, Oxford, gained the Chancellor's Latin Essay Prize and the Ellerton Theological Prize in 1827; son of the late Sir Charles Oakeley, first baronet, formerly Governor of Madras; Prebendary of Lichfield, Incumbent of All Saints', Margaret Street, London, W., and Select Preacher at Oxford University. A priest, Canon of Westminster, at St. John's, Duncan Terrace, Islington, author. (1845.)

Oates, The late William Wilfrid, the publisher.

O'Brien, Mrs. (née Maria C. Procter), wife of F. Lucius O'Brien, formerly an Anglican Sister at East Grinstead. (1866.)

O'Brien, The late James, M.A. Sidney Sussex College, Cambridge, late Vicar of Lyneham. (1856.)

O'Brien, Mrs., wife of J. H. Archer O'Brien, M.R.I.A. (1880.)

O'Brien, Miss, of Windsor. (1875.)

O'Brien, Mrs., wife of William O'Brien, late M.P. for Cork City. (1891.)

O'Callaghan, The Hon. Mrs., daughter of the late Rev. W. H. Williams, M.A., formerly of Wolverhampton, and wife of the late Hon. G. C. G. O'Callaghan, eldest son of Viscount Lismore. (1879.)

O'Connell, Mrs., wife of Daniel O'Connell, late M.P. for Tralee. (1875.)

O'Connor, Mrs., wife of Dr. D. M. O'Connor, of Worksop. (1883.)

O'Connor, Mrs. Alice Marian, wife of Charles O'Connor of Roscommon. (1891.)

O'Connor, The late Michael, formerly Rector of Culdoff, Ireland.

O'Conor, Mrs., wife of the late Denis O'Conor, M.P. for Sligo, brother to The O'Conor Don; and daughter of the late Rev. W. Kevill-Davies, of Croft Castle, Herts.

Oddie, Arthur, of Colney House, Hants.

Oddie, Claude, his brother.

Oddie, Miss Georgina, their sister.

Oddie, Miss Katherine, her sister.

Oddie, Philip, her brother.

Oddie, Mrs., mother to the above.

Oddie, Captain H., late of the 15th Regiment.

Odling, Walter, of Burton-on-Trent. (1875.)

Odling, Mrs., wife of the above, and four children. (1886.)

O'Flaherty, Mrs., wife of Anthony O'Flaherty formerly M.P. for Galway.

Ogden, Booth, of Broadbottom, Manchester. (1899.)

Ogilvie-Forbes, J. C. M., of Boyndlie, Aberdeenshire, J.P., M.A. Keble College, Oxford, formerly an Anglican clergyman in Colombo, Ceylon. (1881.)

O'Gorman, Mrs., daughter of Mervyn N. Crawford, M.D., of Millwood, Co. Fermanagh, and wife to Edmund O'Gorman, of Co. Clare. (1860.)

O'Grady, Mrs., of Onslow Square, London, S.W.

O'Hanlon, Miss, of Manchester.

Okeley, Sebastian, M.A. and Scholar of Trinity College, Cambridge.

Oldaker, Miss Louisa Marian, of Green Lanes, London, N. (1884.)

Oldham, The late Rev. George, M.A. Trinity College, Cambridge, formerly Curate at Dorking, built St. Mary Magdalen's, Brighton. A priest, and first in charge of the above church at Brighton. (1860.)

O'Mahoney, Mrs. William, daughter of Colonel Peisley l'Estrange, and sister-in-law of the late Most Rev. Dr. Marcus Beresford, Protestant Archbishop of Armagh, and Primate of All Ireland.

O'Neil, Arthur, B.A. of Jesus College, Cambridge.

O'Neil, Mrs., of Rotherham.

Orford, The late Horatio William Walpole, fourth Earl, of Trinity College, Cambridge, formerly M.P. for Norfolk and J.P. and D.L. for the same county.

Ornsby, The late Robert, M.A. and Fellow of Trinity College, Oxford, First Class in Classics, late Curate at Chichester, Fellow of the Royal University of Ireland, and sometime Professor of Classics at the Catholic University College, Dublin, author of *Life of St. Francis de Sales*, *Memoirs of the Late James Hope-Scott, Q.C.*, etc. (1847.)

Ornsby, Mrs., wife of the above, and sister to the late Rev. J. B. Dalgairns, M.A. Exeter College, Oxford, and a priest of the Brompton Oratory. (1848.)

Orr, James, B.A. Oriel College, Oxford, late Curate of St. James', Bristol.

Osborne, The late Lord Francis Godolphin, M.A. Trinity College, Cambridge, late Rector of Elm, Frome, and second son of the eighth Duke of Leeds. (1877.)

Osborne, The late Rev. R. B., nephew of the eighth Duke of Leeds; late Vicar of Dunston; a priest of the Brompton Oratory, London, S.W. (1878.)

Ottywell, G. S., a Baptist.

Ottywell, Mrs., his wife.

Ouseley, José-Maria G. T., late an Anglican clergyman. (1894.)

Owen, The late Mrs., wife of the late Canon Owen, an Anglican clergyman.

Owen, Octavius, son of the above.

Owen, The late Rev. William Eddowes, M.A., his brother; a priest.

Owens, Miss, of The Abbey, Denbigh. (1885.)

Oxenford, The late John, poet, dramatic author and critic of the *Times*.

PACKMAN, W. Vance, of Linden Gardens, London, W., formerly editor of the *Church Review* and Assistant-Organising Secretary to the Midland District of the English Church Union; now editor of various trade journals, founder and organiser of the Apostolate of the Press, the Fraternal Society of Converts, and of the Historical Research Society. (1887.)

Packman, Mrs. Vance, wife of the above. (1890.)

Paget, Commander Claude, second son of the late Colonel Leopold Paget and grandnephew of the first Marquis of Anglesea. (1887.)

Paget, The late Miles, son of Captain Catesby Paget, and grandnephew of the first Marquis of Anglesea. (1884.)

Paget, Miss Ruth, his sister. (1894.)

Paine, Arthur Heintz, M.A. Trinity College, Cambridge, late Curate of St. Margaret's, Liverpool. (1896.)

Pakenham, The late Hon. and Rev. C. R., formerly Captain of the Guards, son of the second Earl of Longford, nephew of Arthur, first Duke of Wellington, and at one time Equerry to Her Majesty Queen Victoria; a Passionist Priest. (1850.)

Paley, The late Professor F. A., M.A. St. John's College, Cambridge, grandson of the author of *The Evidences;* at one time Professor of Classics at the Catholic University College, Kensington, London, W., Classical Examiner to the London University, author. (1846.)

Palk, Miss, of Kensington. (1876.)

Palk, Lawrence, received at Florence. (1898.)

Palles, Mrs., of Canada, wife of Andrew Palles, brother of Lord Chief Baron Palles. (1888.)

Palmer, Lieutenant-Colonel, of Alnwick, Northumberland.

Palmer, Charles F. Raymund; a Dominican priest at St. Dominic's Priory, Haverstock Hill, author of *History of Tamworth, Life of Cardinal Howard,* etc.

Palmer, Frederick, a priest of the Order of Charity at St. Peter's, Cardiff.

Palmer, Miss Lizzie, of Solihull, Warwickshire. (1892.)

Palmer, The late William, M.A. and Fellow of Magdalen College, Oxford, formerly an Anglican clergyman, elder brother of the first Earl Selborne. (1845.)

Palmer, William, B.A. Worcester College, Oxford.

Palmer, W. Z., M.A. of Oxford University.

Parfitt, The late Mrs. Anna, mother of the late Right Rev. Monsignor Parfitt, D.D., and family. (1860.)

Parfitt, The late Rt. Rev. Charles, D.D. of Rome, a priest, Monsignor, and Canon Theologian in the Diocese of Clifton. (1839.)

Parke, Miss Elizabeth, of Colchester. (1893.)

Parker, Henry Martyn, M.A. Lincoln College, Oxford, late Curate of St. Bartholomew's, Brighton; a Jesuit Priest at Our Lady of the Assumption, Rhyl, Flintshire. (1877.)

Parker, The late Sir Henry Watson, solicitor.

Parkington, Major Roper, Lieutenant of the City of London.

Parkinson, Claude, of Jesus College, Oxford.

Parkinson, James, of Kensington.

Parkinson, Thomas B., M.A. Queens' College, Cambridge, formerly Incumbent of St. Mary's, Wakefield; a Jesuit Priest, till recently at St. Aloysius', Oxford, now at Stonyhurst College, Blackburn. (1851.)

Parnell, Miss Victoria, of Bayswater, London, W. (1884.)

Parr, Mrs. Catherine, of London.

Parr, Miss Olive, her daughter.

Parry, The late Rev. Charles E., B.A., late an Anglican clergyman; a priest.

Parry, M. Sidney, of University College, Oxford; Hon. Secretary of Newman House, Kennington, London, S.E. (1887.)

Parsons, The late Daniel, M.A. Oriel College, Oxford, late Curate of Marden, Wilts. (1843.)

Parsons, Mrs., wife of the above, authoress. (1843.)

Partridge, Mrs., wife of the late Professor Partridge, of New Street, Spring Gardens, London, S.W., and her three sons and four daughters.

Pasco, Miss, of Plymouth.

Patmore, The late Coventry, poet.

Patmore, Mrs., wife of the above, and daughter of the late Right Hon. Sir John Barnard Byles, the Judge.

Patterson, The late Major-General, brother of the Right Rev. Dr. Patterson, Bishop of Emmaus.

Patterson, Miss Elizabeth, of Liverpool.

Patterson, George Hare, late Unitarian Minister, of Stanhope Street Church, Belfast. (1898.)

Patterson, Miss Gwendoline Josephine, his daughter. (1898.)

Patterson, James Laird, M.A. Trinity College, Oxford, formerly Curate of St. Thomas's, Oxford; some time President of St. Edmund's College, Ware; now Bishop of Emmaus. (1850.)

Paul, C. Kegan, M.A. Exeter College, Oxford, at one time a clergyman of the English Church, and

Assistant Master at Eton; now head of the well-known London publishing firm. (1891.)

Paul, The late Mrs. Alexander, mother of the Revv. Canon and John Paul, priests of the Diocese of Aberdeen.

Paul, W. F., of the Colonial Office.

Paulet, Stuart Etienne, of Dunvegan, Isle of Skye, son of the Rev. C. N. Paulet, of Scarborough. (1874.)

Pauli, Captain, now of the Consular Service. (1852.)

Pauling, George Craig Saunders, of The Lodge, Effingham, Surrey, and family. (1892.)

Pauling, Mrs., wife of the above. (1890.)

Pauling, The late Henry Richard, M.I.C.E., of Holland Villas Road, London, S.W. (1893.)

Paulucci, The late Marchesa.

Paxton, Henry A., of Charsley Hall, Oxford, son of General Paxton, of Midhurst. (1889.)

Payne, A. G., B.A., St. Peter's College, Cambridge.

Payne, Captain J. B.

Payne, John O., M.A. St. Peter's College, Cambridge, late Curate of Linsdale, Bucks.

Payne, Mrs., of Brighton, and her two sons. (1877.)

Payne, Mrs., of Cromwell Place, London, S.W., and her two children.

Peacock, Edward, F.S.A., of Bottesford Manor, Lincoln.

Peacocke, Miss Harriet Elizabeth, sister of the late Sir Joseph Peacocke, Bart.

Pearce, T. G., B.A. Trinity College, Cambridge, late an Anglican clergyman.

Pearse, Captain R. N., of Devonport.

Pearson, The late Rev. E., a priest, and canon.

Pearson, Miss Emma, late nurse of the Red Cross Society during the Franco-Prussian War. (1876.)

Pearson, Mrs. of Notting Hill, and family.

Pearson, Mrs., sister of Mrs. Mordaunt. (1868.)

Pearson, J., M.A. Queen's College, Oxford, late an Anglican clergyman.

Pearson, William, of Hove, Brighton. (1888.)

Peart, Dr., J.P. of Kildare.

Peel, Miss, sister of the late Sir Laurence Peel, Bart. (1850.)

Peel, Edmund, nephew of the late Sir Laurence Peel, Bart. (1850.)

Peel, Miss Emily, niece of the late Sir Laurence Peel, Bart. (1850.)

Peel, William, nephew of the late Sir Laurence Peel, Bart. (1850.)

Peirse, Admiral.

Pelham-Clinton, The late Lord Albert Sidney, fourth son of the fifth Duke of Newcastle. (1884.)

Pennell, Mrs. Croker, daughter of the late Sir William Follet, Bart.

Pennell, Miss, daughter of Admiral Pennell.

Penny, The late Rev. W. G., M.A. Christ Church, Oxford, late Curate of Ashdin, Essex ; a priest. (1844.)

Penrice, Dr.

Penrice, Mrs., wife of the above.

Penrith, Mrs., of Cardiff.

Pepper, The late Professor J. H., F.C.S., A.I.C.S., formerly Professor of Chemistry at the Royal Polytechnic, Regent Street, London, W., author.

Pepys, Lady Mary, daughter of the third Earl of Cottenham. (1895.)

Perceval, The late Hawkshaw, of Knightsbrook, Co. Meath.

Perceval, Mrs., wife of the above.

Perceval, Sir Westby, K.C.M.G., son of the above and Agent-General for Tasmania, and Governor of the Imperial Institute, London.

Perceval, The Misses, daughters of an Anglican clergyman, one a nun.

Perring, Cyril Augustine, son of the Rev. A. Perring, Vicar of Norton-by-Daventry. (1898.)

Perry, Captain, late of the 38th Regiment.

Perry, Miss Mary Anne Agnes, of Midford. (1878.)

Peterkin, Reginald, artist in stained glass.

Petheram, The late Sir William Comer, Chief Justice of the North-West Provinces of India. (1889.)

Petre, The Hon. Mrs. Albert Henry, daughter of the Rev. Prebendary Clarke, of Taunton. (1881.)

Petre, The late Lady Catherine, daughter of the fourth Earl of Wicklow.

Petre, The Hon. Mrs. Frederick, eldest daughter of the Rev. Sir Christopher Musgrave, ninth Baronet, of Edenhall.

Phelan, Colonel, of Indian Army.

Phelan, Mrs., wife of the above, and family.

Philip, John, the publisher.

Philipps, Mrs. Caroline Henrietta, daughter of the late Captain H. J. Lacon, R.N., of Goldrood, Ipswich, niece of Sir Edmund H. K. Lacon, M.P. for North

Norfolk; wife of Owen C. Philipps, of Barham Hall, Suffolk. (1882.)

Philipps, Miss Henrietta, daughter of Sir T. Philipps, Bart, F.S.A., F.R.S.

Philipps, Owen C., B.A. Trinity College, Cambridge, son of the late Charles Philipps, of Barham Hall, Suffolk.

Philips, Mrs. S., of Doncaster.

Phillips, Miss Gertrude, daughter of the Rev. G. P. Phillips, now a nun.

Phillips, Mrs. Lucy, wife of the Rev. G. P. Phillips, M.A., and sister of the Very Rev. Dr. Vaughan, Master of the Temple and Dean of Llandaff.

Phillips, The late Major. (1848.)

Phillips, Robert B., M.A. Trinity College, Oxford, D.L., of Longworth, Hereford.

Phillips, Mrs., wife of the above.

Phillipps-Treby, Edward Mowbray, M.A. St. Mary's Hall, Oxford, J.P., and late Rector of Boscastle, Cornwall. (1895.)

Phillipps-Treby, Miss, sister of the above. (1895.)

Phillpots, Miss, niece of the late Right Rev. Dr. Phillpots, Bishop of Exeter.

Phillpots, Miss Clara, granddaughter of the late Right Rev. Dr. Phillpots, Bishop of Exeter.

Pidcock, Hugh, B.A. Corpus Christi College, Cambridge, formerly Curate of St. Mary's, Paddington, London, W.; now a Jesuit Priest in Ireland. (1882.)

Pidcock, The late Mrs., wife of the above. (1882.)

Pierson, The Misses, of Folkestone, both nuns.

Piggott, Miss, the authoress.
Pigott, Mrs., wife of a Devonshire clergyman.
Pigott, Miss, daughter to the above.
Pigott, William, solicitor, of Portarlington, Ireland.
Pilkington, Leonard, of Bognor. (1898.)
Pinch, Mrs., of Wandsworth, London, S.W. (1886.)
Pinder, Mrs. J. Bourne, daughter of the late Andrew Bathgate, of Liverpool.
Pitman, Mrs., wife of Dr. Pitman, of Highgate, London, N., and her four children.
Pittar, The late Mrs., authoress of *Conversion by My Bible and Prayer-book*, etc. (1843.)
Place, George Godfrey, barrister, of Dublin.
Plaistowe, Edward E., of Loudwater, Bucks. (1878.)
Plater, Edward, of the War Office.
Plomer, The late George Henry, of Birmingham, (1857.)
Plomer, Miss, daughter of the above. (1866.)
Plomer, J. G., solicitor.
Plues, Miss, late Superioress of the Ladies' Home, Kensington Square, London, W. (1866.)
Plumer, late Rev. J., M.A. Balliol College, Oxford. formerly an Anglican curate. (1846.)
Plummer, R., solicitor, of Falmouth.
Plummer, Mrs., wife of the above.
Pollard, William H., of Rugby. (1892.)
Pollen, J. Hungerford, M.A. and Fellow of Merton College, Oxford, F.S. Arts, late Senior Proctor of Oxford University, formerly an Anglican clergyman, brother of the late Sir Richard Hungerford

Pollen, Bart.; till recently on the staff of the British Museum, sometime Professor of Fine Arts at the Catholic University College, Dublin. (1853.)

Pollen, Mrs., wife of the above. (1853.)

Pollen, The late Sir Richard Hungerford, Bart., of Bedenham, Hants. (1853.)

Pollend, Dr. George E., of Corby, Lincolnshire.

Pomeroy, The Hon. Esther, sister of sixth Viscount Harberton.

Poole, Charles Henry, B.L. St. Alban's Hall, Oxford; now Headmaster of St. Joseph's School, Pailton, Rugby.

Poole, Miss, daughter of the above, a nun.

Poole, Miss E., her sister, a nun.

Poole, J. A., B.A. Trinity College, Dublin, late Curate of St. John's, Miles Platting, Lancashire.

Poole, J. R., solicitor.

Poole, Miss L., daughter of C. H. Poole, B.L. of St. Alban's Hall, Oxford; a nun.

Poole, L. H., a Brother of Mercy, late of St. Mary's, Northyde, Middlesex. (1864.)

Poole, Mrs., wife of J. Ruscombe Poole, solicitor. (1846.)

Poole, The Misses, her daughters. (1846.)

Pope, John O'Fallon, M.A. Christ Church, Oxford; a Jesuit Priest at Beaumont College, Old Windsor.

Pope, Miss, sister of the Rev. W. Pope, B.A., late an Anglican clergyman. (1856.)

Pope, Miss L., her sister. (1856.)

Pope, R. V., B.A. of London University, formerly Missionary of the Society of the Propagation of the Gospel in India; at one time master at the Oratory School, Edgbaston, Birmingham.

Pope, Mrs. R. V., wife of the above, and niece of the Very Rev. Dr. Vaughan, Master of the Temple, and Dean of Llandaff.

Pope, Miss S., sister of the Rev. W. Pope, B.A., late an Anglican clergyman.

Pope, T. A., of Wadham College, Oxford.

Pope, Thomas Alder, M.A. Jesus College, Cambridge, late Rector of St. Matthias', Stoke Newington, London, N.; a priest of the Birmingham Oratory. (1856.)

Pope, William, B.A. Christ College, Cambridge, late Curate of Seven Bridges, Bolton, nephew of the late Most Rev. Dr. Whateley, Protestant Archbishop of Dublin; a priest, Canon, at Our Lady and St. Robert's, Harrogate, Yorkshire. (1853.)

Portarlington, The late Alexandrina, Countess of, second daughter of the third Marquis of Londonderry, and sister-in-law of the late Duke of Marlborough, sometime Lord-Lieutenant of Ireland. (1867.)

Porter, Mrs. Elizabeth, wife of John Porter, of Cirencester. (1898.)

Potter, The late Miss Ann, of Tuam. (1852.)

Potter, Dennis, junr., son of Dennis R. Potter, solicitor, of Tuam, and brother of the above. (1852.)

Potter, The late Dennis R., solicitor and Senior Proctor of the Ecclesiastical Court of Tuam. (1852.)

Potter, Miss Edith, only daughter of Thomas Bayley Potter, son of the late Sir Thomas Potter, of Buile Hill, Manchester, formerly M.P. for Rochdale.

Potter, Thomas, M.A. Merton College, Oxford, son of Thomas Bayley Potter, late M.P. for Rochdale.

Powell, Arthur Wentworth, M.A. Corpus Christi College, Cambridge, nephew of Bishop Jones of Washington, U.S.A.; late Rector of Disserth, Wales. (1894.)

Powell, Miss Charlotte, of Liverpool.

Powell, Edward, B.A. and Scholar of Magdalen College, Oxford; a priest at Lydiate, Liverpool. (1865.)

Powell, George, of Llantarnam, formerly a Secularist. (1885.)

Powell, Mrs., of Leominster. (1887.)

Powell, Mrs., daughter of Captain J. Lumsden, of Clova, Aberdeenshire.

Powles, L. D., barrister.

Pownall, A., architect, father of the Rev. A. Pownall, of Clerkenwell.

Pownall, F. H., son of H. Pownall, of Spring Grove, father of the Rev. B. Pownall of Shepherds' Bush, W.

Pownall, Mrs., wife of the above.

Poyer, Charles, a priest, for several years at Rouen; now Private Secretary to His Eminence Cardinal Vaughan, Archbishop of Westminster.

Poynter, William E., M.A., M.L., Queens' College, Cambridge.

Powys, The Hon. Stephen, B.A. Trinity College, Cambridge; son of the fifth Lord Lilford.

Pratt, Mrs., of Folkestone. (1886.)

Prendergast, Colonel Lenox, formerly member of the London School Board.

Prendergast, Mrs., wife of the above, and daughter of the late Neil Malcolm.

Prendergast, Wellesley, of London.

Prentis, Captain W., late of the Scots Greys.

Press, William Henry, son of the late Captain B. M. Press; at one time editor of *Bury Free Press, County Times, Watford Times;* author of *Christmas in Southern Seas, Victorian Triumphs*, etc. (1890.)

Press, The late Mrs., wife of the above, and daughter of Frederick Wood, banker, of Weston-super-Mare. (1890.)

Prestage, Edgar, B.A. Balliol College, Oxford. (1884.)

Prestage, Mrs. Elizabeth M., of Manchester, mother of the above. (1884.)

Prestage, The late Miss Etheldreda, her daughter.

Prestage, Franklin, railway engineer in India. (1897.)

Preston, Mrs., wife of Thomas Preston, uncle of the fourteenth Viscount Gormanston.

Prestwich, Miss, sister of Professor Prestwich, F.R.S.

Price, Miss Edith, of Brighton. (1888.)

Price, Thomas, of Mayfield Lodge, Cashel, Ireland. (1866.)

Prichard, The late Mrs. C. H., daughter of the Rev. Henry Stewart, an Irish clergyman.

Prickett, Mrs., daughter of the late Sir Charles Dodsworth, Bart., and wife of Lieutenant-Colonel Prickett, of Boreas Hall, near Hull, Yorkshire.

Priest, The late Rev. R., a Dominican Priest in Belgium.
Priest, Sarah Anna, of Liverpool.
Priestman, Mrs., of Benwell House, Newcastle-on-Tyne.
Priggett, Thomas, of Brighton. (1886.)
Primavesi, Mrs., of Wellington House, Bournemouth.
Prior, A. R., B.A. Balliol College, Oxford.
Prismall, Edwin, Lieutenant, 2nd V.B. Duke of Cambridge's Middlesex Regiment, of The Old Bank, Brentford, W., and children. (1897.)
Prismall, Mrs., wife of the above. (1880.)
Pritchard, Miss, daughter of the Rev. Professor Pritchard, now a nun.
Probyn, Miss Mary, of Devizes, Wilts, authoress. (1883.)
Procter, The late Miss Adelaide Anne, daughter of the late Bryan Waller Procter, " Barry Cornwall "; the poetess. (1851.)
Proctor, J., a Quaker.
Proctor, The late Richard, a Christian Brother, and formerly on the staff of St. Joseph's College, Clapham. S.W. (1870.)
Prosser, Alfred A., solicitor, of Aberdeen. (1894.)
Prothero, George, B.A. Brasenose College, Oxford.
Prouse, James, of Bideford, Devonshire.
Prouse, Mrs., wife of the above.
Prout, Walter William, of West Hampstead.
Prower, Nelson, M.A. Brasenose College, Oxford, a barrister. (1897.)
Pryor, A. R., B.A. University College, Oxford.

Puckle, Miss, of Sloane Gardens, Chelsea, London, S.W. (1898.)

Pugin, The late Augustus Welby, the reviver of Gothic architecture in England.

Pugin, The late Mrs., wife of the above.

Purbrick, Edward, of Christ Church, Oxford, formerly a solicitor, a Jesuit Priest, sometime Rector of Stonyhurst and Wimbledon Colleges, now Provincial of his Society in America. (1850.)

Purbrick, James, of Christ Church, Oxford, a solicitor, and brother of the above, a Jesuit Priest at Stonyhurst College, Blackburn, Lancashire. (1850.)

Purcell, Mrs. Edmund, youngest daughter of the late Sir F. Desanges, Bart.

Purcell, Mrs. R. Lindsay Dillon, of South Kensington, and aunt of Major Rasch, M.P.

Purdon, James, a priest at Our Lady of the Angels, Worthing, Sussex.

Purdue, William, the architect.

Pybus, Mrs., granddaughter of the sixth Earl of Coventry.

Pye, J. H., M.A. Trinity College, Cambridge, late Rector of Clifton-Campville, son-in-law of the late Right Rev. Dr. Wilberforce, Bishop of Winchester; now a barrister.

Pye, Mrs., wife of the above, and daughter of the late Bishop of Winchester.

Pynsent, Miss Katie, daughter of the late Mr. Justice Pynsent, D.C.L.; now a Benedictine Nun.

Pynsent, Miss Maude, sister of the above, and also a Benedictine Nun.

Pyrrell, Miss Dora, adopted daughter of Mrs. Anne Ramsden Bennett, niece of Sir Thomas Gladstone, Bart., of Fasque. (1870.)

UEENSBERRY, The Marchioness of (Caroline), widow of the seventh Marquis.

Quin, The late Mrs., of Whitelands, Clapham. (1870.)

ADCLIFFE, Captain Godfrey E. A., youngest brother of Sir Joseph Percival Pickford Radcliffe, Bart.

Radcliffe, Sir Joseph Percival Pickford, Bart, of Rudding Park, Knaresborough, Yorkshire.

Radcliffe, Miss Louisa, of Morehampton House, Donnybrook, Ireland.

Radley, Mrs., of Lambute Grange.

Radolinski, The late Countess Lucy, daughter of Colonel T. H. Wakefield, wife of the Prussian peer and diplomatist.

Ram. Mrs. Arthur, the novelist, daughter of the late A. Loftus Tottenham, M.P., of Glenfarne Hall, Co. Leitrim.

Ram, Mrs. (*née* Casamagor), wife of Stephen Ram, D.L., of Ramsfort, Gorey.

Ramsay, David S., a priest and Monsignor in Ayr, Scotland.

Ramsey, H. R., M.A. Exeter College, Oxford; late Vice-Principal of Wells Theological College, now a Benedictine Monk at Downside. (1896.)

Ramsey, Charles George, formerly a clergyman of the English Church.

Ramsey, Mrs. George Dalhousie, of Edinburgh, N.B.

Randall, Giles, formerly a member of the Brotherhood of the Common Life, an Anglican Society at Ramsgill, Yorkshire. (1887.)

Randolph, The late E., M.A. Jesus College, Cambridge, formerly Vicar of St. Clement's, Cambridge. (1857.)

Randolph, Mrs., wife of the above, and family. (1857.)

Randolph, Lieutenant, of the Royal Navy.

Ranken, George Elliot, B.A., and Scholar of University College, Oxford, formerly Captain of the Royal Glamorgan Artillery, Private Chamberlain to the late and present Popes.

Rann, Richard E., M.A. Queen's College, Oxford, late Vicar of Thatcham, Bucks. (1866.)

Ransford, Edward, B.A. St. John's College, Cambridge, (1885.)

Rasch, Miss, late of Brighton, cousin of Major Rasch, M.P.

Rassche, Miss, of Blandford Square, London.

Ratcliffe, Frederick William, of Birmingham.

Ratcliffe, W. H., late Curate of St. Mary Magdalene's, Paddington, London, W.

Raupert, J. Godfrey, formerly Curate at Leyton, Essex, and at Christ Church, Beckenham, Kent, and late Incumbent of a Proprietary Chapel in Bath; author. (1895.)

Ravenscroft, Humphrey, solicitor, of Lincoln's Inn.

Ravensworth, The late Countess of, second wife of the second Earl of Ravensworth. (1879.)

Rawes, The late Rev. Henry Augustus, M.A. Trinity College, Cambridge, D.D. of Rome, a priest, Superior of the Oblates of St. Charles at St. Mary of the Angels, Bayswater, London, W., author.

Rawes, Mrs., of Kensington, London, W.

Rawes, The Misses, her daughters.

Rawlinson, Miss, daughter of the police magistrate.

Rawlinson, Thomas., M.A., brother of Sir Henry Rawlinson, President of the Royal Geographical Society of London.

Rawlinson, Mrs., wife of the above, and family.

Rawson, Miss, sister of the Secretary of the Chiswick Branch of the English Church Union; and Hon. Organist of St. Mary Magdalen's, Chiswick. (1888.)

Rawson, Charles, architect, of Rotherham.

Rayment, G. Richmond, of Colchester. (1888.)

Raymond-Barker, Mrs., wife of the nephew of the late Rev. Dr. Pusey; authoress of *Life of Countess Adelstan, Science and Faith*, etc.; and her two sons (one a Jesuit priest), and two daughters (one a nun).

Rayner, Captain, late of the 5th Royal Lancashire Militia.

Reade, Mrs. Compton, wife of the Rev. Compton Reade, M.A., formerly Chaplain of Magdalen College, Oxford, now Rector of Elton, Stockton-on-Tees, and nephew of the late Charles Reade, the well-known novelist and dramatic author. (1884.)

Reade, Mrs. J. E., niece by marriage of Sir John Chandos Reade, Bart.

Reade, John Edmund, the poet.

Reade, Miss Mary, niece of the late Charles Reade.

Reader, H. Peter, B.A. Merton College, Oxford; a Dominican Priest at Hawkesyard College, Rugeley.

Reay, Miss, sister-in-law of the Rector of Raithby, Lincolnshire.

Redding, Miss, niece of the late Right Rev. Dr. Wilberforce, Bishop of Winchester.

Redman, Charles Ignatius, brother of the late Rev. Dr. Redman; a Jesuit Priest at Ditton Hall, Widnes. (1868.)

Redman, The late John, father of the late Rev. J. W. Redman, D.D. (1868.)

Redman, The late Mrs., wife of the above. (1864.)

Redman, The Misses, her daughters, both Sisters of Charity of St. Vincent de Paul. (1864.)

Redman, John, brother of the late Rev. Dr. Redman; a Jesuit Priest at the Church of the Sacred Heart, Bournemouth. (1864.)

Redman, The late Rev. Joseph W., formerly lay-worker at St. Peter's, London Docks; a priest, D.D. of Rome, and for some time Rector of St. John's, Brentford, London, W. (1864.)

Reed, Mrs., of London.

Reed, Lincoln, barrister, nephew of Sir Charles Reed, M.P. (1891.)

Reed, Mrs., wife of the above, and her four children. (1891.)

Reeves, Major Frederick, late of the 103rd Regiment.
Reid, Charles Aloysius, of North Shields. (1893.)
Reid, Joseph D. Gilzean, late a student for the Nonconformist ministry, son of Sir Hugh Gilzean Reid. (1899.)
Reid, Robert, Banker, of Friockheim, N.B. (1876.)
Remington, Frederick, B.A. Magdalene College, Cambridge, late Rector of Kirkley, Suffolk; now Headmaster of St. Aloysius' School, Bournemouth.
Remington, Mrs., wife of the above.
Remington, Miss., her sister-in-law.
Renouf, The late Sir Philip le Page, of Pembroke College, Oxford, formerly Professor of Ancient and Eastern Languages at the Catholic University College, Dublin, Her Majesty's Inspector of Schools, Keeper of Egyptian and Assyrian Antiquities in the British Museum. (1842.)
Reynolds, Miss Anne, of Manchester,
Reynolds, Miss, of Rotherham.
Reynolds, Mrs., of Ponthir. (1889.)
Reynolds, Reginald, of Brighton. (1879.)
Reynolds, Mrs., wife of the above. (1879.)
Rhetigan, The late Mrs., of London. (1848.)
Rhodes, Matthew J., M.A. Trinity College, Cambridge; author of *The Visible Unity of the Catholic Church*; formerly Lay-Secretary of the Bristol Branch of the English Church Union.
Riband, William, B.A. St. Mary's Hall, Oxford.
Rice, Mrs., wife of the Rev. Howard Rice, M.A., Vicar of Sutton-Courtney.

Richards, George J., B.A. St. Mary's Hall, Oxford.
Richards, Miss H. F. M., of Brighton.
Richards, Walter J. B., of St. Mary's Hall, Oxford, a priest (Oblate of St. Charles) at St. Charles' College, Bayswater, London, W., D.D. of Rome, and Inspector of Schools in the Archdiocese of Westminster. (1857.)
Richardson, The late George, solicitor, of Manchester, brother of the Rev. R. Richardson, of Bexhill-on-Sea. (1837.)
Richardson, John Fryer, of Liverpool.
Richardson, General, of Bath.
Richardson, Richard, a priest of the Order of Charity, at St. Mary Magdalen's, Bexhill-on-Sea. (1840.)
Richie, Miss, of the Radcliffe Infirmary, Oxford. (1888.)
Ricketts, Miss Anne, of Blackburn.
Ricketts, Henry, of Cottles, Wilts. (1861.)
Riley, Charles James, of Brighton. (1879.)
Riley, Mrs., wife of the above. (1879.)
Riley, Miss, her daughter. (1879.)
Ring, William, M.J., D.D. of Rome, a priest in Ireland, formerly in London.
Ripon, The Marquis of (George Frederick Samuel Robinson), K.G., P.C., G.M.S.I., D.C.L., ex-Grand Master of English Freemasons, Chairman of the Catholic Poor School Committee, President of the Society of St. Vincent de Paul, formerly Lord President of the Council, sometime Viceroy of India. (1874.)

Ritchie, William G.B., B.A. Trinity College, Cambridge.

Rivas, Miss, of Brompton. (1882.)

Rivers, Charles Edmund, M.A. Oriel College, Oxford; a priest at Our Lady of Lourdes, Acton, London, W., and Assistant Inspector of Schools in the Archdiocese of Westminster. (1883.)

Rivington, Luke, M.A., and formerly Demy of Magdalen College, Oxford, formerly Curate of All Saint's, Margaret Street, London, W., Superior of the Society of the Holy Ghost, Stoke, Member of the Society of St. John the Evangelist, Cowley, Oxford, for some time Missionary in India and Africa, and once in charge of St. Clement's Church, Oxford. A priest at St. James's, Spanish Place, Manchester Square, London, W., D.D. of Rome, author of *The Inward Part*, *Authority, or a Plain Reason for Joining the Church of Rome*, *Independence or Insecurity of the Anglican Position*, *The Roman Primacy*, etc. (1888.)

Robert, The late Emmanuel Ussher, late Government Surveyor in Queensland and Founder of the Irish Lodge of Freemasons. (1897.)

Robert, Mrs. R., of Cardiff.

Roberts, John, of the War Office.

Roberts, Miss, sister of the Rev. J. Roberts, of Cowley, near Oxford.

Roberts, Miss M., daughter of the late W. Roberts, of Harborne Hall.

Roberts, Miss, of Haverstock Hill, London.

Roberts, W. Pender, M.A. St. John's College, Cambridge, late Vicar of Boscastle, Cornwall.

Roberts, Mrs., wife of the above, and daughter of the Hon. W. H. Yelverton, second son of the second Viscount Avonmore.

Roberts, William H., M.A., of Cambridge University, D.L., and late Recorder of Grantham.

Robertson, James Burton, author of various philosophical works.

Robertson, The late Rev. J. C., M.A. University College, Oxford, formerly Anglican rector in Buckinghamshire; a priest.

Robertson, Miss, late an Anglican Sister at Clewer; now a nun.

Robertson, Miss, formerly of the East Grinstead Sisterhood, now a Carmelite Nun. (1868.)

Robertson, T. C., late Chaplain to the late Duke of Buccleuch. (1858.)

Robins, Miss, of Wimbledon, for several years an Anglican nun at Clewer Convent; granddaughter of Lady Caroline Barham.

Robinson, Charles, of the firm of Ricardo & Robinson, London, E.C., President of the Sodality at Farm Street, London, W. (1885.)

Robinson, Miss, daughter of Captain Robinson, of Armagh, and niece of Sir George Stokes. (1892.)

Robinson, Denham, of St. Hilda's, Hampton Wick; of the War Office. (1860.)

Robinson, Miss F., of Brighton.

Robinson, Miss G., sister of the Rev. W. Croke Robinson, M.A.

Robinson, Miss Harriet, of Dover.

Robinson, Miss Hilda Stapylton, of Bruges. (1897.)

Robinson, Miss Katherine Agnes, of Templeton Place, South Kensington, London. (1896.)

Robinson, Lieutenant T. A., B.A. Corpus Christi College, Oxford.

Robinson, Walter Croke, M.A. and Fellow of New College, Oxford, a priest, and Monsignor, Hammersmith, London, W.

Robson, Francis J. T., of Liverpool.

Robson, Robert, of Her Majesty's Customs, of Upper Clapton, London.

Robson, Mrs., wife of the above.

Rockstro, William S., of Plymouth, musician and composer.

Rodgers, Colonel H. J., of the Royal Engineers.

Rodgers, The late J. T., superintendent of the Bombay Tramway Company, formerly in the Army, and fought in the Crimea.

Rogers, Mrs., wife of General Rogers.

Rogers, Miss, daughter of the late Francis Newman Rogers, Q.C., Recorder of Exeter.

Röhrs, John Henry, M.A. and Fellow of Jesus College, Cambridge.

Rokeby, Miss, of Arthingworth Manor, Northamptonshire.

Rolfe, Frederick William, sometime Master at Grantham Grammar School; journalist. (1887.)

Rolfe, Harry Stephen, of London. (1898.)

Rolfe, Mrs., wife of the above. (1898.)

Rolfe, Miss Neville, of Peterborough.

Rolph, James, of the War Office.

Rooke, Austin M., a Dominican Priest at St. Dominic's Priory, Haverstock Hill, London, N.W.

Rooke, The late Rev. Seton Patterson, M.A. Oriel College, Oxford, late Curate of St. Saviour's, Leeds ; a Dominican Priest. (1850.)

Roope, Charles, of Pembroke Square, Kensington.

Roope, William, a priest, D.D. of Rome, and Monsignor, Bonchurch, Isle of Wight.

Roper, Alfred F. P., M.A. Keble College, Oxford, descendant of Margaret Roper, the favourite daughter of the Blessed Thomas More ; now Headmaster of Ladycross, Bournemouth. (1894.)

Roper, Mrs., wife of the above, and family. (1888.)

Roper, The late Joseph, director of the *Catholic Standard*, of Hobart Town, Tasmania.

Roscommon, The late Earl of. (1850.)

Rose, The late George, M.A., Reader at the Temple Church, son of the late James Rose, and nephew of the late Right Hon. Sir George Rose, Master in Chancery ; a well-known humorous writer under the *nom de guerre* of "Arthur Sketchley," for some time tutor to the Duke of Norfolk, K.G. (1855.)

Rose, Mrs., of York. (1882.)

Rose, Miss, her daughter. (1882.)

Rose, Miss, of Edge Hill, Liverpool. (1880.)

Rose, H., Founder and Superior of the Brotherhood of the Common Life, an Anglican Religious Society at Ramsgill, Yorkshire.

Rose, Sir Philip Frederick, Bart., of Rayners, Penn, Bucks, formerly legal adviser to the late Earl of Beaconsfield, K.G. (1885.)

Rose, Lady, wife of the above, and daughter of the late Rev. William Wollaston Pym, Rector of Willian, Herts; and five children. (1885.)

Rose, William, director of the Submarine Telegraph Cable at Vigo. (1895.)

Ross, John, a Jesuit Priest at St. Walburge, Preston.

Ross, Robert, of Phillimore Gardens, Kensington, art critic and journalist. (1894.)

Ross, Colonel, of Wimbledon, London, S.W.

Ross, Miss Rita, now a nun at the Sacred Heart Convent, Dundrum, Dublin. (1886.)

Ross, Mrs. W. A., of Brixton, London. (1885.)

Ross-of-Bladensberg, The late Hon. Mrs. David, daughter of the ninth Viscount Massereene and Ferrard. (1862.)

Ross-of-Bladensberg, Colonel Edmund, of the Royal Artillery. (1876.)

Ross-of-Bladensberg, Colonel, of Birkenhead.

Ross-of-Bladensberg, Captain F. T., of the Royal Engineers. (1882.)

Ross-of-Bladensberg, Captain John, of the Coldstream Guards. (1880.)

Ross-of-Bladensberg, The Hon. Mrs. John, daughter of the tenth Viscount Massereene and Ferrard. (1879.)

Ross-of-Bladensberg, The late Rev. Robert S., M.A. Exeter College, Oxford, formerly a barrister; a Jesuit Priest. (1875.)

Rossiter, Miss, of Kensington, London. (1884.)

Rossiter, S. J., of Birmingham. (1876.)

Rossmore, Julia, Lady, widow of the third Baron Rossmore. (1879.)

Round, The late Frederick Peel, B.A. Balliol College, Oxford, for forty-two years Gentleman Usher of the Green Rod, son of the late John Round, of Danbury Park, Essex, for many years M.P. for Ipswich and Maldon, and for forty-two years High Steward of Colchester.

Rousby, The late Wybert, the actor, husband of the late Mrs. Rousby, the celebrated tragedienne.

Rouse, Charles, formerly an Anglican Deacon, brother of W. G. Rouse, late Curate of St. John's, Bury St. Edmunds. (1882.)

Rouse, W. G., brother of the above, and late Curate of St. John's, Bury St. Edmunds. (1881.)

Routh, Mrs., wife of the Rector of Tilehurst.

Rowe, The late Rev. James Boone, of St. John's College, Cambridge; a priest of the Brompton Oratory. (1853.)

Rowlands, Miss Lilian Bowen, daughter of W. J. Bowen Rowlands, Q.C. (1896.)

Rowlands, Miss Lucy Bowen, her sister. (1896.)

Rowlands, Miss Teresa Bowen, her sister. (1896).

Rowlands, W. J. Bowen, Q.C., M.A., Balliol College, Oxford, formerly an Anglican clergyman, late M.P. for Cardiganshire, now Recorder of Swansea. (1896.)

Rowlands, Mrs., wife of the above. (1896.)

Rowlatt, C., M.A. of Cambridge University, and late Curate at Thurrocks. (1858.)

Roxburgh, James J. Carnegie, of Bayswater, London, W.

Rudge, Mrs., of Kensington, London. (1876.)

Rudsdell, Miss, daughter of the late Lieutenant-Colonel Sir Joseph Rudsdell, K.C.M.G., of the Grenadier Guards, sometime Chief Secretary to the Lord High Commissioner of the Ionian Islands.

Rudsdell, Miss Mary, her sister.

Rule, Martin Luther, B.A. Pembroke College, Cambridge, late Anglican Curate at Brighton, son of the Rev. Dr. Rule, Wesleyan Minister, author of *The Life and Times of St. Anselm*, etc.

Rumball, Mrs. H., daughter of the late C. Simpson Hanson, and wife of Henry Rumball, Treasurer to H.B.M. Supreme Consular Court at Constantinople, and her five children. (1880.)

Rumbold, The late Sir Arthur, Bart.

Russell, Arthur F. E., son of the late Rev. A. B. Russell, M.A., Rector of Laverton; a priest, Monsignor, Provost and Vicar-General of the Diocese of Clifton.

Russell, Mrs., wife of the Rev. Cyril Russell. (1896.)

Russell, Hon. Mrs. Cyril, *née* Helen Pirie, daughter-in-law of Lord Russell of Killowen. (1898.)

Russell, Miss, sister of the late Sir Charles Russell, Bart., V.C., and formerly M.P. for Westminster.

Russell, Harry Patrick, late Vicar of St. Stephen's, Devonport. (1897.)

Russell, Mrs., wife of the above, and family. (1898.)

Russell, Vernon, B.A. Trinity College, Dublin, late Curate of St. James's, Plymouth. (1888.)

Russell, William M., B.A. Christ Church, Oxford.

Ryan, Mrs., wife of the late Dr. Ryan, of the 56th Regiment. (1860.)

Ryan, Mrs., of Nenagh, Ireland. (1879.)

Ryder, Charles E., son of the late Rev. G. D. Ryder, M.A., formerly Rector of Euston, Hants, a priest at St. Philip's, Smethwick, Birmingham. (1846.)

Ryder, Cyril, brother of the above; a priest of the Redemptorist Order at St. Mary's, Clapham, London, S.W.

Ryder, The late George Dudley, M.A. Oriel College, Oxford, formerly Rector of Euston, Hants, son of the late Bishop of Lichfield, nephew of Henry, the first Earl of Harrowby. (1846.)

Ryder, Mrs., wife of the above, and daughter of the late Rev. J. Sargent. (1846.)

Ryder, George Lisle, C.B., son of the above, late of the Treasury, now Chairman of the Board of Customs. (1846.)

Ryder, Henry Ignatius Dudley, his brother; a priest and Superior of the Birmingham Oratory, D.D. of Rome; author. (1846.)

Ryder, Miss Sophia, daughter of the late Hon. and Right Rev. Dr. Ryder, Bishop of Lichfield; a nun, and superioress of a convent. (1846.)

Ryley, Edward, a Unitarian.

Ryley, Mrs. Edward, niece of Dr. Priestley, and her three sons.

Ryley, Miss, daughter of the above; now a nun.

Ryley, Henry, of Manchester. (1890.)

SAINT, John James Heath, B.A. Christ Church, Oxford, son of the Rev. J. J. Saint, M.A., of Groombridge Place, Kent.

Salamon, The late Madame, daughter of the Hon. W. H. Yelverton, second son of the second Viscount Avonmore, wife of Louis Gaston, Captain in the French Service.

Salt, Mrs. T. H., wife of Colonel Salt, late of the Royal Artillery. (1880.)

Saltiam, Captain, of the Royal Navy. (1881.)

Saltiam, Mrs. E., wife of the above, and daughter of the Rev. W. Forbes, late Rector of Manchester, Jamaica. (1881.)

Samler, Miss Fanny, daughter of the late Major Samler. (1879.)

Sammons, Edward, B.A. Lincoln College, Oxford, a priest at Our Lady of Good Counsel, Brighton.

Sanders, Mrs. Florence, directress of the Beethoven School of Music, Willesden, London. (1889.)

Sanderson, Miss Eliza, daughter of the Hon. J. Sanderson.

Sanderson, R. J., late licensed lay-reader at St. Faith's, Stoke Newington, London. (1884.)

Sanderson, Mrs., wife of the above, and five children. (1884.)

Sands, W. B. B., of London, of Sands & Co., publishers. (1894.)

Sandys, Mrs., wife of the Rev. G. Sandys, M.A., an Anglican clergyman.

Sandys, Miss, sister-in-law of the above.

Sankey, Richard Boyer, M.A. Magdalen Hall, Oxford, formerly Curate of St. Paul's, Leicester; a priest, till lately at St. James's, Spanish Place, London, W. (1881.)

Sankey, William, M.A. Trinity College, Cambridge.

Sankey, Mrs., wife of the above, and two sons.

Sankey, Miss, daughter of the above.

Santley, Charles, the well-known baritone. (1880.)

Sass, Dr. E. E.

Sass, Mrs., wife of the above.

Sass, F. A., surgeon.

Saunders, Colonel Henry G., late of the Bengal Staff Corps. (1880.)

Saunders, Mrs., wife of the above. (1880.)

Savory, Frederick W., of London University, son of Sydney Savory, Head Master of the Nottingham Diocesan College; a priest at St. Joseph's, West Hartlepool, Durham.

Savory, Sydney, Headmaster of the Nottingham Diocesan College.

Savory, Mrs., wife of the above.

Say, Major, of the Bombay Army.

Say, Mrs., wife of the above, and her two sons.

Say, Miss, daughter of the above.

Scargill, Edward, M.A. and Wrangler of Queens' College, Cambridge.

Scarlett, Edward James, of Wolverhampton.

Schenk, William, of Brighton.

Schenk, Mrs., wife of the above.

Schoales, Miss Ellena, of Liverpool.
Schoales, Miss Mable Angelina, her sister.
Schoales, Miss Maria Clementina, her sister.
Schofield, The late Rev. Richard; a Redemptorist Priest. (1850.)
Scholefield, Edward, brother of the late M.P. for Birmingham.
Schomberg, Arthur, of Oriel College, Oxford, son of the late Q.C. (1878.)
Schomberg, Miss, of Oxford. (1886.)
Schomberg, Reginald B., M.A. New College, Oxford, barrister.
Schreiner, Mrs., wife of a German missionary in South Africa, and mother of the Hon. W. P. Schreiner, Q.C., formerly Attorney-General at the Cape, and of Miss Olive Schreiner, the novelist.
Sclater, The late Captain Bertram Lutley, of the Royal Engineers, second son of Philip L. Sclater, Ph.D., F.R.S., and grandson of the late Sir David Hunter-Blair, second Bart. (1897.)
Sconce, Robert K., M.A. Brasenose College, Oxford, late Curate of St. Andrew's, Sydney Australia.
Sconce, Mrs., wife of the above.
Scott, Alexander G., a priest at Our Lady Star of the Sea, Lowestoft, Suffolk.
Scott, Christopher, a priest, Canon and Vicar-General in the diocese of Northampton, at St. Andrew's, Cambridge.
Scott, Mrs. Ernest, daughter of Mrs. Besant. (1895.)

Scott, G. Gilbert, F.S.A. son of the late Sir Gilbert Scott. (1880.)

Scott, Mrs., wife of the above, and family. (1880.)

Scott, Miss, late Abbess of the Protestant convent at Perth. (1881.)

Scott, The late Miss, of Brighton. (1850.)

Scott, Miss Janet May, of Newton Stewart. (1892.)

Scott, General Walter. (1884.)

Scott, W. A., of Leigh House, East Molesey.

Scott, Clement, of Marlborough College, son of the late Rev. W. Scott, M.A., late Incumbent of Christ Church, Hoxton, Vicar of St. Olave's, Old Jewry, and Rector of St. Martin's, Pomeroy; poet, journalist, for many years dramatic critic to the *Daily Telegraph* and sometime editor of *The Theatre*, author of the *Drama of Yesterday and To-day*; now London dramatic critic of the *New York Herald*. (1865.)

Scott-Murray, The late C. R., of Danesfield, M.A. Christ Church, Oxford, formerly M.P. and High Sheriff for Buckinghamshire. (1844.)

Scotts, Miss Amy, of Hayes, Middlesex. (1897.)

Scratton, The late Rev. James, M.A. St. John's, Cambridge, formerly Curate at Sittingbourne, Kent; a priest at the Church of the Immaculate Conception, Deal, Kent. (1846.)

Scratton, The late Thomas, M.A. Christ Church, Oxford, late Curate at Benson, for some time Secretary to the Catholic University College, Dublin.

Seager, The late Charles, M.A. Worcester College, Oxford, late an Anglican clergyman, formerly Assistant-Professor of Hebrew at Oxford, and then Professor of Classics at the Catholic University College, Kensington, London, W. (1843.)

Seager, The late Mrs., wife of the above, and family. (1843.)

Seally, Major A. St. John, of Her Majesty's Artillery Militia, grandson of the late Rev. John Seally, LL.D., Vicar of East Mecon, Herts.

Seally, Mrs., wife of the above.

Seally, The Misses, her three daughters.

Seally, Miss, granddaughter of the late Rev. John Seally, LL.D., Vicar of East Mecon, Herts.

Searle, George M., M.A. of Harvard University, U.S.A., formerly Professor at the Naval Academy, Annapolis; a Paulist Father, now Director of the Vatican Observatory, Rome. (1862.)

Searle, Joseph, a priest, Canon at St. Augustine's, Tunbridge Wells.

Seddon, J., of Manchester. (1889.)

Selle, The late Rev. Edward, a priest.

Sellon, Ernest L., Professor of Literature, formerly a Papal Zouave. (1870.)

Sellon, Marmaduke St. Just, a priest and Canon Regular of the Lateran, at St. Monica's Priory, Spettisbury, Blandford, Dorsetshire, brother of the above and author of *All Roads Lead to Rome*, etc. (1870.)

Sellon, The late William L., the artist, brother of the above. (1876.)

Serle, Philip, B.A. Balliol College, Oxford. (1880.)

Sewell, Harold Edward Bartholdy, of Leamington. (1895.)

Sewell, The late Rev. John; a Jesuit Priest; formerly Major.

Sewell, The late Miss, of Folkestone. (1846.)

Sewell, William, A.R.A.M., formerly organist at Christ Church, Clapham, London, S.W.; now at the Birmingham Oratory. (1883.)

Seymour, Miss Fanny A., daughter of G. E. Seymour, of Forest Hill, Windsor.

Shakespeare, Mrs., wife of Colonel Shakespeare, R.E.

Shakespeare, Miss, daughter of the above.

Shapcote, The late Edward Gifford, B.A. Corpus Christi College, Cambridge, late Curate of St. George's-in-the-East, London. (1868.)

Shapcote, Mrs., wife of the above. (1868.)

Shapter, The late Rev. William, son of Dr. Shapter of Exeter; a Jesuit Priest. (1865.)

Shapter, Miss, sister of the above, now a Poor Clare. (1865.)

Sharpe, Alfred Bowyer, M.A. Christ Church, Oxford, late Vicar of St. Peter's, Vauxhall, London. (1898.)

Shaw, Thomas H., author of *Reasons for Returning to the True Fold, The Roll of Honour*, etc.

Shea, Alexander B., barrister.

Shea, Mrs., wife of the above.

Shears, Dr., of Streatham, London, S.W.

Shelley, The late Arthur John, nephew of the late Sir John Shelley, seventh Bart., of Castle Goring, M.P. for Westminster.

Shelton, The late Captain F., late of the 93rd Highlanders.

Shelton, The late Mrs., wife of the above.

Shepheard, Mrs. H. H., The Adyar, Madras.

Shepheard, Dr. Philip.

Shepheard, The Misses, daughters of the above.

Shepherd, Dr., of Richmond.

Shepherd, Mrs., wife of the above.

Sheppard, James Henry, M.A. Queen's College, Oxford, formerly an Anglican clergyman.

Sherer, The late John Walter, of Radnor House, Bath, late judge in India.

Sherlock, Miss, daughter of the late Colonel Sherlock and sister-in-law of the late Sir John Sutton, third Bart., of Norwood.

Sherrington, Miss, of Bayswater, London, W.

Sherson, The late Lady Anne, sister of the fourth Marquis Townshend and wife of Captain A. N. Sherson.

Sherwood, Frederick William, M.A. and late Scholar of Balliol College, Oxford; barrister.

Shipley, Orby, M.A. Jesus College, Cambridge, formerly an Anglican clergyman, author of *Glossary of Ecclesiastical Terms, Ritual of the Altar, Life of the Holy Virgin, Carmina Mariana*, etc. (1878.)

Shipley, Mrs., wife of the above. (1878.)

Shipman, Miss, now a nun.

Shirley, Mrs. Walter, of Winchester.

Short, John Philip, of Exeter. (1893.)

Shorthouse, A. E., of Birmingham. (1889.)

Shorthouse, Miss, sister of the above. (1889.)

Shortland, The late Rev. John R., M.A. Oriel College, Oxford, late Curate of Kibworth Beauchamp; a priest, Canon of the Cathedral of Plymouth, author. (1851.)

Shuttleworth, Dr. Robert.

Sibley, Arthur Dunstan Fullerton, son of Major-General Thomas H. Sibley, of the Bengal Staff Corps, J.P. and C.C. for Surrey; a Benedictine priest at Fort Augustus, N.B. (1880.)

Sibley, Mrs. Marian Monica, daughter of Captain William Antey, R.N., wife of Major-General Thomas H. Sibley, and mother of the above. (1883.)

Sibthorpe, The late Rev. Richard Waldo, B.D. and Fellow of Magdalen College, Oxford, at one time Rector of St. Mary's, Ryde, Isle of Wight, brother of the late Colonel Sibthorpe, M.P. for Lincoln; a priest. (1841.)

Siccombe, Hewitt, late Sacristan of St. Clement's Church, Boscombe, Bournemouth. (1898.)

Sidebottom, Miss Frances, daughter of an Anglican clergyman.

Sidebottom, Miss, daughter of Joseph Watson Sidebottom, M.P. for the Hyde Division of Cheshire. (1894.)

Sidney, Charles N., of Queen's Square, Wolverhampton. (1891.)

Silk, Mrs., wife of Dr. Silk of Harrow.

Sills, Henry, solicitor, of London.

Simeon, The late Sir John, Bart., M.A. Christ Church, Oxford, J.P. for Southampton, and M.P. for the Isle of Wight. (1861.)

Simeon, The late Lady Jane Maria, wife of the above, her two sons and four daughters. (1851.)

Simeon, The Hon. Lady Catherine Dorothea, sister of Lord Colville of Culross, and second wife of Sir John Barrington Simeon, Bart.

Simmonds, Mrs., wife of Lieutenant-Colonel Simmonds, and eldest daughter of the late Sir Robert Graham, eighth Bart., of Esk.

Simmonds, Mrs., of Clapham, London, S.W. (1882.)

Simmonds, George Parish, of Stoke Newington, London. (1885.)

Simmonds, Robert, son of Lieutenant-Colonel Simmonds, and grandson of the late Sir Robert Graham, Bart.

Simmonds, William Henry, brother of the above.

Simonds, Robert Luckman, of Liverpool.

Simpson, The late Rev. Charles; a Jesuit Priest.

Simpson, Mrs., of Bognor.

Simpson, Miss, daughter of the above.

Simpson, Miss Emily, now a nun.

Simpson, J., M.A. Trinity College, Cambridge, late Curate of Langton, Yorkshire.

Simpson, Miss M. F. M. (1883.)

Simpson, Richard, M.A. Oriel College, Oxford, formerly Vicar of Mitcham, Surrey. (1849.)

Simpson, Mrs., wife of the above. (1849.)

Simpson, The late Rev. Robert, B.A. St. John's College, Oxford; a priest. (1845.)

Simpson, The late William, M.A. Trinity College, Cambridge, Lord of the Manor of Mitcham, Surrey, and descendant of Archbishop Cranmer. (1843.)

Sims, The late Rev. Austin; a Passionist Priest, and Rector of St. Paul's Retreat, Mount Argus, Dublin. (1853.)

Sims, Miss Emily, sister of the above. (1850.)

Sims, Miss S. A., her sister. (1851.)

Skene, A. P., of Durham University.

Skrimshire, Mrs., wife of an Anglican clergyman, and mother of the Revv. Donald and Fenwick Skrimshire, priests.

Slade, Major John Ramsay, of the Royal Horse Artillery, son of the late Admiral Slade, C.B. (1867.)

Slade, The late Major Montagu Maule, brother of the above, of the 10th Hussars; was killed at the battle of El Teb. (1868.)

Slade, Mrs., wife of General Slade, and granddaughter of the late Lord Dalhousie. (1867.)

Slater, John Anderson, of Polsham Park, Paignton. (1885.)

Slatter, William W., B.A. Queen's College, Oxford, son of an Anglican clergyman. (1880.)

Sloane, Mrs., of Villa Medici, Florence.

Smee, Miss F., sister of the Rev. Richard Smee, a Dominican lay-brother. (1867.)

Smee, Richard, son of the late John Smee, of Chelmsford, now a lay-brother of the Order of St. Dominic. (1863.)

Smith, Albert, of Somerset House.

Smith, Bernard, M.A. and Fellow of Magdalen College, Oxford, late Rector of Leadenham. A priest, Canon, Rural Dean of Northampton at St. Peter's, Great Marlow. (1842.)

Smith, Charles William Wenham, Mus. Bac., New College, Oxford, formerly Organist of St. George's Cathedral, Southwark, London, S.E., and Professor of Music at St. Joseph's College, Clapham, London, S.W., now in New York. (1873.)

Smith, Mrs. E., of Brighton. (1878.)

Smith, E. T., B.A. St John's College, Cambridge. (1883.)

Smith, Miss Edna, of Kensington, London, W. (1886.)

Smith, Mrs. F., of Hastings. (1885.)

Smith, F. W., builder, of Aberdeen. (1875.)

Smith, Mrs., wife of Colonel Smith, of Alexandra Park, Manchester. (1873.)

Smith, The Rev. George, of St. Augustine's College, Canterbury, late Curate of St. Mary's, Poplar, London, E.

Smith, James, brother of Dr. W. H. Smith.

Smith, Mrs. Jessie Addison Smith, daughter-in-law of Colonel Smith, of Manchester. (1896.)

Smith, The late John, J.P., of Bangor, Co. Down, Ireland, formerly a Presbyterian. (1894.)

Smith, The late John Campbell, M.A. of Cambridge University, late an Anglican clergyman. (1845.)

Smith, Mrs. Joseph, of Dublin. (1891.)

Smith, Miss K., of Stone, Staffordshire. (1879.)

Smith, Parker, M.A. Trinity College, Cambridge, late Vicar of St. John's, Torquay, Devonshire. (1879.)

Smith, Robert Calder, Secretary of the Chamber of Commerce, Manila, Philippine Isles. (1873.)

Smith, Rutherford, of London.

Smith, Mrs., wife of the above.

Smith, Miss, daughter of the above.

Smith, Miss, daughter of an Essex vicar.

Smith, Sydney F., a Jesuit Priest at The Immaculate Conception, Farm Street, London, W., theological writer. (1864.)

Smith, Thomas, a priest at St. Mary's, Croydon. (1878.)

Smith, Thomas Sydney, brother of C. W. W. Smith, Mus. Bac., New College, Oxford, late Musical Director and Organist at Tooting College, formerly Sub-Organist and Choir-Master of St. George's Cathedral, Southwark, London, S.E. (1870.)

Smith-Dodsworth, Mrs. F., wife of the late Frederic Smith-Dodsworth, son of Sir Charles Smith-Dodsworth, third Bart., of Newland.

Smyth, C. J. Moncrieff, of Christ College, Cambridge; a priest in London; son of the late Dr. Maidstone Smyth, of Gibliston, Fyfe, N.B.

Smyth, Mrs. H. S. More, daughter-in-law of the late Earl of Mount Cashell. (1897.)

Smythe, The late Rev. John Rowley, son of a Presbyterian minister in Co. Derry, formerly a magistrate in Ceylon; a priest, and Military Chaplain in Colombo, Ceylon. (1876.)

Smyth-Pigott, The late J. H., of Brockley Hall, Somerset. (1866.)

Soames, Miss, of Irnham Hall, Grantham.

Soddall, Mrs., an English lady, married to a Swiss federal judge. (1898.)

Somerville, The Misses, daughters of the celebrated Mrs. Somerville, writer on science.

Songe, Mrs. J. A., daughter of Colonel Haffe, of Wigtonshire, N.B.

Soppet, Charles E., for ten years church-warden of St. John's, Hammersmith, London, W. (1895.)

Southerden, William, Associate of King's College, London, late Curate of St. John's, Torquay, Devonshire, and formerly at St. Peter's, London Docks; now Headmaster of St. Joseph's Catholic Home School, Babbicombe. (1885.)

Span, Mrs. J., sister of the Rev. W. T. du Boulay, M.A., Vicar of St. Mary Boltons, West Brompton, London. (1881.)

Sparks, Miss M. A., sister of E. A. Sparks, the barrister.

Sparks, Robert, of Harlesden, London. (1883.)

Sparrow, Mrs. John, of London. (1879.)

Spearman, Mrs. J., of Nenagh, Ireland. (1879.)

Spearman, Mrs., daughter-in-law of the late Right Hon. Sir A. J. Spearman, Bart. (1875.)

Spedding, Carlisle, Queen's College, Oxford. (1881.)

Spedding, J. P. H. Wyndham, Trinity College, Cambridge; of Summergrove, Whitehaven. (1880.)

Speid, Miss Margaret, of Forneth.

Spencer, The late Hon. and Rev. George, M.A., son of the second Earl Spencer, sometime Chaplain to the late Right Rev. Dr. Blomfield, Bishop of London ; a Passionist Priest.

Spencer, George, of Llantarnam. (1887.)

Spencer, Miss, sister of the above. (1887.)

Spender, Hugh S., of Oriel College, Oxford. (1894.)

Sperling, John Hanson, M.A. Trinity College, Cambridge, formerly Curate of St. Mary Abbots, Kensington, London, W. and late Rector of Westbourne, Sussex. (1870.)

Sperling, Mrs., wife of the above, and family. (1870.)

Spode, The late Josiah, J.P. of Hawksyard, Rugeley. (1886.)

Spranger, H. W., B.A. Exeter College, Oxford. (1885.)

Sproston, Samuel, B.A. and late Scholar of Magdalene College, Cambridge, formerly Curate of St. Faith's, Stoke Newington, London, N., and member of the London Diocesan Conference, late Vicar of Winterbourne, Down, Gloucestershire; now private tutor to the sons of the Marquis of Bute, K.T. (1889.)

Sproston, Mrs., wife of the above, and five children. (1889.)

Spurrier, Alfred Henry, L.R.C.P., of Manchester. (1887.)

Stacey, George, of Downing College, Cambridge, cousin of Dean Church ; a priest at Littlehampton.

Staley, Abraham, of Burton-on-Trent.

Staley, Mrs., wife of the above, and her six children.

Stanfield, Francis, a priest, and till lately at Corpus Christi Church, Southampton Street, Strand, London, W.C.

Stanfield, George C., of Brighton. (1879.)

Stanfield, Mrs., wife of the above. (1879.)

Stanfield, The late John, of the firm of Messrs. Stanfield, Leeds.

Stanfield, Mrs., wife of the Royal Academician, and mother of the Revv. Francis and Raymund Stanfield, priests.

Stanfield, Raymund, a priest and chaplain to the Convent of the Good Shepherd, Hammersmith, London, W.

Stanley, The Hon. Algernon C., M.A. Trinity College, Cambridge, fourth son of the second Lord Stanley of Alderley; formerly Incumbent of Holy Cross and St. Anne's, Soho, London, W. Now a priest, Monsignor, Protonotary-Apostolic, and Vatican correspondent to the *Times*, formerly assistant priest at St. James's, Manchester Square, London, W. (1879).

Stanley, George, of Brighton. (1880.)

Stanley, Mrs., wife of the above. (1880.)

Stanley, Miss, of Paris. (1882.)

Stanley, Henry, late a Methodist minister, now a priest at the Cathedral, Northampton.

Stanley, J., of Nenagh, Ireland. (1878.)

Stanley, Mrs., wife of the above, and children. (1878.)

Stanley, The late Miss Mary, eldest daughter of the late Right Rev. Dr. Stanley, Bishop of Norwich, and sister of the late Very Rev. Dean

Stanley, of Westminster; she established a Military Hospital at Koulalee during the Crimean War; authoress of *Flower Missions, True in Life*, etc. (1856.)

Stanton, Henry, B.A. Pembroke College, Oxford. (1878.)

Stanton, Richard M., B.A. Brasenose College, Oxford; a priest at the Brompton Oratory, London, S.W. (1845.)

Stanuel, Mrs., wife of Charles G. Stanuel, solicitor, of Dublin. (1892.)

Stapley, Charles M., M.A., a priest at St. Augustine's, Tunbridge Wells, Kent.

Starr, Miss Eliza Allen, the authoress.

Statter, Miss, daughter of the Vicar of Worminghall.

St. Aubyn, Geoffrey, of London. (1876.)

St. Aubyn, Mrs., wife of the above. (1875.)

Staunton, The late George Staunton Lynch, of Clydagh, J.P. and D.L. for Co. Galway, Ireland.

Staunton, Mrs., wife of the above.

Staunton, Mrs., wife of Captain R. Lynch Staunton, of the Galway Militia.

St. Clare, Miss, daughter of Professor St. Clare, of Edinburgh; lately head of the Catholic Jubilee Institution of Dublin. (1889.)

Steggall, Robert, author. (1888.)

Stenbock, The late Count, of Balliol College, Oxford. (1880.)

Stephens, John, B.A. Trinity College, Cambridge.

Stephens, The late W. H., the actor. (1886.)

Steuart, The late John, of Ballechin, J.P., D.L., Knight of St. Gregory.

Steuart, Mrs., wife of the above, and eldest daughter of Sir Albert Larpent, second Bart.

Stevely, Mrs., of Canterbury. (1883.)

Stevens, The late Thomas, M.A., late Vicar of Hathersage. (1865.)

Stevenson, Henry, of Worthing. (1889.)

Stevenson, The late Rev. Joseph, M.A. of Durham University, formerly Vicar of Leighton Buzzard; a Jesuit Priest at the Immaculate Conception, Farm Street, London, W. (1850.)

Stewart, Miss Alice, daughter of Colonel Stewart, of Folkestone.

Stewart, Ambrose, M.A., formerly an Anglican clergyman.

Stewart, The late Sir Andrew, late Chief Justice of the Province of Quebec, Canada. (1891.)

Stewart, Douglas, grandson of the late Admiral Sir Houston Stewart, G.C.B. (1884.)

Stewart, Francis Hugh, of St. Andrews University, son of R. M. Stewart of St. Andrews.

Stewart, Henry S., late of the Civil Service, son of the Rev. J. A. Stewart, M.A., late Rector of Vange, Essex. (1849.)

Stewart, The late James A., M.A. St. John's College, Cambridge, formerly Rector of Vange, Essex. (1849.)

Stewart, James, M.A. Trinity College, Cambridge, late Curate at Wolverston; Fellow of the Royal

University of Ireland, and Professor at the Catholic University College, Dublin.

Stewart, Miss Margaret Douglas, daughter of the late Douglas Stewart, and granddaughter of the late Admiral Houston Stewart, G.C.B. (1883.)

Stewart, Mrs., wife of Colonel Stewart of Folkestone.

Stewart, Miss, daughter of the late Rev. J. A. Stewart, M.A., late Rector of Vange, Essex. (1849.)

Stewart, Miss Murray, of Edinburgh.

Stewart, R. M., of Hope Street, St. Andrews, N.B.; late parish minister of Galashiels, N.B.

Stewart, R. M., of Balliol College, Oxford, son of the above.

Stewart, The late Thomas, of Aberdeen. (1830.)

Stewart, The late Sir William Drummond, seventh Bart.

Still, The late Robert Trevor, B.A. Trinity College, Dublin, late Vicar of Ken-Yatton, Somerset. (1897.)

Stillwell, The late Edward, of the War Office.

Stillwell, Mrs., wife of the above.

Stingo, William Frederick Aloysius, of Cottles, Wilts. (1855.)

St. John, The late Rev. Ambrose, M.A. Christ Church, Oxford, formerly Curate at East Farleigh; a priest of the Oratory, Birmingham. (1845.)

St. John, Captain St. Andrew, of the Royal Navy.

St. John, Mrs., wife of the above.

St. John, Edward, of Brighton; a priest at Bishop's House, Southwark, and Diocesan Treasurer, formerly private Secretary to the Right Rev. Dr. Butt, late Bishop of Southwark.

Stockley, Professor, B.A. of Trinity College, Dublin, now Professor of Modern Languages at the University of New Brunswick, Fredericton, Nova Scotia. (1894.)

Stockley, Miss Alice Josephine, sister of the above; now a Sister of Charity in Dublin. (1897.)

Stokes, Charles S., B.A. Trinity College, Cambridge. (1855.)

Stokes, F. R., B.A. Trinity College, Dublin.

Stokes, George Frederick, B.A. St. John's College, Cambridge; a priest and Canon of Northampton at Olney.

Stokes, Scott Nasmyth, Scholar and B.A. of Trinity College, Cambridge, one of Her Majesty's Inspectors of Schools. (1842.)

Stokes, The late Mrs., wife of the above, authoress. (1842.)

Stone, Mrs., of York, and her five daughters. (1893.)

Storks, Captain, H. N. R., late of the 97th Regiment.

Storer, John, Mus. Doc., now Organist at St. Patrick's, Soho, London, W. (1877.)

Story, Mrs., wife of Admiral Story.

Story, Commander O., of the Royal Navy.

Story, Mrs., wife of the above.

Stotler, Miss, of Newcastle-on-Tyne.

Stowell, The late Mrs., wife of Anthony Stowell, of the London and County Banking Company.

Strange, A. L., of South Lodge, Champion Hill, London, S.E., midshipman in the Royal Navy.

Strange, C. S., brother of the above, cadet in the Royal Navy.

Strange, Miss Louisa, sister of the above, of Sussex Mansions, South Kensington, London, W.

Strange, Miss M., sister of the above.

Strange, Miss Muriel, sister of the above, of South Lodge, Champion Hill, London, S.E.

Strickland, Mrs. Charles, of London. (1883.)

Strong, Patrick John, of Midford. (1858.)

Strong, Mrs. Templeton, of Rome. (1884.)

Strong, Thomas, of Midford. (1855.)

Stuart, Miss Janet, daughter of the late Hon. and Rev. A. Stuart, M.A., Rector of Cottesmore, Rutland. (1879.)

Stuart, J. H., B.A. St. John's College, Cambridge, late Curate of Bramford. (1850.)

Stuart, Miss, formerly Anglican Sister at Oxford.

Stutler, Mrs., of Birmingham. (1886.)

Superioress, The, and six Sisters, of St. Mary's Anglican Priory, Hackney, all now Catholic nuns.

Surtrees, Miss, of Hamsterley Hall, Durham. (1870.)

Sutcliffe, Joseph George, M.A. and late Scholar of Clare College, Cambridge, formerly Curate at St. Nicholas', Great Yarmouth. (1880.)

Sutcliffe, William Ormond, M.A. and late Scholar of St. John's College, Cambridge; a priest, and Head of St. Edmund's House, Cambridge; brother of the above. (1881.)

Sugden, T. H., of Lincoln College, Oxford.

Suter, Henry, of Midford. (1859.)

Sutton, Francis, of Revell Grange, Sheffield.

Sutton, The late Sir John, third Bart., of Norwood, M.A. Jesus College, Cambridge.

Swabey, Robert Sutton, organist and composer. (1856.)

Swainson, The late Rev. Edward G., B.A. Trinity College, Cambridge; a priest, till lately at St. Mary Immaculate and St. Philip's, Newmarket.

Swan, Mrs., wife of an Anglican clergyman. (1884.)

Swan, Miss Florence, daughter of the above. (1884.)

Swan, The late Rev. S., a priest at Barnet. (1876.)

Sweetman, Mrs. J. M., of London.

Sykes, Lady, daughter of the late Right Hon. G. A. F. Cavendish-Bentinck, M.P., son of the late Lord Frederick Cavendish-Bentinck; wife of Sir Tatton Sykes, Bart. (1882.)

Sykes, Lieutenant Mark, of the 3rd Battalion Yorkshire Regiment, only son of Sir Tatton Sykes, Bart. (1882.)

Sylvester, Walter, F.S.A. (Scot), a priest at St. Charles' College, St. Charles' Square, Bayswater, London, W.

TAAFFE, Mrs. George (*née* Griffiths-Boscawen), wife of George Taaffe of Smarmore Castle and Glen Keiran, Co. Louth, Ireland. (1895.)

Tadman, The late Miss M. F., a nun, and Superioress of the Convent of Our Lady of Mercy, Alderney.

Talbot, The late Hon. and Rev. George, B.A. Balliol College, Oxford, formerly Vicar of Evercreech, Somersetshire, fifth son of the third Lord Talbot de Malahide; a priest, Canon of St. Peter's, Rome, for some time Chamberlain to His Holiness the late Pope Pius IX. (1844.)

Talbot, The late Hon. and Rev. Gilbert Chetwynd, of Christ Church, and Fellow of All Souls' College, Oxford, seventh son of the second Earl Talbot, and great uncle of the present Earl of Shrewsbury; a priest, D.D. of Rome, Domestic Prelate to His Holiness Pope Leo XIII., Monsignor, Canon of Westminster, and Chaplain to the 4th Volunteer Battalion Rifle Brigade. (1838.)

Talbot, The late Sir James, Bart. (1848.)

Talbot, The late Admiral Sir John, G.C.B., of Rhode Hill, near Up-Lynn, Dorsetshire.

Talbot, Marcus, of Ennis, Co. Clare, Ireland.

Talbot, Mrs. Reginald, of Rhode Hill, relative of Admiral Sir John Talbot, G.C.B.

Talmage, Mrs. Susan S., of Falmouth, wife of an Anglican clergyman. (1896.)

Tanner, Dr. Charles, M.P. for Mid Cork. (1897.)

Taplin, Alfred George, of Leamington. (1895.)

Tarleton, F. W., barrister. (1845.)

Tarleton, The late Waldyve Willington, M.A. of Cambridge University, formerly Incumbent at Sydney, Australia. (1894.)

Tasker, The late Countess, of Rotherham. (1855.)

Tatlock, William, M.A. of London University, late Curate of St. James the Less, Liverpool, and of Christ Church Clapham, S.W. (1889.)

Tatum, George Benson, M.A. Christ Church, Oxford, formerly Curate of St. Paul's, Oxford, and Chaplain of Magdalen College; a priest at St. Saviour's, Lewisham, London, S.E. (1883.)

Taunton, Mrs. Alfred George (*née* Osbaldiston-Mitford), of Wimbledon, London, S.W. (1870.)

Taunton, Mrs. Edward, of Liverpool. (1875.)

Taunton, Mrs. Francis H. (*née* Mendoza), of Waterloo, Liverpool. (1894.)

Taunton, Miss L., daughter of the late Sir John Taunton, Bart.

Taunton, Mrs. William, cousin of the Rev. Etheldred L. Taunton. (1868.)

Taunton, Mrs. W. (*née* Newman), of Brockenhurst. (1876.)

Tayler, Archdale William, son of the late Rector of St. Matthias', Stoke Newington, London, N.

Tayler, The late Mrs., wife of the late Rector of St. Matthias', Stoke Newington, London, N. (1843.)

Taylor, Alfred, of Liverpool.

Taylor, The late Captain. (1856.)

Taylor, Miss, who nursed the wounded in the Crimea with Miss Florence Nightingale; Foundress of the Institute of the Poor Servants of the Mother of God and the Poor; authoress of *A Marvellous History, Lost, Tyborne*, etc.

Taylor, The late Rev. Hugh, a priest at Holy Trinity, Stonor, Henley-on-Thames. (1869.)

Taylor, Mrs. Mary Jane, of Cottles, Wilts. (1874.)

Taylor, S. A., of the India Office.

Taylor, Stephen, the barrister.

Tebay, Mrs., wife of Dr. Tebay.

Tebbutt, Henry, of London.

Teevon, Mrs., wife of John Teevon, of Westbourne Terrace, London, W.

Teevon, Mrs., wife of Michael Teevon, surgeon, of Gloucester Terrace, London, W.

Temple, Miss, daughter of Admiral Temple, of Truro.

Temple, Miss, formerly an East Grinstead Sister.

Temple, The late Mrs., wife of the late Charles Temple, of Westminster. (1860.)

Temple, Mrs. Edward (*née* Graham), of Kensington, London, W. (1874.)

Thackray, Percy William Francis, of Leamington. (1895.)

Tharpe, John, of London.

Tharpe, Mrs., wife of the above.

Thatcher, Mrs., of London. (1885.)

Theed, Edward Alexander, M.A. St. John's College, Cambridge, late Curate of All Saints', Plymouth; a priest in Rome. (1895.)

Thewles, Miss, of Brighton. (1880.)

Thomas, Miss Alicia, daughter of Dr. Thomas, of Horsham, Sussex. (1882.)

Thomas, Captain.

Thomas, Capel Stanley, son of Samuel Edward Thomas S.C.L.; journalist. (1887.)

Thomas, Charles, B.A. Exeter College, Oxford, formerly an Anglican clergyman.

Thomas, Mrs. D., wife of an Anglican clergyman. (1872.)

Thomas, David Lloyd, M.A. Jesus College, Oxford, late Rector of Grainsby, near Grimsby, Lincolnshire. (1896.)

Thomas, Mrs., wife of the above, and children. (1896.)

Thomas, Miss F., relative of the late Captain Marryat, R.N., the novelist.

Thomas, Lynall.

Thomas, Mrs., wife of the above, and daughter of the late Captain Marryat, R.N.

Thomas, Miss Mary, daughter of the above.

Thomas, Mrs. (*née* Marryat), of Bruges.

Thomas, Samuel Edward, S.C.L., only son of the late Isaac Thomas, of the Bank of England; journalist, and author of *Albion's Church, or High, Low and Broad Ideas of Essentials, Sketches of the Welsh Clergy in London,* founder of the *Biographical Magazine,* contributor to the *Court Circular,* etc. (1874.)

Thomas, Mrs. Maude, wife of the above. (1897.)

Thompson, Charles, of Tunbridge Wells.

Thompson, The late Edward Healy, M.A. Emmanuel College, Cambridge, late Curate of St. James's, Westminster, author of *Unity of the Episcopate,* and editor of the *Library of Religious Biography,* published by Messrs. Burns and Oates, London, W. (1846.)

Thompson, Mrs., wife of the above. (1846.)

Thompson, Gordon, M.A. and Scholar, Sidney Sussex, College, Cambridge, late Curate of Christ Church, St. Pancras, London, N.W., a priest at

The Holy Name and Our Lady of the Sacred Heart, Bow Common, London, E. (1875.)

Thompson, The late Mrs., wife of the above. (1875.)

Thompson, Henry, late Anglican curate at Ashford, Kent.

Thompson, J. Eyre, B.A. and Scholar of Wadham College, Oxford, a barrister.

Thompson, The late Sir John, S.D., K.C.M.G., Q.C., formerly Conservative Premier of Canada.

Thompson, The late T. J., B.A. Trinity College, Cambridge, father of Lady William Butler, painter of "The Roll Call," etc.

Thompson, The late Mrs., wife of the above.

Thomson, John, printer to the University of Aberdeen. (1865.)

Thorn, Miss Clare Hope, daughter of the late Professor Thorn, of Wellington College. (1897.)

Thornhill, Mrs., wife of the Venerable Archdeacon Thornhill. (1881.)

Thornley, Henry, of Spilsby, Lincolnshire. (1898.)

Thornton, George, C.E., of London.

Thorold, Algar Labouchere, only son of the late Right Rev. Dr. Thorold, Bishop of Winchester; author. (1884.)

Thorold, Mrs., wife of the above. (1898.)

Thorold, Miss Sybil, daughter of the late Right Rev. Dr. Thorold, Bishop of Winchester. (1898.)

Thorp, Sidney Benson, B.A. St. Edmund's Hall, Oxford; formerly Curate of Christ Church, Clapham, then at St. Matthew's, Sheffield. (1890.)

Thorpe, Mrs., of Southampton. (1885.)
Thurstans, Aubrey, of New Inn Hall, Oxford. (1886.)
Thurston, Charles H., surgeon.
Thynne, The late Rev. Lord Charles, M.A. Christ Church, Oxford, late Rector of Kingston Deverell, and Canon of Canterbury, son of the second Marquis of Bath; a priest. (1852.)
Thynne, The late Lady Charles, wife of the above, and daughter of the late Right Rev. Dr. Bagot, Bishop of Bath and Wells. (1852.)
Tickell, G. R., of London. (1878.)
Tickell, The late Rev. George, M.A. University College, Oxford; a Jesuit Priest. (1844.)
Tijou, Herbert E., the architect.
Tijou, Mrs., wife of the above.
Till, F., solicitor, of Folkestone.
Till, Mrs., wife of the above.
Timbrell, William, barrister, of Acton, London, W. (1895.)
Todd, Mrs., daughter of the late Rev. R. Hoare, M.A., an Anglican clergyman, and wife of the late E. Todd, Member of a Colonial Parliament. (1868.)
Todd, The late Rev. William G., M.A. Trinity College, Dublin, formerly Curate at St. James's, Bristol; a priest and Canon. (1851.)
Todhunter, Lieutenant K. W., of the K. O. Scottish Borderers, B.A. of Cambridge University, son of the late Isaac Todhunter. (1894.)
Todhunter, Mrs., mother of the above. (1894.)
Todhunter, Miss, daughter of the above. (1894.)

Toler, George Graham, of Plymouth.

Tollemache, Miss, granddaughter of the late Earl of Dysart.

Tompkins, Mrs. Hattie, of Luddington. (1888.)

Toovey, The late James, publisher, of Piccadilly, London. (1846.)

Toovey, Richard, of London. (1885.)

Topham, Mrs., wife of Dr. Topham.

Tordiffe, T. S., of Bath. (1876.)

Towle, de Lacey, solicitor.

Towne, Arthur Micah, son of the Rev. E. J. Towne, B.A., of New Street Square: was for some time lay-worker in the parish of St Alban's, Holborn, London, E.C.

Towneley, The late Lady Caroline, daughter of the second Earl of Sefton, and wife of the late Charles Towneley, of Towneley.

Townsend, Bruno, a Passionist Priest at St. Joseph's Retreat, Highgate, London, N., author.

Townsend, Charles W., M.A. Keble College, Oxford, late Principal of the Oxford Mission to Calcutta, and for some time previously Vice-President of Salisbury Theological College; a Jesuit Priest at Manresa, Roehampton, London, S.W. (1889.)

Townsend, The late Rev. J. A., a priest.

Townsend, The late Rev. J. W. N., a priest.

Townsend, The late Miss, daughter of an Anglican clergyman. (1843.)

Tozer, A. E., of Norton Road, Hove, Brighton, Mus. Doc. of New College, Oxford, F.R.C.O., Knight of the Pontifical Order of St. Sylvester, composer of *Complete Benediction Manual, Antiphons of the B. V. M.*, etc., etc. (1884.)

Tozer, J. Kellyer, of Clifden, Teignmouth, Devonshire.

Trafford, The late Edward W. S., of Brundell Hall, near Norwich.

Traies, The late Rev. William F., M.A. and Fellow of Merton College, Oxford, late Curate of St. John the Evangelist's, Holborn, London, E.C.; a priest at Holy Cross, Plymouth. (1878.)

Trappes, Mrs. Mary, wife of Robert Trappes, of Clitheroe.

Tredcroft, Lieutenant-Colonel C. Lennox, J.P., late of the Royal Horse Artillery.

Tredcroft, The late Mrs., wife of the above, and daughter of the late Sir William Scott, the sixth Bart., of Ancrum.

Tregena, Charles, B.A. Worcester College, Oxford.

Trelawny, The late Sir Harry, the seventh Bart., of Trelawny, M.A. Christ Church, Oxford, late an Anglican clergyman.

Trelawny, Miss, daughter of the above.

Tremayne, Mrs. W., daughter of Baron de Robeck. (1897.)

Tremenheere, Miss Edith. (1892.)

Tremlett, The late Rear-Admiral S. S. D., a distinguished naval architect, only son of the late Admiral William Tremlett. (1897.)

Trench, F., of Balliol College, Oxford.

Trendell, Captain, of the Ryde Militia.

Trenow, The late Rev. F. D., of St. John's College, Oxford, late Curate at Northfield. A Dominican Priest, and Chaplain to the Convent of Our Lady of Reparation, Carisbrooke, Isle of Wight. (1852.)

Trevelyan, Edwin, M.A. and Scholar of St. John's College, Cambridge, formerly Vicar of Cannock. (1872.)

Trevelyan, Mrs., wife of the above and sister of the late Rev. G. Riddell, M.A., Fellow and Tutor of Balliol College, Oxford, and family. (1872.)

Trevelyan, Mrs., wife of the late Colonel Trevelyan of the 60th Rifles.

Trevelyan, Miss Ada, daughter of the above.

Trevelyan, Mrs. Harrington.

Trevor, Alfred C., Controller of Stamps and Taxes, Edinburgh. (1892.)

Trevor, Mrs., wife of the above, and niece of Lord Loch, G.C.B.

Trevor, Claude, son of General Trevor, C.B.

Trevor, Major F.

Trevor, Hubert, son of General Trevor, C.B.

Trevor, Mrs., daughter of General Trevor, of Plymouth, and wife of General William Cosmo Trevor, C.B.

Trevor, Mrs., of Harrow. (1889.)

Trevor, Miss G., daughter of the above. (1890.)

Trevor, Miss R., sister of the above. (1890.)

Trewd, W. J. P., of Dartmouth.

Trickett, Captain Thomas, of the Royal Navy.

Trotter, The late Charles, of Woodhill, J.P. and D.L. for Perthshire.

Trotter, The late Mrs., wife of the above.

Trotter, The late Lieutenant Charles F. Graham, of the 93rd Sutherland Highlanders, J.P.

Tubb, Charles Edward, a priest at Our Lady of Grace and St. Edward's, Chiswick, London, W.

Tuck, Henry, of Ingateston, Essex.

Tucker, The late Captain. (1848.)

Tucker, S. W., solicitor.

Tucker, William Scott, of London.

Tucker, Mrs., wife of the above.

Tuckwell, Miss, of Headington, Oxford.

Tuckwell, The Misses, daughters of a Methodist minister.

Tuite, The late Sir Mark Anthony, Bart., of Kilruane, Nenagh, Co. Tipperary, Ireland, formerly Captain in the 19th Regiment of the line, and served with distinction. (1897.)

Tuke, Reginald, of King's College, London, formerly Curate of St. John's, Hackney, London, N., a priest, Canon of Westminster at Our Lady of Grace and St. Edward's, Chiswick, London, W.

Tuke, Miss, of Maidstone, niece of the Very Rev. Canon Tuke.

Tunnicliffe, The Misses, of Clapham, London, S.W.

Turnbull, J. T. D., of the Record Office.

Turnbull, The late W. B., D.D., advocate at the Scottish Bar.

Turner, Lady, wife of Sir Charles Turner, R.C.I.E., late Chief Justice of Madras. (1891.)

Turner, Mrs., wife of the Rev. Charles Turner, M.A., late of Hanwell Park, London, W.

Turnerelli, Mrs. Tracy, sister of Thomson Hankey, late M.P. (1856.)

Twiss, H. C., late Sacristan of St. Mary Magdalene's, Chiswick, London, W. (1879.)

Twycross, Dr., of Oxford.

Twycross, Mrs., of Gorton Lodge, Clapham Common, London, S.W.

Twyman, Colonel. (1859.)

Twyman, Captain, late of the Indian Navy.

Twyman, Charles, of Stafford, a solicitor. (1873.)

Twyman, Mrs., wife of the above. (1873.)

Twyman, Mrs., wife of a solicitor at Rugeley.

Tydd, Thomas Henry, M.A. St. Edmund's Hall, Oxford, Classical Medallist, First Classical Honoursman, Second Class in Moral Sciences, and First Class Exhibitioner of Trinity College, Dublin, late Chaplain of Alton Towers (the Earl of Shrewsbury's). (1879.)

Tylee, Edward, of Brasenose College, Oxford, relative of Monsignor Tylee. (1897.)

Tylee, The late General. (1847.)

Tylee, Mrs., wife of the above. (1847.)

Tylee, William, B.A. Oriel College, Oxford; a priest and Monsignor, Chaplain to the Marquis of Ripon, K.G. while Viceroy of India. (1866.)

Tyler, Captain George, of the Royal Engineers, grandson of the late Admiral Sir George Tyler, of Cottrell, Glamorganshire.

Tyrrwhit, Miss M., daughter of the late Rev. St. John Tyrrwhit, an Anglican clergyman.

ULLATHORNE, The late Mrs., mother of the late Archbishop Ullathorne, O.S.B., formerly Bishop of Birmingham.

Uniacke, Mrs., wife of the late Captain Uniacke, of the Rifle Brigade.

Urquhart, The Hon. Mrs., sister of Lord Carlingford, wife of the late David Urquhart, diplomatist and journalist, author of *Turkey and Her Resources*, etc., and family. (1877.)

Urquhart, Arthur Jerome Pollard, of Lincoln College, Oxford, third son of the late William Pollard Urquhart, of Castle Pollard, Westmeath and Craigston, Aberdeenshire; a Benedictine Priest at Fort Augustus, N.B. (1877.)

Urquhart, Francis Gregor. (1877.)

Urquhart, Mrs., wife of the above. (1877.)

Urquhart, The Misses, her daughters. (1877.)

VALE, Henry, late Curate of St. Andrew's, Wells Street, London, W.

Vale, Miss, of Great Malvern.

Vallance, W. H. Aymer, B.A. of Oriel College, Oxford, late Curate at the Annunciation, Brighton, and at St. Bartholomew's, Dover. (1889.)

Valmer, The late Vicomtesse de (*née* Wyndham). (1868.)

Vance, Joseph, of Castletown, Ireland.

Vansittart, Arthur, son of the Rev. Charles Vansittart, M.A., an Anglican clergyman.
Vansittart, Bexley, brother of the above.
Vansittart, Mrs., mother of the above.
Vansittart, Nicholas, son of the above.
Vassall, Oliver Rodie, Balliol College, Oxford; a Redemptorist Priest at Our Lady of the Annunciation, Bishop-Eton, Wavertree, Liverpool, author. (1879.)
Varley, John, of St. Augustine's College, Canterbury.
Vaughan, Miss Ada, of Colchester. (1893.)
Vaughan, E. T., B.A. Christ Church, Oxford. (1880.)
Vaughan, The Hon. George.
Vaughan, Radford, of Merton College, Oxford.
Venables, Thomas H., of New Wandsworth, London, S.W.
Ventris, Mrs., wife of an Anglican clergyman.
Ventris, The Misses, her daughters.
Vere, Langton George, a priest and Dean at St. Patrick's, Soho Square, London, W., author. (1861.)
Verney-Cave, The late Hon. Frances Catherine Sarah, sister of Lord Braye; a nun.
Vernon, Cecil, at one time Assistant Master at St. Joseph's College, Clapham, London, S.W. (1873.)
Vernon, Miss, sister of the above. (1870.)
Vickers, Mrs., of Redgate Hall, Wolsingham, Darlington. (1897.)
Vinall, Miss, now a Dominican Nun.
Vinall, Miss A., formerly an Anglican Sister at Oxford.

Vincent, The late Sir Francis, Bart.
Vinning, Miss, the singer.
Vogt, Mrs., of Liscard.
Voyle, Mrs. M., wife of General Voyle.

ACKERBATH, A. D., M.A. Queens' College, Cambridge, late an Anglican clergyman.

Wadder, Barrett, of London.

Waddy, Cadwalader, of Co. Wexford. (1870.)

Waddy, Frederick, artist.

Waddington, S. P., musical editor of the *Arundel Hymns*.

Wadley, Weston Eskine, of London.

Wadley, Mrs., wife of the above.

Wait, Mrs., daughter of the late Rev. J. C. M. Bellew, S.C.L. of St. Mary Hall, Oxford.

Wait, William T. P., of Newbury.

Wake, The late William, solicitor, of Sheffield, and family.

Walcott, Colonel, of Bournemouth. (1891.)

Walcott, Mrs., wife of the above. (1891.)

Waldie, Ronald James Thorp, of Brighton Grammar School, member of the Institute of Chartered Accountants; a Franciscan Priest and Professor at St. Bernardine's College, Buckingham. (1891.)

Walford, Edward, M.A. and Fellow of Balliol College, Oxford, nephew of the Protestant Bishop of Barbadoes: late an Anglican clergyman, author.

Walford, Frederick, grandson of the late Rev. Henry Clutton, D.D.

Walford, Mrs., of Hatfield Place, near Chelmsford, daughter of the late Rev. Henry Clutton, D.D.

Walford, Miss, sister to the late Rev. J. T. Walford, S.J. (1889.)

Walford, John Berry, M.A. St. John's College, Cambridge, barrister.

Walford, The late Rev. John T., M.A. and Fellow of King's College, Cambridge, at one time an Anglican clergyman and Assistant Master at Eton College; a Jesuit Priest and till lately Professor at St. Beuno's College, St. Asaph, North Wales. (1866.)

Walker, A. J., M.A. Emmanuel College, Cambridge.

Walker, Charles, of Brighton, author of *The Ritual Reason Why*, etc. (1878.)

Walker, Mrs., wife of the above. (1878.)

Walker, Captain Beaumont, of Spilsby, Lincolnshire.

Walker, The late Rev. Henry M., M.A. Oriel College, Oxford, late Curate at Hardenhuish; a priest, till lately at St. Austin's, Kenilworth. (1846.)

Walker, The late Rev. J., M.A. Brasenose College, Oxford, formerly Curate of Benefield; a priest and Canon. (1845.)

Walker, Robert, M.A. Lincoln College, Oxford.

Walker, Rowland, of Engadine House, Torquay.

Walkess, Miss, of Kensington, London, W.

Walkinshaw, Miss, of Cardiff. (1886.)

Wall, Septimus, barrister.

Wall, William M., M.A. Emmanuel College, Cambridge, brother of the foregoing, late Curate at Titteshall, Norfolk; a Benedictine Priest at Fort Augustus, N.B. (1881.)

Wallace, The late Arthur J., M.A. Emmanuel College, Cambridge; a priest.

Wallace, Miss Corry, daughter of Colonel Wallace.

Wallace, Mrs., of Brighton.

Wallace, Henry, of Southampton.

Wallace, Reginald W., of Folkestone.

Wallace, Samuel, of Liverpool.

Wallace, William, late an Anglican clergyman, now a Jesuit novice at Manresa, Roehampton, London, S.W. (1897.)

Wallenger, Henry, of Brighton.

Wallenger, Mrs., wife of the above.

Waller, Henry, the barrister.

Walls, Charles Joseph, B.A. of Durham University, late Curate of Brent Pelham, Herts. (1894.)

Walls, Mrs., wife of the above, and family. (1894.)

Walpole, Lady Dorothy E. M., eldest daughter of the fourth Earl of Orford, married to the Duca del Balzo, only son of the Marquis del Balzo di Galvez, Grandee of Spain of the First Class.

Walpole, Frederick Goulbourne, of London.

Walpole, Mrs., wife of the above.

Walpole, The late Lady Maude, daughter of the fourth Earl of Orford, and wife of the late Prince Palagonia.

Walsh, Miss Caroline, of Lower Wick House, near Worcester.

Walshe, Mrs., wife of Captain Walshe.

Walton, Miss H. E., of Exmouth. (1888.)

Walton, William Hopkins, of Leamington. (1896.)

Wanostrocht, Vincent, of Bath. (1882.)

Warburton, Miss Nona, of Torquay.

Ward, The late Arnold John, of Sheffield. (1849.)

Ward, Mrs. A. H., of London.

Ward, Francis R., brother of the Vicar of St. Saviour's, Leeds.

Ward, Miss Mary, of Midford. (1856.)

Ward, Mrs., wife of the Vicar of St. Raphael's, Bristol.

Ward, The late Rev. Richard, M.A. Oriel College, Oxford, formerly Incumbent at Skipton; a priest and Canon. (1852.)

Ward, The late W. G., M.A., D.Ph., and Fellow of Balliol College, Oxford, formerly an Anglican clergyman, and editor of the *Dublin Review*. (1845.)

Ward, Mrs., wife of the above, daughter of the late Rev. Canon Wingfield. (1845.)

Ward, Mrs., wife of F. R. Ward, and sister-in-law of the Rev. R. Ward, late Vicar of St. Saviour's, Leeds.

Ward, The Misses, daughters of the Hon. and Rev. H. Ward, M.A., Rector, of Killinchy, Co. Down, Ireland, brother of second Viscount Bangor.

Wardell, W. W., the architect.

Wardell, Mrs., wife of the above.

Wardell, Miss, sister-in-law of the above.

Wardroper, H. T., M.A. St. Mary Hall, Oxford, formerly an Anglican clergyman.

Ware, Samuel, M.A. Magdalen College, Oxford, late an Anglican clergyman.

Ware, Titus Hibbert, of Hallbarns, Cheshire.

Waring, Mrs., of London.

Warmoll, Francis James, son of an Anglican clergyman, a priest at Our Lady of Seven Dolours, Stowmarket, Suffolk. (1870.)

Warmoll, The late Rev. John Priestley, B.A. Lincoln College, Oxford, at one time Curate of St. Barnabas', Pimlico, London, S.W., brother of the above; a priest, Provost of Northampton, till lately at The Holy Child Jesus and St. Joseph's, Bedford. (1859.)

Warner, The late Mrs., wife of Charles Warner, the actor.

Warner, Mrs., daughter of an Anglican clergyman.

Warrington, Mrs., wife of the Queen's Counsel.

Warzburg, Baroness, sister of the late Viscount Lyons, K.G., English Ambassador to France, and of the late Dowager Duchess of Norfolk.

Washington, George, B.A. Queens' College, Cambridge.

Wasteneys, William, barrister.

Washbourne, ▓▓▓▓ Robert, the publisher.

Waterall, George S. L., of Manchester. (1893.)

Waterford (Florence), Marchioness of, wife of the fifth Marquis of Waterford. (1870.)

Waters, Mrs., niece of Sir Robert Peel, Bart.

Waters, Miss, daughter of the above.

Waters, J., B.A. St. Mary Hall, Oxford, nephew of the late General Sir J. Waters, K.C.B.

Watkin, Miss Anna, of Liverpool.

Watson, Edward J., M.A. Christ College, Cambridge, formerly Curate at St. Leonard's-on-Sea, a priest in Chelsea, London, S.W. (1876.)

Watson, Ivan W., of Torquay.

Watson, Jabez, M.A. Magdalene College, Cambridge, late Curate at Lostwithiel.

Watson, J. M., M.A. Caius College, Cambridge, formerly an Anglican clergyman.

Watson, Maurice, a Dominican Priest at Woodchester.

Watson-Taylor, The late Emilius, of Headington Manor, Oxford.

Watters, Frank H. E., of Leicester. (1893.)

Watts, C. J., of Cromwell House, Lower Edmonton, formerly a Baptist preacher.

Watts, J. J., of Hawsdale Hall, Cumberland.

Watts, John, of Chester.

Watts, Mrs., wife of the above.

Watts, John Birchley, of Chester.

Watts, Mrs., wife of the above.

Watts, Mrs., of Brighton.

Watts-Russell, David P. (1845.)

Watts-Russell, Mrs., his wife. (1845.)

Watts-Russell, The Misses, her daughters. (1845.)

Watts-Russell, The late Julian, son of the late Rev. Michael Watts-Russell, M.A., Vicar of Benefield; a Papal Zouave. (1845.)

Watts-Russell, Michael, brother of the above; a Passionist Priest, and Superior of the Sacred Heart Retreat, Herne Bay, Kent. (1845.)

Watts-Russell, The late Mrs. M., mother of the above. (1845.)

Watts-Russell, The late Wilfrid, son of the above; a Papal Zouave. (1845.)

Waugh, Mrs., wife of the Rev. Benjamin Waugh, Secretary of the Society for the Prevention of Cruelty to Children.

Waugh, F. J. Norman, son of the above, and a priest at St. Anne's Cathedral, Leeds.

Way, Mrs., of Hastings. (1884.)

Waylen, Mrs., of London.

Waylen, Miss Edith, her daughter.

Waylen, Miss Elizabeth, sister of the above.

Wayte, The late Dr. C. Matthew, brother of the Rev. S. W. Wayte, B.D., late President of Trinity College, Oxford. (1851.)

Wayte, The late S. S., father of the above. (1850.)

Weale, W. H. James, the archæologist, of Clapham, London, S.W.

Webb, Richard, M.A. Lincoln College, Oxford, late Vicar of Hambleton-with-Braunston. (1875.)

Webb, William, of Aylesbury.

Webber, General, C.B.

Webber, Mrs., wife of a London clergyman. (1878.)

Webber, Frederick Glynn Incledon, of Clieglinch Ilfracombe. (1879.)

Wedgwood, Rowland, M.A. Worcester College, Oxford, late an Anglican clergyman. (1879.)

Wegg-Prosser, F. R., B.A. Balliol College, Oxford, Deputy-Lieutenant and late M.P. for Herefordshire. (1852.)

Weguelin, William A., M.A. Trinity College, Cambridge, late Vicar of South Stoke.

Weguelin, Mrs., wife of the above.

Weir, Mrs., of Bristol. (1856.)

Welchman, C. W. F., of Narbonne Avenue, Clapham Common, London, S.W., and of the General Post Office.

Weld-Blundell, Mrs., eldest daughter of the late Hon. Charles D'Arcy Lane-Fox, and wife of Charles Weld-Blundell, of Ince Blundell. (1883.)

Wellesley, Miss, of Kensington, W.

Wellesley, Charles, brother of the above.

Wellesley, Richard J., B.A. Christ Church, Oxford.

Wellington, Augustin, the dramatic author.

Wellington, William P., M.A. (1892.)

Wellington, Mrs., wife of the above.

Wells, Francis, of Torquay, and family. (1860.)

Wells, F. F., M.A. Trinity College, Cambridge, son of Lady Elizabeth Wells. (1845.)

Wells, George, member of the Corporation of Bedford.

Wells, Gresham, M.A. Merton College, Oxford, late Curate of All Saints', Margaret Street, London, W., son of the late Sir Mordaunt Wells, Q.C., now a barrister.

Wells, The late Rev. Thomas, late Curate of St. Martin's, Liverpool; a priest. (1845).

Welman, Charles C. Noel, of Norton Manor, Taunton. (1850.)

Welman, The late Mrs., wife of the above. (1850.)

Welsby, Thomas, of Liverpool.

Wenham, John Alyn, a priest at St. Catherine's, Campden, Gloucestershire.

Wenham, The late Rev. John G., B.A. Magdalen College, Oxford, a priest, Canon, Ecclesiastical Inspector of Schools for Southwark, at St. Mary Magdalen's, Mortlake Surrey, S.W. (1846.)

West, The late Dr., chief physician at the Children's Hospital, Great Ormond Street, London, W.C.

West, Miss, sister of J. R. West, of Alscot Park.

West, Miss Cecilia Georgina. (1881.)

West, Miss Charlotte Elizabeth. (1881.)

West, Miss Elizabeth Anne. (1881.)

West, Miss Ellen Mary. (1881.)

West, Miss Florence Anne. (1881.)

West, Miss Georgina Amelia. (1881.)

West, Miss Sarah. (1880.)

Westall, Rev. Arthur St. Leger, M.A. and Scholar of Queens' College, Cambridge, son of an Anglican clergyman; late Curate at St. Michael's, Brighton, and till recently at St. Saviour's, Croydon. (1897.)

Westall, Mrs., wife of the above, and children. (1897.)

Westermann, Miss, of Kensington, niece of Sir Alexander Grant, Bart., of the University of Edinburgh, and grandniece of the late Miss Ferrier, the novelist.

Western, Major.

Westlake, Frederic, Professor at the Royal Academy of Music, London.

Westlake, Nathaniel, brother of the above.

Westlake, Philip, brother of the above.

Weston, Mrs., of Brighton. (1880.)

Westropp, William, late of Margate College, now Headmaster of Percy House Catholic School, Cliftonville, Margate.

Westropp, Mrs., wife of the above.

Westwood, Mrs., of Bognor.

Westwood, The Misses, daughters of the above.

Whalley, Miss, of Warwick.

Wharton, Arthur, of Kensington, W.

Wharton, Mrs., wife of the above.

Wheeler, The late Rev. William, B.D. and Fellow of Magdalen College, Oxford, formerly Rector of Old and New Shoreham; a priest (Oblate of St. Charles) at St. Mary of the Angels, Bayswater, London, W.

Whelpton, G. B., of Chiswick, late Assistant Secretary of the English Church Union. (1879.)

Whish, Charles, M.A. Christ Church, Oxford, formerly an Anglican clergyman.

Whish, Mrs., wife of the above.

Whitby, J. R. D., of Aldershot. (1879.)

White, H. G., of Canonbury Square, London, N.

White, James Baker, M.A. St. John's College, Oxford, late Curate of St. John the Divine's, Kennington, London, S.E.; a priest (Oblate of

St. Charles), at St. Francis of Assisi, Notting Hill, London, W. (1877.)

White, J. Trevor, late Curate of Norton St. Philip's.

White, Mrs., wife of the above.

Whitehead, Andrew, a Dominican Priest at St. Dominic's Priory, Woodchester, Stroud.

Whitlaw, George, M.A. Christ Church, Oxford, late Curate of St. Stephen's, Clewer, near Windsor. (1881.)

Whitmee, William, a priest of the Order of Charity, and Rector of San Salvatore, Rome.

Wickham, Major H. L.

Wilberforce, Arthur Bertrand, son of the late William Wilberforce, M.P. for Hull; a Dominican Priest at St. Thomas's Priory, Hawksyard, Rugeley. (1850.)

Wilberforce, H. W., M.A. and Fellow of Oriel College, Oxford, and late Rector of East Farleigh, son of the late William Wilberforce, M.P. for Hull, the Slavery Abolitionist. (1850.)

Wilberforce, Mrs., wife of the above. (1850.)

Wilberforce, The late Robert Isaac, M.A. and Fellow of Oriel College, Oxford, late Archdeacon of York. (1850.)

Wilberforce, The late William, sometime M.P. for Hull, eldest son of the slave emancipator. (1850.)

Wilberforce, The late Mrs., wife of the above, and daughter of the late John Owen, founder of the Bible Society. (1850.)

Wilberforce, William, M.A. Oriel College, Oxford, son of the above. (1850.)

Wilcocks, Horace Stone, M.A., late Vicar of St. James-the-Less, Plymouth. (1880.)

Wilcocks, Mrs., wife of the above, and children. (1880.)

Wilcox, J. P., late organist at the Protestant church, Usk, Monmouthshire. (1884.)

Wilde, Captain.

Wilde, Mrs., wife of the above.

Wilderspin, Frederick G., of Cambridge, a priest at SS. Henry and Elizabeth, Sheerness, Kent. (1884.)

Wilderspin, Miss, sister of the above.

Wildman, Miss, daughter of Colonel Wildman.

Wilkin, Miss Catherine, of Colchester. (1894.)

Wilkinson, Miss, of the Fever Hospital, Haverstock Hill, London, N.W.

Wilkinson, Miss Isabel, of Cambridge. (1896.)

Wilkinson, Mrs., wife of the Rev. J. B. Wilkinson, of Lavender Hill, London, S.W.

Wilkinson, Thomas William, B.A. of Durham University, now Bishop of Hexham and Newcastle. (1846.)

Willan, Mrs. Douglas, of Bryderwen, Brecon, South Wales. (1893.)

Willcocks, Thomas Harold, of Clapham, London, S.W.

Willcocks, William R., brother of the above.

Willett, Edmund A., M.A. Trinity College, Cambridge, formerly Anglican vicar in the Diocese of Ely.

Williams, Achilles Leo, grandson of the late Rev. W. H. Williams, M.A., of Wolverhampton.

Williams, Bertie Francis, his brother.

Williams, Miss Clare, their sister.

Williams, Charles Louis, of Winchester.

Williams, Mrs. Evans, of London. (1895.)

Williams, David, a priest at SS. Peter and Paul's, Newport, Shropshire.

Williams, Edwin Vincent, grandson of the late Rev. W. H. Williams, M.A. of Wolverhampton.

Williams, Frederick, brother of the above.

Williams, George Douglas, son of the late G. T. Williams, barrister.

Williams, Rev. John Herbert, M.A. and late Demy of Magdalen College, formerly an Anglican clergyman, author of *Protestant Belief*, etc.

Williams, John J. Paul, son of the late Rev. W. H. Williams, M.A., of Wolverhampton.

Williams, Richard, M.A. Oriel College, Oxford.

Williams, Miss Rita Frances, granddaughter of the late Rev. W. H. Williams, M.A. of Wolverhampton.

Williams, Miss, daughter of the Rector of Bodelwyddan, North Wales.

Williams, Miss, formerly an Anglican Sister at East Grinstead, now a nun.

Williams, Walter R. Francis, son of the late Rev. W. H. Williams, M.A.

Williams, The late Rev. W., a priest and Monsignor.

Williams, The late Rev. W. E., a priest in South Wales.

Williams, William John, B.A. Queen's College, Oxford. (1890.)

Williams, William Vincent, son of the late Rev. W. H. Williams, M.A.

Williamson, Charles David R., B.A. University College, Oxford, only son of Colonel Williamson, of Lawers, Perthshire ; a priest. (1876.)

Willis, Miss Isabel, sister of the late Rector of Bassingham, Lincoln. (1880.)

Willis, Thomas Frederick, B.A. Exeter College, Oxford, late Curate-in-charge of Brooking, Darlington, Devonshire.

Willmott, Alfred, of Liverpool.

Wilmer, Mrs., wife of the late Colonel Wilmer, of the 8th Hussars.

Wilmot, Miss Eliza Harriet, sister of Sir J. Eardley Wilmot, Bart.

Wilson, Arthur, M.A. of Christ Church, Oxford.

Wilson, B., M.A., late Vicar of Fordham.

Wilson, Captain, of Edinburgh.

Wilson, Charles E. P., of Kelso, N.B.

Wilson, Mrs., wife of the above.

Wilson, Miss, till lately an Anglican Sister at Oxford; now a Dominican Nun.

Wilson, Miss Fanny, her sister, also a nun.

Wilson, F. C. Collins, M.A. Trinity College, Cambridge.

Wilson, George, formerly a Quaker, a priest, and Canon of the diocese of Aberdeen, at St. Sylvester's, Elgin, N.B.

Wilson, Harold Lancaster Wilfrid, M.A. Caius College, Cambridge, late Curate of St. Catherine's, Liverpool. (1899.)

Wilson, Mrs., wife of the above. (1899.)

Wilson, James, late Anglican curate at East Dereham, Norfolk. (1896.)

Wilson, John, a Jesuit Priest at St. Aloysius's, Garnet Hill, Glasgow, N.B.

Wilson, The late Rev. William H., M.A. Queens' College, Cambridge, late Curate of Frome Selwood, Somersetshire; a priest. (1870.)

Winchester, William, M.A. Christ Church, Oxford, formerly an Anglican clergyman; Chamberlain to His Holiness Pope Leo XIII.

Winchester, The late Mrs., wife of the above, and sister-in-law to Lord Torrington.

Windeyer, Edward, of King's College, London.

Windeyer, The late Miss, of London. (1850.)

Windle, Mrs., wife of Dr. Windle, Professor and Secretary of Queen's College, Birmingham. (1883.)

Windthrop, The Misses, daughters of Captain Hay Windthrop, R.N.

Wingfield, Philip James, son of the late Rev. Dr. Wingfield, Prebendary of Worcester. (1893.)

Wingfield, William, brother of the above. (1893.)

Wingfield, William, M.A. Christ Church, Oxford, formerly an Anglican clergyman.

Wingham, Miss Agnes Anna, formerly an Anglican nun. (1874.)

Wingham, Mrs. Martha, of Folkestone. (1876.)

Wingham, The late Thomas, Professor at the Royal Academy of Music, London, and Choirmaster of the Oratory, Brompton, London, S.W.

Winter, Ernest Constantine, of Dalston, London, N. (1891.)

Wiseman, Mrs. Harriet, of London. (1894.)

Withers, J. T., the solicitor.

Withers, Mrs., wife of the above.

Withington, John, surgeon, of London.

Witty, R. J., solicitor, of Percy Lodge, East Sheen, London, S.W.

Wodehouse, The Hon. Admiral.

Wolseley, The late Sir Charles, Bart., of Wolseley, Rugeley, Staffordshire, grandfather of the present baronet.

Wolseley, Henry, brother of the above.

Wood, Alexander, M.A. Trinity College, Oxford, F.S.A., author of *The Vatican and the Quirinal*, etc.

Wood, The late Mrs., wife of the Rev. Canon Wood, of Canterbury.

Wood, The late Miss, her daughter.

Wood, The late Miss, of Kensington. (1845.)

Wood, Alfred John Samuel, of Bath. (1854.)

Wood, Charles Henry, late Rector of St. Mary's School Chapel, Hull; a priest, Canon at St. Wilfrid's, Hull.

Wood, Edwin, of Balmoral Terrace, Coatham, Redcar, Yorkshire. (1875.)

Wood, Ernest Holmes, of Midford. (1854.)

Wood, The late Captain Granville, R.N., a Jesuit. (1846.)

Wood, Grenville, the barrister.
Wood, The late Rev. Hubert J., a priest at the Sacred Heart and St. Pancras, Lewes, Sussex. (1857.)
Wood, John Oswald, of Bath. (1849.)
Wood, The late Rev. J. R., a priest.
Wood, Mrs. Munday, of London.
Wood, Reginald, of Willesden, London.
Wood, Richard Somerville, M.A. Exeter College, Oxford, late Military Chaplain of Dum-Dum and Barrackpore, India. (1893.)
Wood, Mrs., wife of the above. (1893.)
Wood, The late Rev. William, a Franciscan Priest.
Woodall, The late Rev. Edward H., M.A. Exeter College, Oxford, late Rector of St. Margaret's, Canterbury; a priest at SS. Mary and Michael's, Settle, Yorkshire. (1859.)
Woodley, Henry, of Belle Vue Terrace, York.
Woodroffe, F. H., Indian District Judge.
Woodroffe, Mrs., wife of the above.
Woodroffe, J. S., barrister.
Woodroffe, Mrs., wife of the above.
Woods, Mrs., wife of Arthur Woods, of Liverpool. (1891.)
Woods, Charles, of Llantarnam. (1886.)
Woods, Mrs., wife of the above, and her seven children. (1886.)
Woods, The late Rev. J. E. Tenison, M.A. Balliol College, Oxford, son of the late J. D. Woods, Q.C.; a priest, and Vicar-General in South Australia, geologist and naturalist, author of the *Discovery and Exploration of Australia*, etc. (1854.)

Woods, The late Mrs., mother of the above. (1860.)

Woodward, The late Jonathan Henry, M.A. Trinity College, Dublin, late Vicar of St. James's, Bristol, an eloquent preacher, son and grandson of dignitaries of the Church of Ireland. (1851.)

Woodward, The Misses, nieces of Viscount Midleton.

Woolett, Mrs., of Stratford.

Woolett, Mrs., wife of George Woolett, J.P.

Woolley, The Misses, daughters of an Anglican clergyman.

Wootten, Mrs. Frances, wife of the late Rev. Dr. Wootten, an Oxford clergyman.

Wordsworth, Charles F., B.A. Magdalen Hall, Oxford, late Private Chaplain to the Marchioness of Bath. (1850.)

Wordsworth, Mrs., wife of the above. (1850.)

Wordsworth, Mrs., the lady who survived the wreck of the *Strathmore*.

Wordsworth, Henry, of Brighton.

Wordsworth, Mrs., wife of the above.

Workman, Walter, M.A. Queen's College, Oxford.

Workman, The late Mrs., of Brighton, wife of the above.

Works, Mrs. W. G., daughter of the late Rev. Dr. Wingfield, Prebendary of Worcester. (1893.)

Worlledge, Charles Wastell, B.A. Trinity College, Cambridge, formerly Curate at St. Mary's, Ipswich, St. Peter's, London Docks, and till lately Chaplain of St. Andrew's Convalescent Home, Folkestone. (1889.)

Worseley, Edward Cayley, of Bognor.

Worswick, Mrs. Worsley, daughter of the Rev. R. Stephens, B.D., Vicar of Belgrave-cum-Bristall.

Woulfe, The late Hon. Mrs., youngest daughter of the second Lord Graves, wife of S. R. Woulfe, son of the Right Hon. Lord Chief Baron Woulfe.

Wrey, The late Sir Bourchier Palk, seventh Bart., of Trebitch ; barrister.

Wrey, Mrs., sister-in-law of the above.

Wright, Joseph, of Keighley.

Wright, Mrs. Leith, cousin of Sir Henry Fletcher, Bart., M.P., and of the Rev. P. Fletcher, M.A., Master of the Guild of Ransom.

Wright, The late Sir Leopold.

Wright, William S., late churchwarden of St. Agnes, Kennington Park, London, S.E. (1891.)

Wyatt, Charles W., of London.

Wyatt-Davies, Ernest R., M.A., Senior in the Historical Tripos, Trinity College, Cambridge. (1888.)

Wymond, Thomas P., the solicitor.

Wyndham, Francis M., M.A. Merton College, Oxford, late Curate of St. George's-in-the-East, London, E., a priest, and Superior of the Oblates of St. Charles at St. Mary's, Bayswater, London, W. (1868.)

Wynell-Mayow, Stanley, son of the Rev. E. M. Wynell-Mayow, M.A., late Rector of Southam, Warwickshire.

Wynne, The late John Henry, B.C.L. and Fellow of All Souls' College, Oxford, D.D. of Rome ; a Jesuit Priest at St. Beuno's College, Wales.

Wynter, Major, son of the Rev. P. Wynter, D.D., late President of St. John's College, Oxford. (1882.)

Wynter, Guy, non-collegiate student of Oxford University, brother of the above, author of various songs and musical settings, for some time Organist of the Birmingham Oratory. (1883.)

Wyse, Mrs., wife of a naval officer.

ARD, Major.

Yard, The late Rev. G. B., M.A. Trinity College, Cambridge, formerly Curate of All Saints', Margaret Street, London, W.; a priest. (1862.)

Yarmouth, Miss, of Torquay.

Yarworth, William V., M.A. St. John's College, Oxford, formerly Curate at Westbury.

Yateman, Miss, of Bournemouth. (1890.)

Yates, Miss, of Brighton.

Yeatman, John Pym, M.A. Emmanuel College, Cambridge, barrister and historical writer, author of *The Shemitic Origin of the Nations of Western Europe*, etc.

Yeatman, Mrs., wife of the above, and family.

Yeoman, Captain C., late of the Indian Army.

Yonge, Dr., of Liskeard.

Yonge, J. F., of Bodmin.

Young, Mr. Deputy, Knight of St. Gregory the Great.

Young, Major.

Young, The late Sir Charles, Bart., brother of Mrs. Bertram Currie, sister-in-law of Lord Currie, British Ambassador in Rome.

Young, Cecil Beadon, M.A. Exeter College, Oxford, late Curate of Burghclere, Hants. (1847.)

Young, Miss, of Brighton. (1882.)

Young, Miss, sister of the above. (1882.)

Younge, Miss Lillian, daughter of the late Major Younge, H.E.I.C.S.

Younge, Miss Olive, sister of the above.

Younger, Mrs., of Haggerstone House.

LIST OF A FEW FOREIGN CONVERTS.

AMERICA.

ADAMS, Henry Austin, M.A., late Rector of the Church of the Redeemer, New York. (1893.)

Adams, John, a well-known Protestant Minister of Iowa. (1884.)

Alexander, Furlow, late Sub-Dean of the Episcopal Cathedral of Fredericton, New Brunswick. (1894.)

Allen, George, LL.D., formerly Episcopalian Rector of St. Alban's, Vermont, and Professor of Greek and Latin in Newark College.

Allen, Miss, of Vermont, granddaughter of the late General Elthan Allen, of the Revolutionary War.

Allen, Mrs. Heman, of New York.

Allen, Miss Mary, of New York.

Allen, Mrs. Mary Withington, and five children.

Anderson, Henry, LL.D., Professor of Mathematics and Astronomy in Columbia College, New York.

Arnold, Miss Emily R., late of the Episcopal Church Settlement House, of New York. (1898.)

Arnold, Mrs. William, of New York. (1898.)

Austin, Charles, barrister.

Austin, Mrs., wife of the above, and family.

Austin, Miss Elizabeth.

Austin, Miss Janet.

Austin, Miss Sarah.

BAKER, The late Rev. Francis, a priest of the Paulist Community, of New York. (1850.)

Bang, Frank, son of the late Henry J. Bang, proprietor of Sturtevant House. (1896.)

Barber, The late Rev. Virgil H., of Vermont, formerly an Episcopalian clergyman, a Jesuit Priest. (1816.)

Barbielini, Countess, of New Bedford, Massachusetts.

Bayley, The late Most Rev. Dr. Bayley, Primate and Archbishop of Baltimore.

Becker, The Right Rev. Dr., Bishop of Wilmington.

Becker, Rev. Francis A., formerly an Episcopalian clergyman, now a priest.

Berrian, Chandler, son of the Rev. Dr. Berrian, Episcopalian minister, and Rector of St. John's, New York.

Betzhover, Mrs., of New York.

Betzhover, daughter of the above.

Bissell, Miss Josephine, of Illinois. (1860.)

Bissell, The late William H., Governor of Illinois. (1854.)

Blair, Mrs. James, of New York. (1884.)

Blake, Henry, the banker.

Bolognetti-Cenci, The Marchesa (*née* Lorillard-Spencer), of New York.

Bowns, George M. P., late a minister of the New York Methodist Episcopal Church. (1898.)

Boyle, Mrs. Stephen, of Philadelphia.

Bradshawe, Miss Catherine, of Chicago.

Bristead, Mrs. Astor, of New Orleans.

Bristead, Henry Arthur, her son.
Brown, The late Rev. Lewis G., a priest of the Paulist Community, New York. (1856.)
Brownson, The late Orestes A., LL.D., the distinguished reviewer whom Lord Brougham styled "the master-mind of America".
Bryant, Dr. John D., of Philadelphia, author.
Buckey, Edward L., late Rector of St. John the Evangelist's, Newport, Rhode Island. (1897.)
Burnet, Hon. Judge, of Ohio, author.
Burnett, The late Peter H., lawyer and first Governor of California.
Burnett, Miss Ruth, a Nun of the Sacred Heart.
Butterworth, Miss E. Jay, niece of John Jay, late American Minister to Vienna.

CALDWELL, Rev. J., of San Francisco, late an Episcopalian minister, now a priest.
Carter, The late Very Rev. Charles Ignatius Hardman, of Kentucky, at one time Vicar-General of the Archdiocese of Philadelphia. (1822.)
Carroll, Mrs. Royal Phelps, wife of R. P. Carroll, a descendant of Charles Carroll, of Carrolltown, one of the signatories of the Declaration of Independence. (1896.)
Cassidy, Mrs., wife of General A. S. Cassidy.
Cavalotti, The Marchesa, now of Rome. (1861.)
Chandler, The late Hon. Joseph R., member of Congress, United States Minister to Naples, and formerly a prominent Freemason of Philadelphia. (1850.)
Chase, Thomas, of Detroit, an Episcopalian.

Chitty, Edward, of Jamaica. (1847.)

Church, The late Rev. Charles, a priest in the Yorktown Diocese of Adelaide.

Church, Miss, sister of the above.

Churchill, Miss, an Episcopalian.

Churchill, General Clark, of Phœnix, Arizona, formerly Attorney-General of Arizona Territory, and a prominent Freemason. (1896.)

Churchill, Mrs., wife of the above. (1896.)

Clapp, Rev. Walter Clayton, late an Episcopalian minister in New York. (1894.)

Clark, Mrs. Frank B., who was the Minnesota Representative on the World's Fair Commission in connection with the Chicago Exhibition. (1894.)

Clark, Rev. James, of Georgetown College, a priest, and army chaplain.

Clarke, General D. W., of Vermont.

Claxton, Mrs., daughter-in-law of Admiral Claxton.

Coleman, Alexis Irene du Pont, of Oxford University, late Rector of St. Michael's, Wilmington, son of the Right Rev. Dr. Leighton Coleman, Bishop of Delaware. (1897.)

Coles, Miss, of New York.

Colt, Anson T., late Missionary of Church Mission to Deaf-Mutes, and in charge of the Protestant Episcopal Mission of St. David's, Woodbine Street and Knickerbocker Avenue, Brooklyn, New York, a nephew of the late Right Rev. Dr. Brown, Bishop of Fond du Lac. (1892.)

Colville, Joseph, of Washington.

Conrad, The Hon. Mrs., of New Orleans, daughter of the Marchesa Cavalotti, of Rome. (1881.)

Cooke, Mrs. Laura Wheaton Abbott, daughter of Admiral Abbott.

Cooke, Dr. Nicholas Francis.

Cooper, The late Rev. Charles, of Virginia, a priest. (1807.)

Copeland, Charles C., a lawyer and attorney to the late Cyrus McCormick, the founder and supporter of the McCormick Theological Institute, the great Presbyterian Seminary of the West, at Chicago, Illinois.

Cowles, Miss Ellen, daughter of the editor of the *Cleveland Leader*.

Cowper, Miss, of Jamaica. (1880.)

Curd, Rev. Thomas J., formerly a Methodist, now a priest, and army chaplain.

Cutts, Colonel James Madison, nephew of ex-President James Madison.

Cyrill, Rev. F., late an Episcopalian minister, now a Passionist Priest.

DALY, Mrs. Philip (*née* Jenny Joyce), of New York. (1896).

Daner, Miss Angela Henrietta, of Boston.

Daner, Miss Charlotte, of Boston.

Davidson, George (Brother Aloysius), late Superior of the Order of the Good Samaritan, New York. (1898.)

Dawson, Miss Ellen, an Episcopalian of Cincinnati.

Dawson, Miss Mary E., of Ohio.

De Camp, Miss, daughter of Admiral de Camp.
De Charette, The Baronne.
De Normandie, The late Mrs. Maria, daughter of a Unitarian minister. (1892.)
Dent, The Hon. Judge, of Washington, brother-in-law of the late President Grant.
Depew, Harold, of New York. (1896.)
Deshon, Rev. F., Superior-General of the Paulists, formerly Professor at West Point Military Academy. (1851.)
De Schauensée, Baroness Frederic Meyer (*née* Toland), of Philadelphia, wife of an officer of the Swiss Papal Guards. (1898.)
Desprez, Madame, daughter of the late General George B. McClellan, and wife of Paul Desprez of the French Legation, Washington. (1893.)
Dillon, The Hon. Henry C., of Los Angelos, California. (1898.)
Dishon, Rev. George, of New London, Connecticut, now a priest and army chaplain.
Doane, Rev. George H., son of the Right Rev. Bishop Doane, of the Protestant Episcopal Church; a priest, Vicar-General and Prelate of the Papal Household, Newark, New Jersey. (1855.)
Dommett, Miss Harriet, now a nun.
Dorsay, Professor Oswald.
Douglas, The late Stephen, the statesman.
Dunne, The Hon. Chief Justice, of Arizona.
Dutton, Charles E., late an officer in the American Army, now attending the Lepers, at Molokai. (1896.)

Dutton, Rev. Francis, late an Episcopalian minister of Massachusetts.
Dutton, Mrs., wife of the above, and family.
Dwyer, Rev. W. J., an Episcopalian, now a priest.

ECCLESTON, The late Most Rev. Dr., Primate and Archbishop of Baltimore.
Edes, Miss Ella, niece of the Right Rev. Bishop Wainwright, of the Episcopal Church of New York.
Edis, Miss Ellen B.
Elbert, Nicholson, of Detroit, an Episcopalian.
Elbert, Mrs., wife of the above.
Elliot, Rev. Walter, a priest of the Paulist Community of New York.
Emery, Miss J., of Dorchester, an Episcopalian.
Emmet, Dr., of New York, grandnephew of the Irish Patriot.
English, Miss Alice, daughter of the poet Dr. Thomas Dunn English, of Newark, New Jersey. (1896.)
Everett, Rev. William, late an Episcopalian minister, relative of Edward Everett, at one time United States Minister in England; now a priest in the Archdiocese of New York.
Ewing, The Hon. Thomas, Senator from Ohio, and for sometime Secretary of the United States Treasury.

FILLICCHI, Madame (née Mary Cowper, of Boston), wife of Chevalier Philip Fillicchi, first Consul of the United States at Leghorn.
Filling, Charles M., of New Jersey.

Fisher, Rev. J., late a clergyman, now a priest.
Florence, The Hon. Thomas B., of Philadelphia, member of the United States House of Representatives.
Forbes, the late Edward, D.D., formerly Rector of St. Luke's Episcopal Church, New York. (1849.)
Foster, General, of the Engineers.
Frenfanelli-Cibo, Countess (*née* Mary Seton Wilkes), of New York.
Frost, Professor, of the Friends' Central School, Philadelphia. (1894.)

Gardner, Miss Ellen, now a nun.
Garesche, Colonel J. P.
Gerdes, Captain, of the Geographic Corps.
Gilmour, Right Rev. Dr., Bishop of Cleveland.
Graham, General.
Grainger, Rev. A., of Fort Wayne, a priest.
Greeley, The late Horace.
Griffin, Charles, late an Episcopalian minister, son of one of the most distinguished lawyers of his day in New York. (1851.)
Grimes, Mrs. (*née* James), of New York.
Grouside, The late Rev. George Edmund, formerly an Episcopalian minister of New Jersey, at one time Chaplain and Secretary to the late Bishop Hobart, of New York. (1820.)
Guernsey, Miss Julia, of Detroit, an Episcopalian. (1897.)
Gurney, Miss Marion F., of the Episcopal Church, Settlement House. (1897.)

Hagan, Mrs. E. P., wife of the late senator. (1896.)
Hall, Oakley, late mayor of New York. (1896.)
Hall, Mrs., wife of the above. (1896.)
Hamersley, Mrs., wife of the late Louis Hamersley. (1884.)
Harden, General D.
Hardin, General M. D.
Hardin, Mrs., wife of the above.
Hardy, General James.
Handley, Marks White, secretary to George W. Cable, the author, of Northampton, and nephew of Governor Marks, of Tennessee. (1894.)
Haskins, Rev. George T., late an Episcopalian minister, a priest and founder of the "House of the Holy Guardian Angel," Boston, author. (1846.)
Hassard, John R. G., of New York, journalist and author.
Hastings, Miss, of Philadelphia.
Hecker, The late Rev. J. J., a priest and founder of the Paulist Community.
Henry, Rev. Thomas, a priest.
Hewitt, Rev. A. F., a priest of the Paulist Community.
Higgins, Mrs. Eliza, of New York.
Hoyt, Rev. F., son of the Rev. W. H. Hoyt, an Episcopalian Rector at Vermont, a priest.
Hoyt, Mrs., mother of the above.
Hoyt, The Misses, her daughters.
Hudson, Rev. David, O.S.C., of Notre Dame, Indiana.
Hudson, Percival, of New York. (1894.)
Huntington, The late Dr. Jedediah Vincent, author of *Rosemary* and other works.

Huntington, Dr. Joshua, author of *Gropings After Truth*, etc.

IRWIN, Robert, of Springfield, Illinois.
Ives, The late Right Rev. Dr., late Protestant Bishop of North Carolina. (1850.)
Ives, The late Mrs., wife of the above, and daughter of Bishop John Henry Hobart, of New York, and goddaughter of the late Mrs. E. A. Seton. (1850.)

JAMES, Robert, of Boston, brother of Professor James, Harvard University, and of Henry James, the novelist. (1896.)
Jones, Charles Taylor, a Methodist, of New York.
Jones, The late General George W., son of the late Chief Justice Jones, of the Supreme Court of Missouri. (1859.)
Jones, Nathaniel S., a Methodist, of New York.
Jones, Miss, daughter of Chancellor Jones, now a nun, and Superioress of the Sacred Heart Convent.

KANE, The Misses, sisters of the Rev. J. Kane, Chaplain to the United States Navy, both nuns.
Kane, Colonel Delancey Astor, of New York. (1897.)
Kearney, Mrs., wife of the late Major-General Philip Kearney. (1866.)
Kearney, The Misses, her daughters. (1866.)
Keen, Gregory B., of Philadelphia.
Kehoe, Mrs., wife of Colonel Kehoe, of North Carolina. (1894.)

Kelly, Mrs. Mary, daughter of Dr. Niles.

Keyes, Dr., of New York.

Kilpatrick, General Judson, at one time United States Minister to Chili. (1882.)

King, The late Crow, one of the prominent leaders of the Sioux Tribe. (1884.)

Kinney, William C., of New York.

Klein, Mrs. Adrian, of New York.

LAPTHROP, The late George Parsons, LL.D., a well-known writer. (1891.)

Lapthrop, Mrs., wife of the above. (1891.)

Lay, Henry, son of the Protestant Bishop of Maryland.

Lee, Governor Thomas Sims, of Maryland. (1860.)

Lee, Mrs., wife of Charles Carroll Lee, of Maryland. (1865.)

Lenicke, The late Rev. Henry, formerly a Lutheran minister, a Benedictine Priest. (1823.)

L'Hommedien, Miss Alma, of Cincinnati, an Episcopalian.

L'Hommedien, Mrs. Stephen, of Cincinnati, an Episcopalian.

Lincoln, Mrs. T. D., of Cincinnati, an Episcopalian and relative of the late President Lincoln.

Lindsey, Mrs., wife of ex-Congressman James G. Lindsey, of Kingston, New York. (1895.)

Livingston, Miss, of New York.

Livingston, Vanbrugh, at one time United States minister to Russia, an Episcopalian, and author of controversial works.

Locke, Rev. Jesse Albert, till lately assistant minister at the Protestant Episcopal Church, New York. (1893.)

Lowe, Mrs., wife of Governor Lowe, of Maryland.

Lyman, The late Rev. Edward Dwight, late an Episcopal Rector, a priest, and Rector of St. Mary's, Govanstown.

Lytton, Miss Gertrude, of Chicago.

MACKAY, George D., ex-president of the Church Industrial Alliance.

Mason, Miss Emily, niece of Senator Mason, of Virginia.

Matthews, Mrs. Nathan, of Boston.

Matthias, Rev. F., formerly a Presbyterian minister, now a Passionist Priest.

Maxwell, Miss Carrie, of New York. (1894.)

May, The Hon. Henry, one of the leaders of his party in the United States House of Representatives.

McBride, Miss, daughter of a Presbyterian minister.

McCall, Rev. Father, of Baltimore, late a clergyman of the Episcopal Church, now a priest.

McCarty, John H., United States Marshal. (1897.)

McEnery, Mrs., of New Jersey, daughter of the British Consul at Richmond, granddaughter of Bishop Moore, of Virginia, and wife of Colonel McEnery.

McHenry, The Hon. Walter, son of Judge McHenry, of Iowa. (1899.)

McLeod, Rev. Donald, formerly a Presbyterian minister, now a priest.

McMaster, James, formerly a Presbyterian, of Pennsylvania, editor of the New York *Freeman's Journal.*

Meath, P. G., late a Baptist minister. (1895.)

Meathe, Rev. Father, of Detroit, Michigan.

Meriwether, Dr. William A., now a priest in Charlestown Diocese.

Metcalf, Miss, of Boston, daughter of the Hon. Judge Metcalf.

Metcalf, Miss Julia, her sister.

Metcalf, Theodore, her brother.

Miles, Professor George H.

Millar, Mrs. William, of Baltimore, an Episcopalian.

Miller, Miss, daughter of Joaquin Miller, poet of the Sierras.

Mills, Lewis, of Cincinnati.

Monk, The Hon. Cornwallis, Justice of Appeal for Lower Canada. (1867.)

Monk, Rev. Lewis Wentworth, son of the above, a priest. (1867.)

Monroe, Rev. F., of Virginia, near relative of President Monroe, now a Jesuit in New York.

Montgomery, The late Mrs., of Philadelphia. (1807.)

Montgomery, Colonel L. Morton.

Morris, Mrs. Isabel T., of Jamaica, West Indies.

Nemis, Rev. A. R., a priest of the Paulist Community in New York.

Nevada, Mdlle. (Emma Wixon), the American *Prima Donna.* (1884.)

Newton, General J. (who blew up "Hell Gate").

Newton, Mrs., wife of the above.

Nicol, Robert Thomas T., a clergyman, of Trinity College, Toronto, Canada. (1899.)

Nichols, Dr., of New York.

Nichols, The late Mrs. Mary S. Gore, author of *A Woman's Work in Water-cure*, etc., contributor to the *Athenæum*, *Frazer's Magazine*, *Household Words*, etc., wife of the above.

Niles, Dr. Addison, of Quincy, Illinois.

Niles, Mrs., wife of the above, and daughter of Colonel Whiting, of Bath.

Northrop, Right Rev. Dr., Bishop of Charleston, South Carolina.

ODOLI, The Marchesa, of New York.

Olmstead, General W. A., now a Priest of the Order of Charity.

Ord, General Edward O. C., who distinguished himself during the late Civil War.

PARKER, Mrs. S., of Boston.

Pelly, F. W., late Principal of St. John's College, Qu'appelle, Canada, and Pastor of St. Andrew's Episcopal Church. (1896.)

Peshin, Rev. George, a priest of the Paulist Community of New York.

Peter, Mrs. Sarah, of Cincinnati, an Episcopalian.

Peterson, Alfred, of Philadelphia.

Phillips, Rev. J. A., of Philadelphia, late an Episcopalian Rector.

Pike, General, of New York.

Pollard, Rev. J., formerly an Episcopalian Minister.

Pope, Miss Amy, daughter of W. H. Pope, Judge in Prince Edward's Island.

Powell, Charles, of New York. (1894.)

Powell, Miss Maud, of New York. (1894.)

Powell, Mrs. Sarah, of New York. (1894.)

Prescott, Miss Harriet, well-known in American literary circles. (1884.)

Preston, Right Rev. T. A., late a minister of the Episcopal Church, a priest, Monsignor and Chancellor of the Archdiocese of New York.

Pugh, Edward L., eldest son of Senator Pugh, of Alabama. (1898.)

RAMM, Rev. Charles A., of the University of California late Assistant Pastor of St. Mary's Cathedral, San Francisco, California.

Rathbone, Lawrence, stepson of the Hon. Judge Harris, United States Senator.

Ratz, Emilio Hugo, of Mexico. (1898.)

Reed-Lewis, William, late American Consul at Tangiers. (1894.)

Revere, General Joseph Warren, of Boston, grandson of Paul Revere, of Revolutionary fame, and of General Joseph Warren, who was killed at Bunker Hill. (1851.)

Richards, Henry Raymond, of New York. (1894.)

Riordan, Mrs., wife of Dr. Riordan, of Delhi, Iowa.

Robbins, Mrs. Mary Utley, widow of the Hon. Judge Robbins.

Robertson, The late Rev. John, connected with the Cowley Fathers in America, a Jesuit Priest. (1875.)

Robinson, Rev. Henry, descendant of the first minister settled in the Boston Colony, now a priest.

Robinson, Rev. Thomas V., a priest of the Paulist Community at New York.

Rodgers, Rev. Dr., late an Episcopalian Rector.

Rodgers, Mrs., of Rome, wife of Randolph Rodgers, the sculptor.

Rosecrans, Henry, brother of the General and Bishop, late a Methodist.

Rosecrans, The late Right Rev. Dr. S. H., Bishop of Columbia, formerly a Methodist.

Rosecrans, General W. S., brother of the Bishop, late a Methodist.

Rosecrans, Mrs., wife of the above, formerly an Episcopalian.

Rosecrans, Miss, daughter of the above, an Episcopalian.

Russ, Dr., a distinguished savant and author, of New Mexico.

Russell, Rev. J. C., late a Protestant clergyman, of Baltimore, and his five children. (1880.)

Ryan, Rev. A. A., "the Poet Priest".

Ryckmann, Mrs. Garrett, of New York.

Sanderson, Miss Sybil, the celebrated singer. (1897.)

Sands, Admiral, of Virginia.

Scammon, General E. P., an Episcopalian.

Scammon, Mrs., wife of the above, an Episcopalian.

Schofield, Mrs., wife of General Schofield.
Schumann, Charles, an officer in the 3rd Artillery, Tampa, Florida. (1898.)
Scott, Dr. R. T., of Houston, Texas. (1898.)
Scott, The Hon. Judge T. Parkin Scott, of Baltimore.
Sedgwick, Miss Jane, of Stockbridge, Massachusetts.
Seton, The late Mother, foundress of the Sisters of Charity in America.
Seton, The late Miss Cecilia, of New York. (1806.)
Seton, The late Miss Henrietta, of New York. (1809.)
Seton, The late Mrs. John Curzon, of Boston, and two children. (1816.)
Seton, Mrs., wife of William Seton, of New York, and sister of Mrs. C. Carroll Lee. (1866.)
Settle, Rev. M., formerly an Episcopalian minister, a priest.
Sherman, Frederick, late Chaplain to the United States Navy and Assistant Curate of the Church of the Advent, Boston, son of the Hon. Judge Edgar J. Sherman. (1896.)
Shields, Mrs. Walter, of New York. (1898.)
Shimman, Miss M. Parker, of Boston.
Simmons, Rev. W. J., a Priest of the Paulist Community at New York.
Sinderson, Mrs., wife of General Sinderson.
Smalley, Mrs. Sarah A., and five children.
Smith, General George, of Chicago.
Smith, J. Wesley, of New York.
Smith, General K., of Tarrytown.

Smith, Mrs. Leonard, niece of John Hay, late American minister to Vienna.

Spaulding, James Field, D.D., late an Episcopalian minister and Rector of Christ Church, Cambridge, Massachusetts. (1893.)

Stanley, General.

Stevens, Miss A. de Grasse, of New York.

Stevens, The late Thaddeus, the statesman.

Stobinger, Rev. J., a priest.

Stobinger, Mrs., mother of the above. (1882.)

Stone, Rev. James Kent, late President of Hobart and Kenyon College, a Priest of the Paulist Community.

Storer, The late Bellamy, United States Minister to Belgium. (1897.)

Storer, Mrs., of Cincinnati, wife of the above. (1895.)

Symms, Mrs. Americus, of Louisville, an Episcopalian.

Smyth, The Hon. Judge Frederick, of the Supreme Court of New York, an Episcopalian. (1898.)

Smyth, Miss, daughter of the above. (1896.)

Temple, James, of Montgomery.

Temple, Mrs., wife of the above.

Tenbroeck, Miss, now a nun.

Tenney, The Hon. Judge, of New Jersey, author.

Thayer, Henry Adams, of Cambridge, Massachusetts. (1883.)

Thom, The late Royal H., of Syracuse. (1897.)

Thompson, Mrs. Charles, a descendant of General Putnam, of Connecticut.

Thompson, Mrs. Edgar T., daughter of the late Senator Benjamin Hill, of Georgia, and family. (1893.)

Thompson, Miss Florence, niece of the Right Rev. H. C. Potter, Bishop of New York. (1896.)

Throop, Francis H., of Baltimore. (1894.)

Tillston, The late Rev. Robert, a priest of the Paulist Community at New York.

Tinker, Miss, of New England, authoress.

Tinsley, James H., of Brooklyn, New York. (1894.)

Tracey, Charles, of New York.

Tracey, Miss, his daughter.

Tracey, Miss Eustace, her sister.

Treviño, Madame, daughter of General Edward O. C. Ord, and wife of General Treviño, of Mexico.

Tucker, Captain, of Burlington, Vermont.

Tucker, Mrs., wife of the above.

Turner, The late Lieutenant James H., of the Alaska Squadron. (1894.)

Turner, Rev. John Spencer, of New York. (1898.)

Turner, Mrs. Sarah K., mother of the above. (1894.)

Tyler, The late Right Rev. Dr., Bishop of Hartford.

Tyler, Mrs., wife of Ex-President Tyler, her daughter, and her granddaughter. (1880.)

VAN BUREN, Dr. W. H., one of the leading surgeons in the United States, nephew of Ex-President Van Buren.

Van Dyke, James A., of Detroit.
Van Hoffmann, The Baroness (*née* Ward).
Van Rensselaer, Miss, sister of an Episcopalian minister, now a Sister of Charity.
Victoria, Sister, of St. Vincent's Sanitarium and Orphan Asylum, Sante Fé, New Mexico, formerly a Methodist.
Voorhees, Miss, daughter of Senator Voorhees. (1893.)

WADHAMS, The Right Rev. E. P., Bishop of Ogdenburg, formerly an Episcopalian.
Walff, Rev. Professor, ex-Lutheran minister, author.
Walker, Charles, the celebrated lexicographer.
Walworth, Rev. Clarence, son of the late Chancellor Walworth, of New York; a priest.
Walworth, Mrs., mother of the above.
Walworth, Mrs. E. Harden, and five children.
Ward, Captain J. W., of the United States Navy.
Wayne, General Henry.
Wheaton, Homer, late of Poughkeepsie, of New York, first a lawyer and then a Protestant minister.
Whipple, General Amiel W., who distinguished himself during the late Civil War.
White, The late Calvin, of New Jersey, first a Presbyterian minister, then an Episcopal layman, grandfather of Richard Graham Grant White, of New York, author and Shakesperian scholar.
Whitfield, The late Most Rev. Dr., Primate and Archbishop of Baltimore.

Wilkins, The Hon. Judge, of Detroit, formerly a Methodist.

Wilson, The Very Rev. F., late an Episcopalian, now a Dominican Priest and Superior of his Order in Ohio.

Withington, Miss Lydia Mary, of New York.

Witzell, Mrs., of New York. (1884.)

Wolff, The late Rev. George D., formerly Pastor of the German Reformed Church, late editor of *Philadelphia Catholic Standard*. (1871.)

Wood, The late Most Rev. Dr., Archbishop of Philadelphia.

Woodman, Rev. Clarence S., a priest of the Paulist Community of New York.

Worthington, Mrs. George, of Cleveland.

Worthington, Lewis, of Cincinnati.

Worthington, Mrs., wife of the above.

Wyman, Rev. H. M., a priest.

YOUNG, Rev. Alfred, a priest of the Paulist Community of New York.

Young, The late Right Rev. Dr. J. M., formerly a Unitarian, late Bishop of Erie.

DENMARK.

Count Holstein Ledreborg, at one time leader of the majority in the Danish Parliament.

Rev. Pastor Hanssen, formerly a Protestant clergyman of note in Copenhagen.

Rev. L. von Hammerstein, ex-clergyman of the Danish Church, a Jesuit Priest at Limburg, Holland.

FRANCE.

The late Cardinal de Bonnechose, Archbishop of Rouen. (1830.)

Rev. M. A. Bermaz, formerly Protestant Pastor at Lyons. (1846.)

The Vicomte de Bussière.

The late Comtesse d'Avry, daughter of the late Duke of Brunswick.

The late John Daniel Blavignac, formerly a Methodist, and Freemason.

The late Mdlle. d'Haussonville, great-granddaughter of the celebrated Mme. de Staël, and only sister of Comte d'Haussonville, of the French Academy.

Rev. Charles Lachat, late Protestant Pastor at Bordeaux.

The late Rev. Paul Laval, formerly Protestant Pastor at Condé-sur-Noireau. (1825.)

Rev. Georges Michand, late Protestant Pastor at Marseilles. (1870.)

The Baronne d'Ordred. (1854.)

The Countess O'Connell (*née* Princesse Nonia Bertong), Lady of the Order of the Sepulchre, and wife of

Count O'Connell, of Paris, Chamberlain to His Holiness Pope Leo XIII. (1879.)

The Marquis de Poix. (1865.)

The Princesse Alexandre de Wagram (*née* Berthe de Rothschild), daughter of Baron Charles de Rothschild. (1882.)

The Comtesse Zute. (1854.)

Ferdinand, Brunetière, editor of the *Revue des Deux Mondes*, member of the French Academy, and author of the *Bankruptcy of Science*, etc. (1898.)

GERMANY.

Her Majesty the late Queen of Bavaria, Princess of Prussia. (1875.)

H.R.H. Prince Henry von Hanau, son of the Elector and Landgrave of Hesse-Cassel, and grand-nephew of His Imperial Majesty the late Emperor William I. of Germany. (1884.)

H.R.H. the late Count of Ingenheim, brother of the then King of Prussia. (1826.)

H.R.H. the Princess of Ingenheim. (1852.)

H.R.H. the late Duke of Saxe-Gotha, a relative of King George III. of England.

H.R.H. the late Prince Adolf Frederick, of Mecklenburg-Schwerin. (1818.)

H.R.H. the late Princess Charlotte Frederic, wife of a former Crown Prince of Denmark.

H.R.H. the late Prince Henry Edward of Schönburg. (1822.)

H.R.H. the late Countess of Brandenburg, daughter of the late King William II. of Prussia.

H.R.H. Prince Alexander zu Solms-Braunfels. (1865.)
H.R.H. Prince Isenburg-Birstein. (1861.)
H.R.H. Princess Isenburg-Birstein. (1861.)
H.R.H. Count Isenburg-Birstein. (1861.)
H.R.H. Prince Leopold von Löwenstein-Wertheim.
H.R.H. Prince von Wittgenstein.
Count Frederick Leopold zu Stolberg-Stolberg.
Count Franz zu Stolberg-Wernigerode.
Count Charles Schönburg-Vorderglanchau. (1869.)
Countess Schönburg-Vorderglanchau. (1869.)
Count Schönburg-Vorderglanchau, their son. (1869.)
Count Von Schönburg-Glanstan.
Count Götz Christoph von Degenfeld-Schönburg. (1853.)
Countess von Degenfeld-Schönburg. (1853.)
Count Ferdinand Hahns-Newhans. (1858.)
The late Countess Frederica Solms-Baruth. (1826.)
Countess Lützow, wife of Count Francis Lützow, of the Austrian Embassy in London. (1882.)
The late Countess Natalie von Kielmansegge. (1841.)
The late Countess Ida von Hahn-Hahn, the celebrated authoress. (1850.)
The late Count Hermann von der Schulenberg, a Capuchin Monk. (1855.)
Baron Frederick von Berlithingen. (1865.)
Baron von Eckstein.
Baron von der Kettenburg.
Baron Rochns von Rockow. (1852.)
Baron von Romberg.
Baron von Suchow.

Baron von Vogelsang.

Baroness von Donop, daughter of the late Baron de Reuter.

Clemens Brentano, the celebrated romantic writer. (1842.)

Rev. Gustavus Bicknell, formerly a Lutheran clergyman, now a priest, and Professor of Oriental Languages at the University of Innsbruck.

The late Dr. Henry Eisenbach. (1833.)

Rev. Pastor Hager, ex-Lutheran minister.

Fraulein Louise Hänsel, the distinguished poetess.

Rev. Hugo Linmer, ex-Lutheran minister, now a priest and canon.

Herr Gfrörer, the historian.

Herr Klopp, the historian.

Herr Adam Müller, Aulic Councillor.

Fraulein Emilie Ringens, the distinguished painter.

The late Herr Nepilly, one of the leading old Catholics of Prussian Rhineland. (1883.)

The late celebrated painter Overbeck.

Herr Frederick Schlegel, the savant.

The late Herr Zacharius Werner, the celebrated writer and poet, a priest. (1823.)

SWEDEN.

The late Count Hamilton, senator, and descendant of an old Stuart family.

Baroness van Klinkowström.

www.ingramcontent.com/pod-product-compliance
Lightning Source LLC
Chambersburg PA
CBHW031340230426
43670CB00006B/392